THE ORIGINS OF BOWING

THE ORIGINS OF BOWING

and the development of bowed instruments up to the thirteenth century

WERNER BACHMANN

Translated from the German
by Norma Deane

London

OXFORD UNIVERSITY PRESS

New York   Toronto

1969

Oxford University Press, Ely House, London W. 1

Glasgow New York Toronto Melbourne Wellington
Cape Town Salisbury Ibadan Nairohi Lusaka Addis Ababa
Bombay Calcutta Madras Karachi Lahore Dacca
Kuala Lumpur Singapore Hong Kong Tokyo

Originally published under the title
Die Anfänge des Streichinstrumentenspiels,
first edition 1964, second edition 1966,
by VEB Breitkopf & Härtel, Leipzig

Printed by VEB Breitkopf & Härtel, Leipzig, Germany

CONTENTS

PLATES

(The plates will be found between pages 80 and 81).

Plate 1

*Four musicians 'habentes citharas dei', and seven
angels with the seven plagues, illustrating Revelation XV, 1–4.* Mozarabic manuscript, *S. Beati
de liebana explanatio in apokalypsis S. Johannis*,
Biblioteca Nacional, Madrid, Hh 58, fol. 127 r.
Spain, *c.* 920–30 (Photograph: Biblioteca
Nacional, Madrid.)

Plate 2

Joculatores. Miniature from the Mozarabic
Romance Beatus manuscript, British Museum,
London, Add. 11695, fol. 86. Originated in
Santo Domingo de Silos, near Burgos, be-
tween 1073 and 1091. Miniatures completed
by 1109. From J. Dominguez Bordona, *Die
spanische Buchmalerei vom 7. bis 17. Jahrhundert*,
Vol. I (Munich, 1930), Plate 61 A.

Plate 3

*The Lamb of God on Mount Zion, and four
players of the 'cithara dei', illustrating Revelation
XIV, 1–3.* Mozarabic/Romance manuscript,
Beato de San Millán, Academia de la Historia,
Madrid, Sig 33, fol. 177. Spain, 10th century.
Illustrated, early 11th century. (Photograph:
Biblioteca Nacional, Madrid.)

Plate 4

King David with musicians. Detail of a Byzantine
miniature from a Greek psalter manuscript,
Vatican Library, MS. graec. 752, fol. 23 v.
11th century. (Photograph: Vatican Library.)

Plate 5

King David with dancers and musicians. Detail
of a Byzantine miniature from a Greek psalter

manuscript, Vatican Library, MS. graec. 752,
fol. 3 r. 11th century. (Photograph: Vatican
Library.)

Plate 6

Statues of muses. Detail of a Byzantine miniature
in the Pseudo-Nonnus Commentary, Patriarchal Library, Jerusalem, Codex Taphou 14,
fol. 100 r. 11th century. (Photograph: Professor Kurt Weitzmann, Princeton University.)

Plate 7

Eight musicians, surrounded by dancing girls.
Pictorial representation of the eight ecclesi-
astical modes. Byzantine miniature from a
Greek psalter manuscript, Vatican Library,
MS. graec. 752, fol. 449 v. 11th century.
(Photograph: Vatican Library.)

Plate 8

Minstrel. Byzantine fresco in the North tower
of the Cathedral of St. Sophia in Kiev,
c. 1050. From *Geschichte der russischen Kunst*,
Vol. I (Dresden, 1957), p. 108, Plate 92.

Plate 9

Boy on an acanthus leaf. Relief on a Byzantine
ivory casket, Museo Nazionale, Florence,
Coll. Carrand, No. 26. 10th or early 11th
century. (Photograph: Professor Friedrich
Behn, Mainz.)

Plate 10

Corybants making music. Detail from a representation of the birth of Zeus. Byzantine miniature from the Pseudo-Nonnus Commentary,
Patriarchal Library, Jerusalem, Codex Taphou
14, fol. 310 v. 11th century. (Photograph:

Professor Kurt Weitzmann, Princeton University.)

Plate 11

Detail from a group of musicians. Byzantine miniature from a psalter manuscript. British Museum, London, Add. 19352, fol. 191. Written in 1066 in the Monastery of St. Basil at Caesarea for the Abbot of the Studion Monastery in Constantinople. (Photograph: British Museum, London.)

Plate 12

Corybants dancing and playing (detail from a representation of the birth of Zeus). Byzantine miniature from the Codex graecus 1947 in the Vatican Library, fol. 146 r. 11th/12th century. (Photograph: Professor Kurt Weitzmann, Princeton University.)

Plate 13

Banquet scene. Detail from a hunting tableau. Lacquer painting on the belly of a lute (*p'i-p'a*) in the Japanese Imperial Treasure-house, the Shōsōin, Nara, 9th/10th century. (Photograph: Shōsōin, Nara.)

Plate 14

Musician. Detail from the Airtam Frieze, discovered in 1932 near Termez (Uzbekistan). 1st century B.C.–3rd century A.D. The Hermitage, Leningrad, Central Asiatic Section. From K.V.Trever, *Pamjatniki greko-baktrijskogo iskusstva* (Moscow, 1940), Plate 48.

Plate 15

Musicians on a shard from Central Asia. 8th/9th century. The Hermitage, Leningrad, Central Asiatic Section, Petrovski Collection, Inv. No. 266. From J. Strzygowski, *Altai-Iran und die Völkerwanderung* (Leipzig, 1917), Plate 213.

Plate 16

Miniature from the Stuttgart Psalter. Württembergische Landesbibliothek, Stuttgart, Cod. bibl. folio 23, fol. 125 r. 10th century. From E. T. Dewald, *The Stuttgart Psalter* (Princeton University, 1931).

Plate 17

Musician from King David's retinue. Psalter in the Biblioteca Capitolare, Ivrea, Cod. 85, fol. 23 v. End of first millennium. From L. Magnani, *Le Miniature del Sacramentario d'Ivrea* (Vatican City, 1934), Plate 46.

Plate 18

Asaph, musician in King David's suite, with 'cythara'. Miniature (detail) from the glossed Psalter manuscript in the Bibliothèque municipale at Amiens, fonds l'Escalopier, MS. 2, fol. 2. First half of the 11th century. From C. V. Leroquais, *Les Psautiers manuscrits latins des Bibliothèques publiques de France* (Macon, 1940/1941), Plate 26.

Plate 19

Musician with pandora. Mosaic in the Byzantine Imperial Palace (Constantinople). First half of the 5th century A.D. From H. G. Farmer, 'An Early Greek Pandore', *Journal of the Royal Asiatic Society* (1949), p. 177.

Plate 20

Musician with p'i-p'a. Relief from the tomb of Wang Chien at Ch'êng-tu, Sech'uan Province. From the Five Dynasties (907–913 A.D.). From *Wang Chien mu fon tiao* (Peking, 1958), Wen-wu ch'u-pan-shê.

Plate 21

Fresco in the Palatine Chapel, Palermo. Early 12th century. From U. Monneret de Villard, *Le Pitture Musulmane al Soffitto della Cappella Palatina in Palermo* (Rome, 1950) Fig. 209.

Plate 22

Musicians. Detail from a scene representation the worship of a golden statue. Miniature from a Catalan Bible, in the Vatican Library, MS. lat. 5729, fol. 227 v. Originated in the Monastery of Santa Maria in Ripoll at the beginning of the 11th century. From A. Boeckler, *Abendländische Miniaturen bis zum Ausgang der romanischen Zeit* (Berlin and Leipzig, 1930), Plate 60.

Plate 23

King David with musicians. Detail from a miniature from the Brunonis Psalterium in the Bibliothèque Nationale, Paris. MS. lat. 2508, fol. II v. Northern Italy, beginning of the 12th century. (Photograph: Bibliothèque Nationale, Paris.)

Plate 24

Dancing musician. Detail of a miniature (Initial B) at the beginning of Psalm 1, Catalan Bible manuscript, Museo Diocesaro, Barcelona, MS. 8011, *c.* 1100. From. H. Anglès, *La musica a Catalunya fino al ségle XIII* (Barcelona, 1935), Fig. 15.

Plate 25

King David and musicians tuning their instruments. Miniature from a Catalan psalter, in the Bibliothèque Nationale, Paris, MS. lat. 11550, fol. 7 v. Mid-11th century. (Photograph: Bibliothèque Nationale, Paris.)

Plate 26

King David with musicians. Miniature from a Lombard psalter manuscript, Biblioteca Civile, Mantua, MS. C. III. 20, fol. I r. Abbey of San Benedetto di Polirone, 12th century. From P. d'Ancona, *La Miniature Italienne du Xe au XVIe siècle* (Paris and Brussels, 1925), Plate VI, fig. 6.

Plate 27

Musicians dancing, with the legend 'Consonancia cuncta musica'. Miniature from a manuscript in the Bibliothèque Nationale, Paris, MS. lat. 9449, fol. 34 v., Gradual of Nevers, about 1060.

Plate 28

The angels bring the Christmas message to the shepherds. Fresco in the Crypt of San Urbano alla Caffarella, near Rome. Executed in 1011. From G. Ladner, 'Die italienische Malerei im 11. Jahrhundert', *Jahrbuch der kunsthistorischen Sammlung in Wien*, N. F. 5 (Vienna, 1931), Plate 73.

Plate 29

King David with musicians. Miniature from a Bible manuscript in the Gräflich Schönbornsche Bibliothek, Pommersfelden, Cod. 2777, fol. I. Rhineland, *c.* 1070. (Photograph: Gräflich Schönbornsche Bibliothek, Pommersfelden.)

Plate 30

Detail from a group of musicians. Miniature from a psalter in Leipzig University Library, MS. 774, fol. 31. Soignes (Hainault), second half of the 11th century. (Photograph: Leipzig University Library.)

Plate 31

Musician from King David's suite. Detail from a miniature from a psalter manuscript, British Museum, London, Cotton MS. Tib. C. VI, fol. 30 v. Southern England, *c.* 1050. (Photograph: Bildarchiv der Deutschen Akademie der Künste, Berlin.)

Plate 32

Musician. Detail of initial T. Passionale of Augustine. British Museum, London, MS. Arundel 91, fol. 218 v. Canterbury, *c.* 1100. From F. Wormald, 'Survival of Anglo-Saxon Illumination after the Conquest', *Proceedings of the British Academy*, XXX (1944), p. 127, Plate 5 b.

Plate 33

Musician. Detail from an initial V, Biblia Mazarinea, Bibliothèque Nationale, Paris, MS. lat. 7, fol. 125 v. Languedoc (Southern France), *c.* 1200. (Photograph: Bibliothèque Nationale, Paris.)

Plate 34

Musician. Detail from an initial B. Psalter manuscript in Trinity College Library, Dublin, MS. 53, fol. 151, 12th/13th century. (Photograph: Trinity College Library, Dublin.)

Plate 35

King David with musicians. Detail from an initial B. MS. in the Bibliothèque municipale, Douai, MS. 250, fol. 2 v. Marchiennes, mid-12th century. From A. Boeckler, *Abendländische Miniaturen bis zum Ausgang der romanischen Zeit* (Berlin and Leipzig, 1930), Plate 96.

Plate 36

Miniature. From a Kalendarium in the Seminary Library, Strasbourg, MS. 78 (I, Scr. 10), fol. 79 r. Executed at the Augustinian Monastery in Marbach (Northern Alsace), in 1154. (Photograph: Seminary Library, Strasbourg.)

Plate 37

Detail. From a miniature from the psalter manuscript in the Biblioteca Laurenziana, Florence, Plut. XVII, Cod. 3, fol. 24v. From Marturi, an abbey near Florence, *c.* 1100. (Photograph: Biblioteca Laurenziana, Florence.)

Plate 38

Miniature. From a tonar in the British Museum, London, MS. Harl. 4951, fol. 297v. Etienne (Toulouse), 12th century. (Photograph: British Museum, London.)

Plate 39

Detail from a pictorial representation of secular music. English psalter manuscript, St. John's College Library, Cambridge, MS. B. 18, fol. 1. Second quarter of the 12th century. From F. W. Galpin, *Old English Instruments of Music* (London, 1910).

Plate 40

King David's musicians. As shown on a capital from the church of Notre Dame de la Dourade, Toulouse. Augustinian Museum, Toulouse. *c.* 1100. (Photograph: Marburg 32817.)

Plate 41

King David. Sculpture on portal of side nave, left-hand lintel bracket, St.-Sernin, Toulouse, *c.* 1100. (Photograph: Marburg 32490.)

Plate 42

Animals making music. Third capital at the West door of the Church at Meillers. 12th century. (Photograph: Marburg 40114.)

Plate 43

Apocalyptic kings. Detail from the tympanum above the main door of the Church of St. Pierre in Moissac, *c.* 1120. From F. Marcou, *Musée de sculpture comparée*, Vol. I, Plate 19.

Plate 44

Musical instrument held by one of the Apocalyptic kings. Detail from the tympanum above the main door of the Church of St. Pierre, Moissac, *c.* 1120. (Photograph: Marburg 30762.)

Plate 45

Apocalyptic king. Sculpture on central part of West door, second archivolt on the left, Abbey Church of St. Denis, *c.* 1140. Considerably restored. (Photograph: Marburg 36994.)

Plate 46

King David Capital of a pillar in the Cathedral at Vienne (France) (Photograph: Marburg 36840.)

Plate 47

One of King David's musicians. Miniature (detail) from the Notker Labeo Psalter in the Stiftsbibliothek at St. Gall, Cod. 21, Pgm. 2°. 12th century. (Photograph: Stiftsbibliothek, St. Gall.)

Plate 48

Minstrel. Detail from a miniature from the Bible manuscript in the Staatliche Bibliothek, Bamberg, MS. bibl. 59 (B–I–10), fol. 2v, *c.* 1200. (Photograph: Staatliche Bibliothek, Bamberg.)

Plate 49

The worship of the golden calf. Detail from the Gebhard Bible, Stiftsbibliothek, Admont, MS. 4, Vol. I, fol. 44. Second third of the 12th century. From P. Buberl, *Die Stiftsbibliotheken zu Admont und Vorau* (Leipzig, 1911), p. 23.

Plate 50

Miniature. From the *Vocabularium latinum* in the Stiftsbibliothek, Admont, Hs. 3, fol. 540, 12th century. (Photograph: Oesterreichische Nationalbibliothek, Vienna.)

Plate 51

King David with musicians. Miniature from an English Psalter manuscript in the Library of St. Godehard, Hildesheim, Albani-Psalter, fol. 447r. St. Alban's Abbey, early 12th century. (Photograph: H. Wehmeyer, Hildesheim.)

Plate 52

Musician. Detail from an inital E, Manuscript in the Deutsche Staatsbibliothek, Berlin, now in the Staatsbibliothek, Marburg, MS. lat. theol. fol. 379, fol. 245 v. Germany, 13th century. (Photograph: Deutsche Staatsbibliothek, Berlin.)

Plate 53

Initial E with musicians. British Museum, London, MS. Arundel 157, fol. 71 v. England, early 13th century. (Photograph: British Museum, London.)

Plate 54

King David. Miniature from an English psalter manuscript. Library of St. Godehard, Hildesheim, Albani-Psalter, fol. 56 v. St. Alban's Abbey, early 12th century. (Photograph: H. Wehmeyer, Hildesheim.)

Plate 55

King David with musicians. Detail from an ivory carving on a book cover, British Museum, London, MS. Egerton 1139. Origin: Byzantium/Jerusalem, 12th century. From O. M. Dalton, *Catalogue of the Ivory Carvings of the Christian Era* (London, 1909), Plate 15.

Plate 56

Musicians at the feet of King David. Miniature from the Bible of St. Etienne Harding, Bibliothèque publique, Dijon, MS. 14, Vol. III, fol. 13 v. Abbey of Cîteaux, 1109. From C. Oursel, *La Miniature du XIe siècle à l'abbaye de Cîteaux d'après les manuscrits de la Bibliothèque de Dijon* (Dijon, 1926), Plate VI.

Plate 57

King David with musicians. Miniature from a Latin manuscript in the Vatican Library, Pal. lat. 39, fol. 44 v. Southern Germany, 12th century. (Photograph: Vatican Library.)

Plate 58

King David with musicians. Miniature from the Lambertus Treatise, Bibliothèque Nationale, Paris, MS. lat. 6755 (2), fol. Av. 13th century. (Photograph: Bibliothèque Nationale, Paris.)

Plate 59

King David with musicians. Initial B. Koninklijke Bibliotheek, The Hague, MS. 76 E 11 (formerly y 421), fol. 2 r. France, first half of the 13th century. (Photograph: Koninklijke Bibliotheek, The Hague.)

Plate 60

Musicians at the feet of King David. Miniature from a psalter manuscript in the Hunterain Museum, Glasgow (University), MS. 229 (U. 3.2.). England, *c.* 1170. From: *The Burlington Fine Arts Club, Exhibition of Illuminated Manuscripts* (London, 1908), Plate 30.

Plate 61

King David with musicians. Miniature from a Bible manuscript in the British Museum, London, MS. Harley 2804, fol. 3 v. Germany, about the middle of the 12th century. From *British Museum Reproductions from Illuminated Manuscripts*, Series IV (London, 1928), Plate XI.

Plate 62

King David, initial E. Trinity College Library, Cambridge, MS. 0.4.7., fol. 112 r. 12th century. (Photograph: W. G. Rawlings, Cambridge.)

Plate 63

King David, initial D. Bible manuscript, Bibliothèque Nationale, Paris, MS. lat. 11509, fol. 5 r. 12th century. (Photograph: Bibliothèque Nationale, Paris.)

Plate 64

Apocalyptic kings. Portal sculpture from the Cathedral of Sainte-Marie, Oloron, outer archivolt, right. 12th century. (Photograph: Marburg 52691.)

Plate 65

Detail from a procession of female musicians. Miniature from the Velislav Bible, Prague University Library, MS. 412, fol. 72 r, *c.* 1340. From A. Buchner, *Musikinstrumente im Wandel der Zeiten* (Prague, 1956), Plate 104.

Plate 66

Musicians at the feet of King Wenceslas of Bohemia. Miniature from the *Manessische Liederhandschrift*, Heidelberg University Library, Cod. pal. germ. 848, 14th century. (Photograph:

Bildarchiv der Deutschen Akademie der Künste, Berlin.)

Plate 67

Minstrel. Wood carving. Choirstall in the Cathedral at Erfurt. 14th century.

Plate 68

Reinmar the fiddler and a dancing girl. Miniature from the *Manessische Liederhandschrift*, Heidelberg University Library, Cod. pal. germ. 848, fol. 312r. 14th century. (Photograph: Bildarchiv der Deutschen Akademie der Künste, Berlin.)

Plate 69

Musician. Detail from a miniature from the glossed psalter manuscript in the Bibliothèque municipale at Lunel, MS. I, fol. 6. England, first half of the 12th century. From C. V. Leroquais, *Les Psautiers manuscrits latins des bibliothèques publiques de France* (Macon, 1940/41), Plate 35.

Plate 70

Minstrel. Sculpture, detail from the tympanum above the West door of the Baptistery in Parma, 1169. (Photograph: Marburg 1635.)

Plate 71

Minstrel, with the legend 'Nicolo da la viola fiorentino'. Miniature from the *De Musica* of Boethius in the Biblioteca Ambrosiana in Milan, Cod. C. 128, Inf., Plate 3a. 10th century manuscript. miniature added later, 13th/14th century. From G. Cesari, 'Tre tavole di strumenti in un "Boezio" del X secolo', in *Festschrift G. Adler zum 60. Geburtstag* (Vienna, 1930), Plate 3a.

Plate 72

Minstrel. Stained glass. Detail from a window in the Florentius Church in Niederhaslach (Alsace), 1370. From H. Wentzel, *Meisterwerke der Glasmalerei* (Berlin, 1951), Plate 147.

Plate 73

Musician in King David's suite. Detail from a miniature in St. Elizabeth's Prayerbook, fol. 295, Cividale del Friuli, Museo Archeologico Nazionale. Saxon-Thuringian school of paint-

ing, *c.* 1200. (Photograph: Bildarchiv der Deutschen Akademie der Künste, Berlin, No. 720.)

Plate 74

Detail from a painting representing music and dicing. Miniature from a Bible manuscript belonging to St. Louis, in the Oesterreichische Nationalbibliothek, Vienna, Cod. 1179, Bl. 316, fol. 86r. Paris, *c.* 1250. (Photograph: Oesterreichische Nationalbibliothek, Vienna.)

Plate 75

Angel with fiddle. Detail from a Aragonese reliquary triptych, in the Academia de la Historia, Madrid, 14th century.

Plate 76

Musician. Detail from a miniature from the Boethius manuscript *De Musica*, 14th-century copy in the Biblioteca Nazionale, Naples, Cod. V. A. 14. From A. Carta, C. Cipolla, and C. Frati: *Monumenta Palaeografico-Artistico* (Turin, 1899), Plate 66.

Plate 77

Apocalyptic kings with hurdy-gurdy. Capital in the transept of the Abbey of Saint-Georges de Boscherville, near Rouen. Mid-12th century. Rouen Museum.

Plate 78

Apocalyptic kings with hurdy-gurdy. Soria, Santo Domingo, West door, inner archivolt, *c.* 1150. From A. Kingsley Porter, *Romanesque Sculpture of the Pilgrimage Roads*, Vol. VI, Illustrations (Boston, 1923), Plate 798.

Plate 79

Apocalyptic king with hurdy-gurdy. Sculpture on the St. Anne door, Cathedral of Notre-Dame, Paris, *c.* 1160. Considerably restored. From J. Roussel, *La sculpture française, époque romane*, Plate 30 (3).

Plate 80

Apocalyptic kings with hurdy-gurdy. Sculpture on the Pórtico de la gloria of the Cathedral at Santiago de Compostela, 1168–88. From A. Kingsley Porter, *Romanesque Sculpture of the Pilgrimage Roads*, Vol. VI, Illustrations (Boston, 1923), Plate 826.

Plate 81

Initial B with musicians. Miniature from Robert de Lindesey's Psalter, Society of Antiquaries, London, MS. 59, fol. 38 v. Peterborough, 1214–22. (Photograph: Society of Antiquaries, London.)

Plate 82

Musicians. Miniature from the *Cantigas de Santa Maria*, Escorial Library, Madrid, MS. T-i-I. Second half of the 13th century. From J. Ribera, *La musica de las Cantigas* (Madrid, 1922).

Plate 83

Musician. Detail of a miniature from the Luttrell Psalter, in the British Museum, London, Add. MS. 42130. *c.* 1330. From E. G. Millar, *The Luttrell Psalter* (London, 1932).

Plate 84

Miniature. From the Luttrell Psalter in the British Museum, London, MS. Add. 42130, fol. 81 v. *c.* 1330. From E. G. Millar, *The Luttrell Psalter* (London, 1932).

Plate 85

Initial B. Miniature from the Bible manuscript in Munich University Library, MS. 24, 4°, fol. 2 r. 13th century. (Photograph: Munich University Library.)

Plate 86

King David at the organ, with an organ-blower and a musician playing the hurdy-gurdy. Miniature from a psalter manuscript in the library at Belvoir Castle. England, around the middle of the 13th century.

Plate 87

Some of King David's musicians. Miniature from the *Weltchronik* of Rudolf von Ems, in the Zentralbibliothek, Zürich, MS. Rh. 15, fol. 218. South-Western Germany, *c.* 1360. (Photograph: Marburg 67071.)

Plate 88

Angel with hurdy-gurdy. Detail from a painting on an Aragonese reliquary triptych in the Academia de la Historia, Madrid. 14th century.

Plate 89

King David with musicians. Miniature from a psalter manuscript in the library of the Augustiner-Chorherrenstift, Klosterneuburg, Cod. 987, fol. 11 v. Hildesheim, 11th century. (Photograph: Oesterreichische Nationalbibliothek, Vienna.)

Plate 90

King David. Ivory carving on the binding of the Lothar Psalter (Psalter of St. Hubert d'Ardennes), British Museum, London, MS. Add. 37768. Originated in the St. Bertin region *c.* 1100. (Photograph: British Museum, London.)

Plate 91

King David. Miniature from a *Troparium*, once the property of the Abbey of St. Martial at Limoges, now in the Bibliothèque Nationale, Paris, MS. lat. 1118, fol. 104r. Originated in the Auch region in the 11th century. (Photograph: Bibliothèque Nationale, Paris.)

Plate 92

Asaph, one of King David's musicians. Detail from a miniature from a psalter manuscript in the University Library, Cambridge, Ff. I. 23, fol. 4v. England, 11th century. (Photograph: University Library, Cambridge.)

Plate 93

Musician. Relief in St. Finian's Church, Waterville, Co. Kerry, South-West Ireland, *c.* 1200. *Journal of the Royal Society of Antiquaries of Ireland* (1908), p. 383.

Plate 94

Musicians at the feet of King David. Miniature from the Psalter in the Staatsbibliothek, Berlin, MS. theol. lat. Fol. 358, fol. 1v. Originated in the Monastery at Werden on the Ruhr in the 11th century. (Photograph: University Library Tübingen.)

Plate 95

Miniature. From a manuscript in the Bayrische Staatsbibliothek, Munich, Cod. lat. 2599, fol. 96 v. 13th century. From G. Kinsky, *Ge-schichte der Musik in Bildern* (Leipzig, 1929), p. 39, Plate 5.

Plate 96

Musician. Capital in the transept of the Gross-münster in Zurich, *c.* 1200. (Photograph:

Bildarchiv des Deutschen Vereins für Kunst-wissenschaft, Berlin.)

Plate 97

Musician. Sculpture from Trondheim Cathe-dral. End of the 12th century. From *Lesbøk,* XXIIth year (1947), p. 1.

ABBREVIATIONS

AfMf	*Archiv für Musikforschung*
AfMw	*Archiv für Musikwissenschaft*
AMl	*Acta Musicologica*
CS	Coussemaker, Edmond de, *Scriptorum de musica medii aevi novam seriem a Gerbertina alteram collegit nuncque primum edidit, Paris 1864–76*
GS	Gerbert, Martin, *Scriptores ecclesiastici de musica sacra potissimum*, St. Blasien 1784
GSJ	*The Galpin Society Journal*
JAMS	*Journal of the American Musicological Society*
JIFMC	*Journal of the International Folk Music Council*
JNChBRAS	*Journal of the North Chinese Branch of the Royal Asiatic Society*
JP	*Jahrbuch der Musikbibliothek Peters*
JRAS	*Journal of the Royal Asiatic Society*
KmJb	*Kirchenmusikalisches Jahrbuch*
Md	*Musica disciplina*
Mf	*Die Musikforschung*
MfM	*Monatshefte für Musikgeschichte*
MGG	*Die Musik in Geschichte und Gegenwart*
ML	*Music and Letters*
MQ	*Musical Quarterly*
NMz	*Neue Musikzeitung*
PRMA	*Proceedings of the Royal Musical Association*
RBM	*Revue Belge de Musicologie*
R d'E	*Revue d'Ethnographie*
RM	*Revue Musicale*
RMI	*Rivista Musicale Italiana*
SIMG	*Sammelbände der Internationalen Musikgesellschaft*
STMf	*Svensk Tidskrift för Musikforskning*
SvglMw	*Sammelbände für vergleichende Musikwissenschaft*
VfMw	*Vierteljahrschrift für Musikwissenschaft*
ZfE	*Zeitschrift für Ethnologie*
ZfI	*Zeitschrift für Instrumentenbau*
ZfM	*Zeitschrift für Musik*
ZfMw	*Zeitschrift für Musikwissenschaft*
ZföV	*Zeitschrift für österreichische Volkskunde*

INTRODUCTION

'The historical evolution of bowed instruments has still to be explored, not only in respect of specific details but also in respect of major problems.' This statement by Struve[1] is particularly true in relation to the origin of bowing which, despite the existence of numerous publications on the development of the bow and the antecedents of the modern violin, still remains obscure. The present work may, it is hoped, help to clarify this important problem.

In view of the vastness of the field and the multiplicity of problems involved, it has been necessary to restrict the period covered in this inquiry. The end of the twelfth and the beginning of the thirteenth centuries was selected as *terminus ante quem*, since by 1200 bowed instruments were already beyond the early stages of tentative experiment, and had established themselves as a permanent constituent of the European family of instrument. Only a few lines of development will be followed to the late Middle Ages or to the present, in order to demonstrate continuity of development.

Because bowed instruments occupy a privileged position in the modern orchestra, the question of the origin of bowing has assumed prominence in the field of organological studies. The large volume of literature devoted to this problem offers a variety of conclusions, often mutually contradictory. In order to obtain a firm basis for further studies it has been necessary to evaluate publications already available and to make a critical analysis of their results. The dating and interpretation of their sources has had to be checked, and the principles underlying their methods examined. The present work begins with a summary of the present state of research, which surveys both the development of organology in general and changes in methods of investigation.[2]

Early chroniclers of the history of bowing frequently confined their field of enquiry to Europe. This led to mistaken or biased conclusions, especially as attempts were often made to bolster up preconceived ideas by careful selection of corroborative material. In consequence, the impression was given that only European peoples were capable of significant cultural achievements. Other learned contributions to this subject, acknowledging that the evolution of European musical instruments was constantly influenced by the old cultures of Western and

---

[1] B. A. Struve, *Prozess formirovanija viol i skripok* (Moscow, 1959), p. 32.   [2] Chapter I,

Central Asia, put forward the hypothesis of an oriental origin of the bow. They were not, however, able to furnish conclusive evidence in support of their contention. In the present work, special consideration will be given to non-European predecessors of our bowed instruments.[3] In addition to medieval Arabic, Byzantine, Chinese, and Indian sources,[4] the evidence to be considered will include archaeological materials from the peoples of Central Asia.[5]

Previous works dealing with the early stages of bowed instruments have considered them almost exclusively from the morphological or structural point of view. The present study, however, also examines playing techniques and the musical use of medieval bowed instruments, in the context of their social function and not isolated from man and human society.[6] These aspects of the problem steer our research into seas still uncharted so far as the Middle Ages are concerned, and draws it further than ever before into the domain of historical musicology. The development of bowing, for example, leads us to infer a change in the concepts of sonority and performance, and above all allows us to draw conclusions about the manner of performance of secular music, of which virtually nothing is otherwise known. A thorough investigation is necessary to determine how closely the origin of bowing was related to the widespread medieval use of drones or similar embryonic forms of polyphony.[7]

The problem of interaction between musical instruments and musical style is also one of considerable significance. 'The exigencies of society lead to the development of a new content in music. To express this, an ever-increasing variety of new instrumental qualities is required, involving changes in sonority and technique and yielding new musical possibilities.'[8] Within the limits of contemporary technical development, men create musical instruments which embody the contemporary urge for expression as nearly as possible, in regard both to sound and to technique. If the expressive potential of instruments no longer corresponds to the musical requirements of a particular epoch, they either die out or are modified. Many examples can be quoted where the construction of instruments was unable to keep pace with the development of musical culture, as a result of which the shortcomings of the instruments imposed limitations on performance. On the other hand, there are also examples where the discovery of new instruments or the reorganization and modification of the instruments already available opened up new fields of musical expression, so that the expressiveness and the stylistic and formal structure of the music benefited considerably.

Any study concerned with early bowed instruments must examine them in the context of the music and the social climate of their time. Organological evidence can in fact considerably amplify and correct our conception of music and musi-

---

pp. 5 ff.   [3] Detailed description in Chapter II, pp. 24 ff.   [4] Both pictorial representations and medieval written sources have been considered, insofar as these have been translated or already evaluated.   [5] Chapter II, pp. 50 ff.   [6] The question of the allocation of medieval musical instruments to particular social strata is discussed in Chapter IV, pp. 117 ff.   [7] Chapter III, p. 93 ff. and Chapter V.   [8] E. H. Meyer, *Musik im Zeitgeschehen* (Berlin, 1952), p. 74.

cians in medieval times – imperfect as this is and biased by the preponderance of ecclesiastical sources. Furthermore, research into the origins of bowing, the problems of which seem so far removed from those of the present, can contribute to our understanding of certain traditions and practices in the folk music of our own time. Various practices of folk fiddlers emerge in this way as traditions dating back for about a thousand years, and preserved in certain remote areas almost unchanged. These studies can also help us to understand the general developmental process which bowed instruments have undergone through the centuries.

The sources on which this inquiry rests vary in quality; and their evaluation calls for a few remarks on general principles. To date, the scattered archeological discoveries of medieval bowed instruments, though affording information on construction and the nature of the materials used, do nothing to help us decide how they were played.[9] More important are medieval literary sources. Because of the unsympathetic attitude towards musical instruments and musicians adopted by the Church in the Middle Ages, instruments are only casually mentioned in Latin treatises on music. References mostly consist of brief lists, following the example of Cassiodorus's *De artibus ac disciplinis liberalium litterarum*, and Isidor of Seville's *Etymologiarum*, Book III. Only in Aegidius Zamorensis, John Cotton, and Jerome of Moravia, do we find a few organological references. Secular medieval vernacular literature is more productive, particularly the Arabic treatises[10] on music. But although these sources yield numerous details of importance, they are inadequate for an overall picture of medieval bowed instruments.

Thus we have to depend chiefly on visual representations of musical instruments, of which numerous examples exist in miniatures, frescoes, and sculpture of the period. Single pictorial representations are of relatively slight documentary value. Since medieval artists were rarely concerned to achieve a true likeness of any object, instruments were represented carelessly and inaccurately, and often in a stylized manner. Often, too, the sculptor's difficulties in handling fragile or brittle materials, or the miniaturists' lack of space, precluded any great attention to detail. In many instances, the instruments illustrated have a purely symbolic function, and serve as attributes, demonstrating the relationship to music of the person holding the instrument. In accordance with the traditionalism of medieval art,[11] illuminators or sculptors often worked from older models, which they either copied or, prompted by a taste for the grotesque, fantastically transformed. A variety of improbable representations do of course stem from the artist's inadequate knowledge of instruments. Illustrations of this type, however, are comparatively rare. By far the greater part of the available iconographical evidence shows

---

[9] From the remains of lyres and fiddles, or of lutelike chordophones, it is never clear for instance whether the strings were bowed or plucked. [10] Various preliminary studies are already available in this field: cf. Bibliography for works by F. Dick, J. F. Finlay, J. Levy, G. Schad, M. I. S. Sorensen, D. Treder and D. Droysen, and a Dissertation of F. Brücker, *Die Blasinstrumente in der altfranzösischen Literatur* (Giessen, 1926). The medieval Arabic musical treatises are particularly informative, and have been evaluated organologically, above all by H. G. Farmer. [11] R. Hamann,

I*

that the artists had a clear mental image of what he was depicting. He concentrated, however, on emphasizing the essentials of the object and on reproducing it in a simplified form.[12]

The general validity of medieval pictorial representations as evidence is substantiated by the agreement between different documents. Many questions indeed concerning ergological features of the instruments can only be answered by reference to the entire range of iconographic materials. The fundamental problem of when, where, and how chordophones were first made to sound by means of a bow, cannot be solved on the basis of only a few iconographical sources come across by chance. In order, therefore, to lay a firm foundation for this study, it has been necessary to assemble all available contemporary representations and to procure the best possible photographs of the most important of these.

The iconographical method suffers from certain limitations when used to investigate techniques of playing medieval bowed instruments. Representations can often be interpreted in several ways, and we are reduced to guesswork. Only when results in the field of ethnomusicology are also taken into account, do we have a reliable basis for comparison. Here the completeness or incompleteness of the material is less important than the existence of typical examples that agree with the medieval sources. Of particular interest are those archaic techniques and types of instrument that have survived in certain remote areas for hundreds of years, often virtually unchanged, and which therefore permit inferences to be drawn regarding the practice of bowing in the Middle Ages. One must disregard evidence of the use of the bow outside the European area, where the influence of modern European bowing-techniques is clearly perceptible. But with this proviso musical folklore and ethnomusicology supply observations and comparative materials essential to the understanding and reliable interpretation of the medieval sources.

This book offers a new interpretation of a complex and much-debated chapter in the history of musical instruments, broadly based on comparative studies and on a critical appraisal of all available sources.

NOTE

The various medieval words used to describe bowed instruments were somewhat confused in their own day, and have remained so ever since. It has therefore been decided to refer to them all in this book where necessary by the generic word *fiddle*.

Geschichte der Kunst, Vol. II (Berlin, 1957), pp. 207 ff. (Carolingian Art).   [12] The question of how far medieval musical illustrations should be regarded as true-to-life documentary evidence is answered by H. Besseler in 'Spielfiguren in der Instrumentalmusik', *Deutsches Jahrbuch für Musik-wissenschaft, 1956*, I. Jg. (Leipzig, 1957), pp. 23 ff., with the help of numerous pictorial examples.

I

THE PRESENT STATE OF RESEARCH

Older Literature

With the awakening sense of history and growing interest in *musica antica* since the end of the sixteenth century, the question of the origin and age of particular musical instruments has also been raised. In historical studies of this sort the bowed instruments figure prominently,[1] in view of their special importance from the Middle Ages onwards. 'Non diffitemur tamen inter omnia plectrorum genera praestantissimum fuisse arculi inventum, cuius mihi auctor ignotus' wrote Giovanni Battista Doni.[2] Vincenzo Galilei[3] also considered the question of the origins of bowing, and concluded that Italy was probably the original home of bowed instruments.

As early as the treatise *Ars musica*, written about 1270 by the Franciscan friar, Johann Aegidius Zamorensis,[4] there is an attempt to catalogue musical instruments in the chronological order of their invention. The latter section of his list is devoted to those instruments which – 'postremo inventa' – came into being in the immediately preceding centuries. Apart from the trapezoidal psaltery (canon = *qānūn*) and the guitar, these are primarily the bowed instruments such as the rabr (= *rabāb*). Some two centuries later, Johannes Tinctoris, in his treatise *De inventione et usu musicae*,[5] attempts to derive viola, rebec, guitar, cetula, tambura, and similar stringed instruments of his time from a common lute-like ancestor, 'quid sit lyra populariter leutum dicta'.[6] He suggests that these special forms were evolved from the prototype at different times and in different countries.[7] In this context his comment on the relatively recent advent of bowing is especially interesting. In antiquity, he claims, only the plectrum (*pecten*) was used, not the bow; while in the Middle Ages both the quill (*penna*) and the bow (*arculus*) were used to draw sound from stringed instruments.[8]

[1] Medieval evidence for the popularity of the fiddle and the esteem in which it was held is listed in Chapter IV, pp. 118 ff. [2] *Lyra Barbarina*, ed. Gori and Passeri (Florence, 1763), p. 44. [3] *Dialogo della musica antica et della moderna* (Florence, 1581), p. 147. [4] *GS* II, p. 388 b. [5] The text of his treatise was published by K. Weinmann, *Johannes Tinctoris und sein unbekannter Traktat 'De inventione et usu musicae'* (Regensburg and Rome, 1917); cf. also Weinmann's contribution to the *Riemann-Festschrift* (Leipzig, 1909), pp. 267 ff, and the essay by A. Baines, 'Fifteenth-century Instruments in Tinctoris' *De Inventione et Usu Musicae*', *GSJ* III (March, 1950), pp. 19 ff. [6] K. Weinmann, *Johannes Tinctoris*, p. 40. [7] Loc. cit., 'Quid sit lyra populariter leutum dicta; quid etiam quelibet instrumentalis species ex ea producta: utpote (iuxta linguam vulgarem) viola: rebecum: ghiterra: cetula: et tambura.' [8] Loc. cit., 'Cuiusmodi apud nos sunt penna et arculus: apud antiquos

This important statement by Tinctoris, who based his conclusions on tradition and his own experience and research rather than on the testimony of the preferred authorities of the Middle Ages, was forgotten (or at least set aside as untenable and out-of-date) when, around 1600, there was a turning towards the music of antiquity as a pattern for certain Renaissance musical ideals. In view of its own high regard for bowed instruments, the seventeenth century could not believe that Greek music – the superiority of the Greeks being undisputed – lacked the sound of bowing. Consequently most authors of treatises on instruments in the seventeenth and eighteenth centuries sought to trace the development of the use of the bow back into antiquity. In searching through Greek texts, names and brief descriptions of stringed instruments, together with legendary accounts of their origins, were found and these were collected together in mythical histories of instruments. Limited knowledge of such instruments and of representations of these on ancient monuments frequently led to faulty interpretations of the available texts. *Plektron* (or *pekten*) was carelessly translated by 'bow',[9] and the Greek poetess Sappho – according to tradition the first to use the *plektron*[10] – was credited with having discovered the use of the bow. This opinion was held by various Italian authors of the seventeenth and eighteenth centuries, among them Lorenzo Penna, Zaccaria Tevo, and Daniele Bartoli.[11]

In addition, it was an accepted fact during the seventeenth and eighteenth centuries that the ancient Hebrews used the bow. Their instruments had excited particular interest since medieval times – witness the many attempts to interpret the names of instruments mentioned in the Bible.[12] However, these studies tended to base their textual interpretations on the range of instruments available in their own time, since archaeological knowledge of instruments of the ancient East was still virtually non-existent.

The often cited descriptions of Hebrew bowed instruments were based chiefly on the treatise of Schilte Haggibborim,[13] which appeared in Mantua in 1612. In the author's opinion, the *neghinot* had three gut strings, over which a bow strung with horsehair was drawn.[14] These details were repeated by

pecten.'   [9] Various authors have sought support for this theory in A. Calmet's *Dissertatio in musica instrumenta Hebraeorum*, included in Blasio Ugolino's *Thesaurus antiquitatum sacrarum* (Venice, 1767), Vol. 32, pp. 775 ff.   [10] Those ancient writers who credited Sappho with the 'invention' of the plectrum are mentioned in the article 'Plectrum' in the *Realenzyklopädie der klassischen Altertumswissenschaften*, edited by A. Pauly, revised by G. Wissowa (Stuttgart, 1894ff.).   [11] Lorenzo Penna, *Li primi Albori musicali per li principianti della musica figurata* (Bologna, 1672). Zaccaria Tevo, *Musico Testori* (Venice, 1706). Daniele Bartoli, *Del suono de'tremori armonici e dell'udito* (Rome, 1679 and Bologna, 1680). This notion of the bow's use in ancient Greece is still maintained in a few recent works on the history of instruments. A synopsis of the various arguments in favour of such an assertion is given, for instance, in Isaia Billé, *Gli strumenti ad arco e i loro culturi* (Rome, 1928), Chapter I, pp. 3 ff.   [12] The most important 17th and 18th-century works on the music and instruments of the Hebrews are listed in Vol. 32 of Blasio Ugolino's *Thesaurus antiquitatum sacrarum* (Venice, 1767).   [13] An extract from this Hebrew treatise appeared in a Latin translation in Ugolino, op. cit., Vol. 32, pp. IIff.   [14] 'Et Neghinot, inquit, fuerunt instru-

Kircher[15] whence they were taken by Forkel.[16] Printz,[17] who paid particular attention to Hebrew music, also referred to Schilte Haggibborim when discussing the use of the bow in relation to the instruments known as *minnim, michol,* and *schalasim.* Marpurg[18] and Hawkins[19] also subscribed to the view that the Israelites were familiar with the use of the bow. After various authors[20] had expressed doubts about the translation of *plektron* by 'bow', in the latter part of the eighteenth century, new studies,[21] drawing to a considerable extent on archaeological material, finally discredited the theory that the ancient Hebrews used the bow.

During the late seventeenth and eighteenth centuries, several short works appeared which for the first time dealt specifically with the origins of bowing. They gave a comprehensive account of what was known at that time and offered, in addition, new and original information. In 1687 there appeared in Paris the *Traité de la viole, qui contient une dissertation curieuse sur son origine,* written by the gambist and violist Jean Rousseau. The author is convinced that the viol is one of the oldest instruments, possessing a peculiarly high degree of naturalness and perfection by virtue of the similarity between its sound and that of the human singing voice. Not content with crediting the ancient Greeks and Hebrews with knowing and playing bowed instruments,[22] he advances the somewhat curious hypothesis that Adam himself would certainly have made a viol if he had wanted to make a musical instrument.[23]

More carefully considered judgements are expressed in eighteenth-century treatises. Among these are the essays of Paul Gemsage, *Origin and Introduction of the Violin,*[24] and Le Prince le jeune, *Observations sur l'Origine du Violon.*[25] They expressed the view that, although the actual origins of bowing were still completely obscure, they should clearly be sought in the Middle Ages. The French author in particular is persuaded that the use of the bow was unknown in ancient times. Bernard Lamy (1640–1715)[26] held the same view, based on the fact that

menta lignea longa et rotunda et subtus ea multa foramina tribus fidibus constabant ex intestinis animalium, et cum vellent sonare ea, radebant fides cum arcu compactu ex pilis caudae equinae fortiter astrictis.' A. Kircher, *Musurgia universalis* (Rome, 1650), Vol. I, p. 48. [15] Loc. cit. [16] J. N. Forkel, *Allgemeine Geschichte der Musik* (Leipzig, 1788), Vol. I, p. 87. [17] W. C. Printz, *Historische Beschreibung der Edelen Sing- und Kling-Kunst* (Dresden, 1690), p. 27. [18] F. W. Marpurg, *Kritische Einleitung in die Geschichte und Lehrsätze der alten und neuen Musik* (Berlin, 1759), p. 32. [19] J. Hawkins, *A General History of the Science and Practice of Music,* Vol. 1 (London, 1776, republ. 1875), p. 91, note and illustration 18 and p. 92. [20] Among them Forkel, op. cit., p. 202. [21] Cf. dissertation by E. Kolari, *Musikinstrumente und ihre Verwendung im Alten Testament* (Helsinki, 1947), and M. Wegner, *Die Musikinstrumente des Alten Orients* (Münster, 1950), both of which quote further specialist literature. [22] P. 7 f. On p. 16 the use of the bow among the ancient Hebrews is again referred to: 'outre que nous avons veu que l'Archet tel que nous l'avons aujourd'huy estoit en usage parmy les premiers Hébreux.' [23] '... si Adam avoit voulu faire un instrument, il auroit fait une Viole' (p. 3). [24] Published in *The Gentleman's Magazine* (London, 1757), pp. 560 ff. [25] In *Journal Encyclopédique ou Universel* (November 1782), pp. 489 ff. [26] His *Dissertatio de Levitis Cantoribus* was published by Ugolino in his *Thesaurus antiquitatum,* Vol. 2, pp. 572 ff. The passage reads as follows (p. 592f): 'illud autem, quo nunc pulsantur nos violons, violes, & appellamus archets ignotum fuit primae aetatis Musicis. Etenim non conveniebat

on ancient instruments all the strings lay in the same plane; this, in his opinion, would have precluded the use of the bow. Eventually, towards 1800, it became generally accepted that bowing was unknown to the Mediterranean peoples of classical antiquity.[27]

Theories of the Nordic and Indian origin of bowed instruments

In the nineteenth century, the question of the origin of bowing became increasingly prominent. Many specialized studies set out to clarify the problem by means of new and scientific methods[28]. Their guiding principle was the theory of evolution, with its stress on the steady progress of humanity throughout history towards a higher stage of development, better and more complete. The simple was regarded as the older, the compound and complex as the more recent. If we set out to trace a bowed instrument back to its origin, says Fétis,[29] we must find the most primitive form it can take. The quest for rudimentary types of bowed instruments led to the Welsh crwth and the Indian *ravanastron*, both regarded as the ancestor of our violin. It was thought that these stringed instruments originated in prehistoric times,[30] and had been played with the bow from the outset. It followed that the bow must have originated either in Northern Europe or the East—South Asia in particular. The rival theories provoked incessant controversy.

The North European origin of the use of the bow was postulated by Fétis[31] during the 1830s and was taken up, with certain reservations, by a number of other authors,[32] who reinforced it to some extent with new arguments. According to this view, the Western ribbed fiddle, with its clearly defined neck, evolved

fidibus, quarum nervi, chordae . . . in antiquis instrumentis omnes in recto plano tensae erant. In illis instrumentis nullus usus potest esse hodierni plectri, quod vocamus l'archet.' [27] This view is upheld in the following works: R. G. Kiesewetter, 'Über die musikalischen Instrumente und die Instrumentenmusik im Mittelalter', *Caecilia* XXII (Mainz, 1843), p. 198; F. Zamminer, *Die Musik und die musikalischen Instrumente* (Gießen, 1855), p. 41f.; E. de Coussemaker, *Essai sur les instruments de musique au moyen âge, Annales archéologiques par Didron Ainé*, Vol. III (Paris, 1845), p. 150. [28] Cf. works by the following authors, as listed in the bibliography: H. Abele; E. H. Allen; G. E. Anders; A. Bottée de Toulmon; E. de Coussemaker; C. Engel; F. Fétis; L. Grillet; R. G. Kiesewetter; J. Rühlmann; W. Sandys and S. A. Forster; L. A. Vidal. [29] *Antoine Stradivari* (Paris, 1856, p. 2). [30] The invention of the *ravanastron* is acribed to Ravanon, legendary ruler of Ceylon, a huge monster with ten heads, said to have lived about 3000 B.C.; cf. C. Engel, *Researches into the early History of the Violin Family* (London, 1883), p. 10f. [31] *Résumé philosophique*, supplement to the *Biographie universelle des musiciens* (Brussels, 1837), Vol. 1 p. 83, and *La Musique mise à la portée de tout le Monde* (Brussels, 1839), p. 121. [32] The following works support the theory of the nordic origin of bowed instruments: H. Riemann, *Musiklexikon* (2nd ed., Berlin, 1929), the articles entitled 'Chrotta' and 'Streichinstrumente'; A. W. Ambros, *Geschichte der Musik* (3rd ed., Leipzig, 1891), Vol. II, p. 36f.; R. G. Kiesewetter, 'Über die musikalischen Instrumente und die Instrumentenmusik im Mittelalter', *Caecilia* XXII (Mainz, 1843), p. 198; O. Andersson, 'Altnordische Streichinstrumente', *Report of the 3rd Congress of the International*

from the crwth of the Welsh bards, the yoke having been discarded as an impediment to bowing. Apart from the Welsh crwth, the Russian *gudok*[33] and the pear-shaped bowed 'lyra'[34] with only one string, copied by Gerbert[35] from a medieval miniature, were also cited as examples of original forms, to strengthen the opinion that Europe was the birth-place of bowed instruments.

The theory that the bow originated in India was formulated about the middle of the last century, under the influence of that interpretation of history which sought to derive all Western culture from the East.[36] In 1855 Friedrich Zamminer[37] expressly suggested that bowed instruments came from the East. In the following year Fétis published his monograph on Stradivarius, prefaced by a historical introduction on the antecedents of our bowed instruments. He had now completely shifted his ground vis-à-vis the origins of bowed playing. Having further exhaustively studied the Welsh crwth he concluded that its form was too complex for it to be an original form, while the gudok also told against the Northern provenance of bowed instruments because of its Oriental origin. Fétis believed he had found the original ancestor of our bowed instruments[38] in the simply-constructed Indian *ravanastron*. The use of the bow must therefore have spread from India across Persia and Arabia – whose bowed *kamanja* and *rabāb* he regarded as related to the Indian *ravanastron* – until it finally reached Europe. Fétis also held that direct links must have existed between Indian and Northern European bowed instruments because of racial affinities between Indian peoples and the Celtic tribes of North-Western Europe who brought the bow with them on their immigration from Asia.

This theory of the Indian origin of our bowed instruments quickly gained ground,[39] despite some objections. Rühlmann[40] protested that Fétis had not proved the Indian instrument in question to be 'either old, original, or primitive'. On the contrary, he believed that the bow originated independently in different places, among peoples of high cultural level.[41] Engel and Hammerich, though at the outset opposed to Fétis's 'Indian' theory,[42] were nevertheless converted later to his view.

Music Society (Vienna, 1909), p. 259; H. W. Schwartz, *The Story of Musical Instruments* (New York, 1938), p. 38 f.; C. Dolmetsch, 'The crwth', *The Consort* (1956), p. 23.   [33] F.-J. Fétis, *Résumé philosophique*, p. 83.   [34] H. Riemann, *Präludien und Studien*, Vol. II (Leipzig, 1901), p. 218. [35] *De cantu et musica sacra*, Vol. II (St. Blasien, 1774), Plate XXXII.   [36] F.-J. Fétis, *Antoine Stradivari*, p. 11; 'rien dans l'Occident qui ne vienne de l'Orient.' Salomonis van Til, in his *Cantus Poeseos*, included in Ugolino's *Thesaurus antiquitatum*, Vol. 32, p. 266, was already convinced that our bowed instruments came originally from the Orient: 'certior vero opinio est, violinum extisse orientale.'   [37] *Die Musik und die musikalischen Instrumente*, p. 41 f. and p. 379.   [38] *Antoine Stradivari*, pp. 2 ff., and *Histoire générale de la musique* (Paris, 1869–76), Vol. II, pp. 291 ff.   [39] This view is adopted in most historical works dating from the second half of the 19th century, for example, L. A. Vidal, *Les instruments à archet*, Vol. I (Paris, 1876), p. 3; L. Grillet, *Les ancêtres du Violon et du Violoncello*, Vol. I (Paris, 1901), p. VIII ff.; E. H. Allen, *Violin-making, as it was and is* (London, New York, 1884), pp. 37 ff.; C. Engel, *Researches*, pp. 10 ff.   [40] J. Rühlmann, *Die Geschichte der Bogeninstrumente* (Brunswick, 1882), p. 11.   [41] *Op. cit.*, p. 6.   [42] C. Engel, *The*

Philological Considerations

Attempts were made to strengthen both the 'Indian' and the 'Nordic' theories with philological and etymological arguments. These were frequently based on the assumption that the name of a medieval or a more modern bowed instrument has been at all times applied to a *bowed* instrument. Thus it was believed that the terms *lira joh fidula*, mentioned in Otfrid von Weissenburg's ninth-century Gospel poem *Krist*,[43] and *chrotta*, described by Venantius Fortunatus[44] in the sixth century as the favourite instrument of the Britons, referred already to bowed instruments, because instruments of the same name were later bowed. O'Curry[45] and Grattan Flood[46] in particular tried to prove that the instruments described as *fidil*, *timpan*, and *cruit* in old Irish texts were already bowed instruments, and hence that the bow had been in use in Ireland since the sixth century.[47] Such arguments overlooked the fact that in connection with the list of musical instruments in Otfrid von Weissenburg's *Krist* there is an express reference to the playing of these chordophones by plucking: 'thoz spiel, thaz seiton fuarit joh man mit hanton ruarit'; that the *fidla* is mentioned in the Norse sagas as a plucked instrument;[48] and that many sources lead to the conclusion that in the early Middle Ages *fidula* was employed as a general term to describe any instrument with strings.

Fétis had based his argument for the Indian origin of the bow on three Sanskrit words, all allegedly meaning 'bow'. The words are *koṇa*, *śarika*, and *parivāda*. At Hammerich's instigation Dines Andersen, Professor of Sanskrit at Copenhagen University, checked this evidence, and established that there was no reason to believe that the three words occur with that meaning in earlier periods.[49] Andersen's conclusion was verified by a further examination of the relevant sources. Sanskrit dictionaries from the seventh to the twelfth centuries[50] interpret the term *koṇa* (which appears already in the *Nâtyaśâstra*, Chapter XXIX, 119, 121, of Bharata) as an objects with which musical instruments were struck, and they apply the term to the beater and plectrum of stringed instruments, as

---

Literature of National Music, p. 70f.; A. Hammerich, 'Zur Frage nach dem Ursprung der Saiteninstrumente', *Report of the 2nd Congress of the International Music Society* (Leipzig, 1907), pp. 225 ff. [43] Most recent works treat this quotation from Otfried's *Evangelienharmonien* (*Krist* V, 23, verse 198) as proof that the bow was used in the 9th century. [44] The reference reads: 'Romanusque lyra plaudat tibi, Barbarus harpa, Graecus achilliaca, chrotta Britanna canat.' [45] O'Curry, *On the Manners and Customs of the Irish*, Vol. I, Introduction, p. 521 and Vol. III, pp. 364ff. [46] *The Journal of the Royal Society of Antiquaries of Ireland* (1908), p. 381; this theory has also been put forward by A. Fleischmann, *Music in Ireland* (1952), p. 1. [47] The significance of these sources has been questioned particularly by F. W. Galpin in his *Old English Instruments of Music* (London, 1910), p. 68. [48] *Grove's Dictionary of Music and Musicians*, 5th Edition (London 1954), article 'Folk Music'. [49] O. Andersson, *Altnordische Streichinstrumente*, p. 225; A. K. Coomaraswamy, 'The Parts of the Vina', *Journal of the American Oriental Society*, Vol. 50 (1930), p. 348. [50] Halāyudha's *Abhidhānaratnamālā*, edited by Th. Aufrecht (1864), Part I, V. 98; *Kosha* or *Dictionary* by Umura Singha, edited by H. T. Colebrooke (Serampore, 1825), I, 6, p. 46; Hemakandra's

well as to the drumstick.[51] Not until the thirteenth century was the meaning of this word so expanded that *koṇa* came to be used synonymously with *dhanuh* (bow) to denote the sound-producing apparatus used on friction instruments. The earliest example of the use of *dhanuh* in the sense of 'bow' occurs in the *Saṃgītaratnākara* (Book VI, 401, 415) by the Kashmiri-born Brahmin Niḥśanka Śārṇgadeva (thirteenth century).[52]

Also somewhat suspect are attempts to prove that the earliest sources for the names *kamānja*, *rabāb*, and *ikliq* are evidence of bowed instruments, deriving the first of these names from the Persian word *kaman* (the bow), the second from the Arabic verb *rabba* (to bind together – that is, the notes), and the third to the Uigurian *oklu kobuz* (bowed *kobuz*).[53] The same line of reasoning sees a possible etymological connection between the Nordic term *fidil* and the old Irish *fidh* – tantamount to 'a curved stick' – confirming the theory that the *fidula* was from the outset played with a bow.[54] Equally disputable are the attempts to show that the stringed instrument known as *smyk*, mentioned in the old Russian *Chronicle of the Patriarch*[55] (1068), was a bowed instrument, on the grounds of etymological relationship with the Old Slavonic verb *smyzati*,[56] meaning 'to draw' or 'to smooth'.[57]

These and similar efforts serve to show the limited value of philology – both the etymological interpretation of words and comparative linguistics – as a tool for investigating the subject of this book.

In more recent times Curt Sachs[58] has cited medieval texts which seem to prove that playing with the bow was known in different places as early as the ninth century: 'Looking for the first evidence of a bow, we find the first mention in Persia in the ninth century; in China, a bowed zither is spoken of in the ninth or tenth century.' In both cases the instruments mentioned are certainly known to have been played with the bow in later centuries; but in neither quotation is there any reference to the actual use of a bow. The Persian source is obviously the account of the journey made in the ninth century by the Persian-born Ibn Khurdādhbih, and related by him at the court of the Caliph al-Muʿtamid,[59] wherein he merely states that the Byzantines played a musical instrument called a *lūrā*, made of wood and having five strings, which corresponded to the *rabāb*. Curt Sachs's quotation from the Chinese is taken from the older T'ang annals, Book 29 of the *Chiu T'ang Shu*, written in the first half of the tenth century. In the course of a description of a Mongolian orchestra at the Chinese court, this source lists,

---

Abhidhānakintamāni, edited by O. Boehtlingk (St. Petersburg), 1847, p. 49.   [51] *Koṇa* occurs in the same sense in the *Saṃgītaratnākara*, Book VI, 824.   [52] Cf. p. 60.   [53] A. Hammerich, *Zur Frage nach dem Ursprung der Saiteninstrumente*, pp. 227 ff.; H. G. Farmer, *The origin*, p. 776 f. and M. R. Gazimihāl, *Asya ve anadolu kaynaklarında ıklığ* (Ankara, 1958).   [54] O. Andersson, *The Shetland Gue*, p. 20.   [55] Quoted in L. Ginzburg, *Istorija violončel'nogo iskusstva*, Vol. II (Moscow, 1957), p. 10.   [56] In modern Russian the generic term for a bowed instrument is still *smyčkovye instrumenti*.   [57] L. Ginzburg, op. cit., p. 10, note 2.   [58] *The History*, p. 216.   [59] Published in an English translation by H. G. Farmer: 'Ibn Khurdādhbih on musical instruments', *JRAS* (1928),

among other instruments, the elongated, many-stringed board zither, the *chêng*.[60] The name of the instrument is prefixed by the syllable *ya*, which is tantamount to saying that it was 'made to sound by scraping, scratching, rubbing or stroking'.[61] However, this reference to the *ya chêng* does not necessarily prove the use of a bow, a fact which has led to a reappraisal of medieval Chinese source material summarized in the following chapter.[62]

It may be said, therefore, that in any research into the origins of bowing the philological evidence is only of value where the bow is specifically mentioned, as for instance in the quotations from the Arabic compiled by Farmer,[63] to which further reference will be made in the course of this study.[64]

In more modern times, works devoted to the history of bowing frequently accept the old theory of the Indian origin of the bow. Like Kinsky and Galpin,[65] van der Straeten in his two-volume history of bowed instruments also regards India as the birthplace of bowed instruments: 'The only facts which appear fairly certain are that it [the bow] originated in India, whence it was taken to Persia.'[66] The same viewpoint is upheld by Dräger, in his standard work on the history of the bow: 'The origin and early development of the bow lie in the East, probably in India.'[67] To begin with, Curt Sachs shared this view,[68] and in a special study devoted to the musical instruments of India and Indonesia he touches, among other things, on this problem: 'The question of its [the bow's] country of origin was already answered by Fétis with: India. And today, after a temporary loading of the scales in favour of the Northern Germanic countries, the answer is still the same and we, too, can reply: India.' Later, however, Sachs was to revise this opinion. In his *History of Musical Instruments*,[69] which appeared in 1940, he again discusses the country of origin of the bow, and this time suggests that in all probability neither India nor Scandinavia qualifies as the country of origin, but that the bow most likely stems from Central Asia. Bessaraboff[70] reached a similar conclusion. Basing his arguments on the evidence of comparative philology, Mahmud Ragib Gazimihāl[71] recently claimed that the bow originated among the Uigur and was brought to us by the Huns as they pressed forward into Europe. He based his argument on etymological relationships between the names of bowed instruments in the Turkish dialects of Anatolia and corresponding words in the languages of Turkish peoples of Central Asia. The evidence advanced

pp. 509 ff. [60] Quoted in A. Lavignac, *Encyclopédie de la musique et dictionnaire du conservatoire*, first part, *Histoire de la musique (antiquité — moyen âge)* (Paris, 1913), p. 181, No. 145. [61] For the significance of the Chinese syllable '*ya*' cf. F. W. Galpin, *A Textbook*, p. 133. [62] Pp. 64 ff. [63] H. G. Farmer, *The origin*, pp. 775 ff. [64] In Chapter II, pp. 24 ff. [65] G. Kinsky, *Musikhistorisches Museum von Wilhelm Heyer in Cöln*, Catalogue, Vol. II (Cologne and Leipzig, 1912), p. 309; F. W. Galpin, *Textbook*, p. 134 f. [66] E. van der Straeten, *History of the Violin, its ancestors and collateral instruments, from earliest times to the present day*, Vol. I (London, 1933), p. 17. [67] H.-H. Dräger, *Die Entwicklung des Streichbogens und seine Anwendung in Europa (bis zum Violenbogen des 17. Jahrhunderts)* (Dissertation, Berlin, 1937), printed in Cassel, 1937, p. 10. [68] *Die Musikinstrumente Indiens und Indonesiens* (Berlin, 1915), p. 107. [69] P. 216. [70] N. Bessaraboff, *Ancient European Musical Instruments* (Cambridge, Boston, 1941), p. 250. [71] *Asya ve Anadolu Kaynaklarinda*

dates, however, from a time when bowing is known to have been long established in Europe.

Despite this and similar studies in recent times, the Indian theory in this field of the origin and early history of bowing has not yet been factually disproved and is still the subject of discussion.

Ethnomusicological Considerations

Earlier scholars had maintained that certain categories of stringed instruments were from the outset played with the bow while others were invariably plucked, and that bowed and plucked instruments existed side by side at all periods, having evolved from two different ancestral types. At the beginning of this century, however, it came to be accepted that bowed instruments had developed from plucked instruments, or had diverged from them. The theory was that, initially, stringed instruments were all plucked, then beaten, then rubbed, and finally bowed.[72] Thus most of the bowed medieval instruments, such as the crwth (rote), fidel, or rebeck, were allegedly exclusively plucked instruments at first, and only gradually came to be played with the bow. 'We know', writes Behn,[73] 'that from the beginning the crwth or chrotta was, like the cithara, a plucked instrument, and the transference to it of the technique of bowing gives the impression of a not very happy contamination [of one instrument by another].'

If the bow was 'invented' at a certain point of historical time, it was important to know when and where the bow was first used to draw sound from stringed instruments. According to Behn,[74] the date at which it could be proved that bowed chordophones were in use ushered in 'a new era in musical history'. In 1918, Sachs[75] had already expressed his opposition to this theory: 'It seems almost as though an attempt were being made to divide up the whole development of musical instruments into two great periods – a bowless period of lesser importance, and one of greater maturity following the advent of the bow'. In his view 'the demarcation of a boundary between techniques of plucking and bowing is a matter of ethnology, not of chronology'.[76] The whole problem of the bow, including its introduction and application, ought therefore to be resolved by the methods of comparative musicology. Wallaschek,[77] the first to attempt a general

---

Iklığ (Ankara, 1958). [72] This 'transition' theory is put forward in most of the recent works on the subject. [73] F. Behn, *Musikleben im Altertum und frühen Mittelalter* (Stuttgart, 1954), p. 165. This view is also supported by K. Schlesinger, *The Instruments of the modern Orchestra and early Records of the Precursors of the Violin Family*, Vol. II (London, 1910); A. Hammerich, *Zur Frage nach dem Ursprung der Saiteninstrumente*, p. 227, and many other authors. [74] Op. cit., pp. 162 ff.; Behn adopts the same position in his 'Miszellen zur Musikgeschichte', III. *Der Streichbogen*, *NMz* XXXIX (1918), part 7, pp. 104 ff. [75] 'Die Streichbogenfrage', *AfMw* I, 1918, p. 3. [76] Op. cit., p. 5. [77] R. Wallaschek, *Anfänge der Tonkunst* (Leipzig, 1903), p. 146; see also C. Sachs, *The Rise of Music in the Ancient World East and West* (New York, 1943), p. 197: 'With the rise of

survey of the musical instruments of primitive peoples, had already indicated the importance of this field: 'The total neglect of ethnology', he writes, 'has nowhere led to such ill-founded views as in the history of the violin.'

More than anyone else, Curt Sachs infused new life into the quest by considering the results and methods of ethnomusicological studies in his own work.[78] Sachs began by establishing where the bow appears in its most rudimentary form: the musical bow used by certain primitive tribes still culturally in the Stone Age.[79] In the light of the historical development of man, he reaches the conclusion that the bow was known from the earliest times. A number of doubts arise, however, at the point where he goes on to deduce from this the antiquity of bowing, and when he claims the primitive musical bow as the ancestor of our own modern bow. These primitive one-stringed chordophones are surely *musical instruments*, unlike the friction bow, which is a *tool*, serving to generate sound on stringed instruments.[80]

From the distribution of the various bowed instruments, Sachs endeavoured to draw conclusions as to their age, based on the theory of 'cultural zones', and with the aid of the 'geographical method' used in ethnomusicology.[81] He reached the conclusion that 'the oldest type of bowed fiddle' can be placed 'between the 16th and 21st layers; that is to say, about the beginning of the Christian era.'

According to Norlind,[82] the use of the bow is a cultural matter. Whereas the more primitive races frequently played their stringed instruments with the bow, he writes that 'civilized peoples had a decided aversion to bowing'.[83] 'Every composite chordophone', he says, 'was played with the bow, except where an advanced form of civilization had been established.' Sachs stresses repeatedly[84] that whereas some peoples preferred bowing, others used plucked chordophones exclusively. Whereas the classical peoples of the Mediterranean at their first appearance in history possessed only plucked instruments, the Northern races showed a predilection for bowed instruments from the beginning.[85] It would seem, therefore, that whether the sound of bowed or plucked strings was preferred depended on which type of sound corresponded to the ideal sonority of the individual races. Thus the different techniques or methods of performing were regarded as a 'criterion of race'.[86]

comparative musicology, it has dawned on us that music historians of early generations were doomed by their ignorance of Oriental music to misinterpret the sources.' [78] *Geist und Werden der Musikinstrumente* (Berlin, 1929). [79] Op. cit., pp. 87 and 183 ff. Cf. also Dräger, op. cit., pp. 28 ff. [80] Equally doubtful is the attempt made occasionally in earlier studies to derive the musical bow from the archer's bow. [81] Op. cit., p. 187. [82] T. Norlind, 'Beiträge zur chinesischen Instrumentengeschichte', *STMf* 15 (Stockholm, 1933), p. 75. [83] Op. cit., p. 74. [84] *Die Streichbogenfrage*, pp. 4 ff; also *Handbuch der Musikinstrumentenkunde* (Leipzig, 1920), p. 206. [85] *Handbuch der Musikinstrumentenkunde* (2nd ed., Leipzig, 1930). [86] Marius Schneider, 'Die musikalischen Beziehungen zwischen Urkulturen, Altpflanzern und Hirtenvölkern', *Zeitschrift für Ethnologie*, Vol. 70 (1938), p. 287, puts forward the hypothesis that 'the *method* of performance is a question of race, but the style of performance is a question of culture'. This is criticized by J. Kunst in *Ethnomusicology* (The Hague, 1955), p. 45, on the grounds that the demarcation line between the

While von Schlosser[87] expressed doubts about this theory, based as it was on the very shaky and scientifically unsound theory of race, Fleischer[88] firmly rejected Sachs's thesis, maintaining that the use of the bow had nothing whatever to do with 'race', and was not inborn. 'For the bow only appeared in Europe in about the eighth to the tenth centuries, and prior to that all peoples, including the Northern races, had only plucked stringed instruments.' Furthermore, there can be no question of any fundamental racial prejudice on the part of the Mediterranean peoples against bowing, since Italy was a great centre of bowing in the fifteenth, sixteenth, and seventeenth centuries. Bose[89] has recently pointed out that sonority ideals, as for instance a preference for the sound of plucked as opposed to bowed strings, are governed by fashion and contemporary taste, and are therefore liable to change. Thus they can never be firmly linked with racial differences.[90] A further point is that musical instruments and accessories (for example, plectrum or bow) are readily exchanged between peoples,[91] and hence can only be regarded as ethnic criteria under certain conditions.

Comparative musicology has, however, proved of value in the search for the origins of bowing, in that it has brought non-European bowed instruments, and thus instruments from many different levels of culture, within the scope of the investigation. Light has been shed on various types of instruments and performing techniques, and this in turn has led to valuable conclusions relating to bowing in the Middle Ages. Sachs,[92] for example, by comparing the earliest illustrations of bowed instruments with those of today, was able to draw certain parallels with Turkestani, Georgian, Greek, and near-Eastern instruments. Further investigations have been pursued along these lines, in particular by Schaeffner[93] and Hickmann,[94] but with regard to bowed chordophones their studies have yielded only isolated points. While Andersson[95] revived the suggestion that Northern Europe was the original home of bowed instruments, basing his arguments on hitherto little-known ethnographic source material, there can today be little doubt that, in Hickmann's words,[96] 'the bowed, stringed, instruments *rabāb* and *kamanja* of the Turks, Persians, and Arabs, together with the Graeco-Byzantine pear-shaped *lyra*, must be regarded as their predecessors.'

two is extremely hard to draw. [87] J. v. Schlosser, *Unsere Musikinstrumente, eine Einführung in ihre Geschichte* (Vienna, 1922), p. 18. [88] Quoted from H. Matzke, *Unser technisches Wissen von der Musik, Einführung in die musikalische Technologie* (Vienna, 1949), p. 258, note 3. [89] F. Bose, *Musikalische Völkerkunde* (Freiburg, 1953), pp. 53ff. and 80. [90] See also the following articles: R. Lach, 'Das Rassenproblem in der vergleichenden Musikwissenschaft', *Berichte des Forschungsinstituts für Osten und Orient*, III (Vienna, 1923), pp. 107ff., and F. Blume, 'Musik und Rasse, Grundlage einer musikalischen Rassenkunde', *Die Musik*, XXX (1938), pp. 736ff. [91] On the interchange and spread of folk instruments see E. Gerson-Kiwi, 'Migrations and mutations of oriental folk instruments', *Journal of the International Folk Music Council*, 4 (1952), pp. 16ff. [92] *Handbuch*, 2nd ed., pp. 175ff.; *Geist und Werden*, pp. 184 and 242f. [93] A. Schaeffner, *Origine des instruments de musique* (Paris, 1936), pp. 222ff. [94] H. Hickmann, article 'Fidel' in *MGG*, and also *Quelques précurseurs égyptiens du luth court et du luth échancré* (Cairo, 1949). [95] *The Shetland Gue, the Welsh Crwth, and the Northern Bowed Harp* (Budkavlen, 1954), pp. 1ff. [96] Article 'Fidel'

More intensive research is clearly necessary. But it must be borne in mind that in questions relating to the origins of bowing, ethnomusicology can only offer subsidiary aid, that is to say it can only be brought in to corroborate and strengthen evidence drawn from medieval sources. At all costs the temptation 'to try and make musical history wise before its time, on the basis of apparently illuminating rapprochements between the exotic and the historic,'[97] must be avoided.

Iconographical Considerations

No proper foundation could be laid for a historical approach to organology until the pictorial material made available by archaeological and historical research had been thoroughly investigated and scientifically assessed. Up to the second half of the eighteenth century, ancient and medieval illustrations had little place in musical literature; and if, by chance, illustrations *were* included, so as to throw light on the actual appearance of the instruments of an earlier age, these were either fanciful pictures – as for instance the illustrations of antique instruments in Virdung's *Musica getutscht und ausgezogen*[98] and Praetorius's *Syntagma musicum*,[99] based on medieval illustrations to Hieronymus's *Dardanus Letter*[100] – or drawings made by the artist from his own conception in the light of descriptions in the text.[101] Numerous representations of bowed instruments, cited as pictorial evidence for the use of the bow in ancient times, have proved to date from the Renaissance.[102] Silvestro Ganassi, in his *Regola Rubertina*,[103] which appeared in 1542, refers to a 'discovery from antiquity' made in Rome, representing the figure of a musician with a 'viola d'arco'. On closer investigation, however, this was found to be the work of a Renaissance artist. The statue of Apollo with a bowed instrument, now in Florence, was frequently quoted as evidence:[104] but this piece of allegedly classical sculpture is in reality a product of the seventeenth century. Thus, early attempts at research in organology, insofar as they incorporate pictorial evidence from ancient times, are of little value for the purposes of histo-

---

in *MGG.* [97] J. Handschin, *Musikgeschichte im Überblick* (Lucerne, 1948), p. 61. [98] (Basle, 1511), C, IIIff. [99] Vol. II (Wolfenbüttel, 1618), Plate XXXIIff. [100] This treatise, presumably written in the 8th or 9th century by a monk named Hieronymus, is included in J. P. Migne's *Patrologia latina*, Vol. 30, col. 214ff. Many medieval manuscripts containing this text also have illustrations describing the instruments. The most important illustrated manuscripts of the Dardanus letter are cited in E. Buhle, *Die musikalischen Instrumente in den Miniaturen des frühen Mittelalters* (Leipzig, 1903), p. 48, note 4, and in R. Hammerstein, 'Instrumenta Hieronymi', *AfMw* 16 (1959), pp. 117ff. [101] Cf. illustrations in the following publications: A. Kircher, *Musurgia universalis*, Vol. I, p. 48; W. C. Printz, *Historische Beschreibung*, Plate I; F. W. Marpurg, *Kritische Einleitung*, Appendix; J. N. Forkel, *Allgemeine Geschichte der Musik*, Vol. I, Plates Iff.; Ch. Burney, *A General History of Music*, Vol. I (London, 1776), illustrations in Appendix. [102] Cf. E. Winternitz: 'Archeologia Musicale del Rinascimento', in *Rendiconti della Pontifica Academia Romana di Archeologia*, 27 (1952). [103] Part I, Ch. VIII. [104] As for instance in Hawkins, op. cit., Vol. I, p. 91, illustration 18 and note. Similar representations are mentioned by Burney, op. cit., Vol. I, p. 512, and Le

rical study, in view of their author's lack of archaeological knowledge.[105] In 1782, Le Prince le jeune made the first critical analysis of the 'ancient' illustrations of bowed instruments,[106] and concluded that it was not until medieval times that the bow became an established feature of paintings and illustrations.

Since the end of the eighteenth century the tremendous importance of works of art of all periods as source materials for research on instruments has become increasingly recognized. Gerbert,[107] whose publications laid the foundations for the study of medieval music, included several illustrations of musical instruments from medieval codices in his work *De cantu et musica sacra*, while Edmond de Coussemaker[108] illustrated his *Essai sur les instruments de musique au moyen âge* with many more medieval representations of musical instruments of all kinds. Since the second half of the nineteenth century, numerous specialized studies in the history of our bowed instruments have appeared, based for the most part on pictorial source materials. By and large, however, scholars have had to make do with a relatively small number of widely-known illustrations, reproduced from one book to another. The information contained in such works is therefore based on a few fortuitously available illustrations, from which the authors generalize. In consequence, their conclusions have not infrequently been invalidated, or at least modified, by the discovery of fresh pictorial material. 'Particularly with bowed instruments', says Edward Buhle,[109] 'the largest possible number of pictorial examples should be sought, so that the representations can be completed with respect to details, as well as precise dating and the location of the monuments concerned.'

Grillet, Rühlmann, Panum, Schlesinger, and Dräger[110] have contributed much valuable new material towards the history of bowed instruments, while Galpin and Sachs[111] have drawn on hitherto unknown pictorial evidence for their general organological studies. Among the papers left by Buhle[112] are many illustrations of stringed instruments culled from medieval miniatures, which he had no opportunity to assess.

Droysen's dissertation[113] presents a systematic account of medieval chordophones, based on iconographic material, with special emphasis on necked instruments. For future organological research a work of immense value will be the as yet unpublished *Index of Christian Art*, compiled by the Department of Art

Prince le Jeune, *Observations*, pp. 489f. [105] Notably F. Bonanni, *Gabinetto armonico* (Rome, 1722), and F. Bianchini, *De tribus generibus instrumentorum musicae veterum organicae dissertatio* (Rome, 1742). [106] *Observations*, pp. 489ff. [107] M. Gerbert, *De cantu*, Vol. II, Plate XXXII. [108] *Essai*, pp. 147ff. [109] 'Über den Stand der Instrumentenkunde', *Report of the 2nd Congress of the International Music Society* (Leipzig, 1907), p. 221. [110] L. Grillet, *Les ancêtres du Violon*; J. Rühlmann, *Geschichte der Bogeninstrumente*; H. Panum, *Middelalderens Strengeinstrumenter* (Copenhagen, 1915–31); K. Schlesinger, *The Instruments of the modern Orchestra*; H.-H. Dräger, *Die Entwicklung des Streichbogens*. [111] F. W. Galpin, *Old English Instruments*; C. Sachs, *Geist und Werden* and *History of Musical Instruments*; in his *Handbuch* Sachs mentions a great many illustrations, but reproduces only a few. [112] The papers left by E. Buhle are preserved in the Deutsche Staatsbibliothek, Berlin. [113] D. Droysen, *Die Saiteninstrumente des frühen Mittelalters (Halsinstrumente)*

and Archaeology of Princeton University, in which, under various subject-headings, thousands of illustrations bearing on music have been collated from the whole field of Christian Art.

An exhaustive examination of the archaeological evidence led ultimately to the realization that the bow was not used in antiquity. This conclusion was based initially only on illustrations drawn from the Mediterranean area.[114] Recent research, systematically weighing up all the available pictorial evidence from various localities, has reached out further, to embrace the Near, Middle, and Far East as well as the ancient civilization of America. Here, as elsewhere, the evidence points to the existence in early times of only plucked chordophones. Thus in Indian paintings and sculptures – which include a vast number of musical scenes – the bow only figures subsequent to the end of the seventeenth century, a fact which emerges from the detailed study undertaken by Marcel-Dubois[115] and is confirmed by my own survey of Indian sources. Thus all the available pictorial evidence flatly contradicts the theory which regards India as the original home of bowed instruments and attempts to trace the evolution of the bow back into the grey mists of Indian pre-history.

As Kunst's research[116] showed, there is no evidence yet that the bow was used in ancient times either in Indo-China or in the Malay Archipelago. Among all the many representations of musical instruments in the Temple of Borobudur, built in the ninth century A. D., there is not a single example of a bowed instrument. Similarly Arno Huth,[117] whose dissertation discussed the early medieval illustrations of musical instruments in Eastern Turkestan up to the eleventh century, notes that there is no sign that bowed instruments existed during this period, even though the great trade routes linking the Near and Far East traversed the country. An examination and evaluation of Chinese pictorial sources has given the same results. Although at an early date – and more particularly during the T'ang and Sung periods – musical instruments and also larger instrumental ensembles were frequently depicted, not one bowed instrument appears in any source prior to the fourteenth century.[118] Research based on iconographical

(Dissertation, Hamburg, 1959). [114] E. de Coussemaker, *Essai*, p. 150: 'L'archet n'était point connu des peuples de l'antiquité.' [115] C. Marcel-Dubois, *Les instruments de musique de l'Inde ancienne* (Paris, 1941), p. 91. See also K. Schlesinger's article on the bow in the *Encyclopaedia Britannica*, 11th ed. (Cambridge, 1910). [116] J. Kunst, *Hindoe-Javaanische Muziek-Instrumenten speciaal die van Oost-Java* (= *Studien over Javaanische en andere indonesische Muziek*, Part II) (Koninklijk Batav. Genootenschap van Kunsten en Wetenschappen, 1927). On p. 23 Kunst says that the *ravanahasta*, a bowed lute, was originally a plucked instrument. [117] *Die Musikinstrumente Ost-Turkistans bis zum 11. Jahrhundert n. Chr.* (Dissertation, Berlin, 1928). [118] It is clear that bowing spread gradually from Central Asia to China. This view is supported by Farmer in his 'Reciprocal Influence in Music 'twixt the Far and Middle East', *JRAS* (1934), p. 329: 'Perhaps the use of the bowed instruments in China was due to this cultural contact' (with the Middle and Near East); and by Norlind, 'Beiträge zur chinesischen Instrumentengeschichte', *STMf* 15 (1933), p. 76: 'bowed instruments were never included in the court orchestra, and the cultured aristocracy would have none of them. All the bowed instruments were labelled "barbaric" and

evidence seemed therefore to support the theory of the European origin of bowing, since in Asia, as in other continents, illustrations showing the bow appeared
significantly later than in Europe, where there is unambiguous pictorial evidence
from the eleventh century[119] for the existence of different types of bowed instruments.

Most authors of more recent organological studies go appreciably further as
regards dates. From pictorial evidence they attempt to trace the origins of bowing in Europe back to the ninth century, or even earlier. However, their very
early evidence, when put to the test, invariably turns out to be inadmissible, or
else to be wrongly dated.[120] For example, the pen-and-ink drawing from Notker
Labeo's Psalter manuscript,[121] placed by Schlesinger and Abele[122] in the
tenth century, dates from the twelfth, while Buhle's[123] supposedly tenth-century
miniature from the Codex latinus 774 (Leipzig University Library) belongs to
the second half of the eleventh century. Behn's[124] dating of the ivory carving on
the binding of the Lothar Psalter, depicting King David holding a bowed rote,
places it from two to three centuries before its time. Again, the illustration from a
miniature in the Anglo-Saxon Psalter manuscript Cod. Tib. C VI (British Museum), showing a musician with bow and dating from about 1050, has been
wrongly attributed to a tenth-century source by a number of authors.[125] Andersson[126] mistakenly back-dates the eleventh-century illustration of King David,
again with a bowed rote, which appears in an illumination now in the Bibliothèque Nationale in Paris (MS. lat. 1118), to the ninth century. Likewise the
'Lyra' with bow, copied by Gerbert[127] from a manuscript since destroyed by fire
in the Library at St. Blasien, is from the thirteenth century, not from the eighth
or ninth, as several authors have assumed.[128] Similar misconceptions have arisen
in the cases of many other representations, wrongly thought to date from the
second half of the first millenium A. D.

As my own research has shown, not one Western illustration dates from before the beginning of the second millennium. The only illustration of a bow mentioned in the literature, which demonstrably dates from the tenth century, is of
Mozarabic provenance, and shows Oriental influence.[129] There is some doubt as

___

are still classified as such.'   [119] Cf. Chapter II of this book.   [120] I have examined all the literary
descriptions or illustrations of bowed instruments claimed to have originated before the end of
the 10th century. From this vast mass of material, only the most important examples have been
selected for inclusion here.   [121] St. Gall, Stiftsbibliothek, Cod. 21.   [122] *The Instruments of the
Modern Orchestra*, Vol. II, p. 280, and *Die Violine, ihre Geschichte und ihr Bau*, 2nd ed. (Neuburg a.
D., 1874), p. 3.   [123] Op. cit., p. 15, note 3; cf. also Schlesinger, op. cit., p. 401, Fig. 149.   [124] *Mis-
zellen*, III, p. 104; also *Musikleben*, p. 155.   [125] E. g. Behn, *Miszellen*, III, p. 104; Moser, *Das
Streichinstrumentenspiel im Mittelalter*, p. 1; W. Sandys and S. A. Forster, *The History of the Violin*
(London, 1864), p. 51.   [126] *Altnordische Streichinstrumente*, pp. 255 and 259.   [127] *De cantu*, Vol. II,
Plate XXXII, 18.   [128] Among them de Coussemaker, *Essai*, p. 150; Fétis, *Antoine Stradivari*,
p. 32, Fig. 3; Abele, *Die Violine*, p. 3; L. Grillet, *Les ancêtres du Violon*, p. 24; H. Riemann, *Präludien und Studien*, Vol. II (Leipzig, 1901), 'Zur Geschichte der Instrumente', p. 218; K. Schlesinger, op. cit., p. 282; W. Sandys and S. A. Forster, op. cit., p. 51,   [129] This illustration is

2*

to the date of a much-cited bas-relief on an ivory Byzantine casket in the Museo Nazionale, Florence, Coll. Carrand, No. 26,[130] carved either in the tenth century or in the first half of the eleventh. This Byzantine illustration, however, comes from outside the Western cultural zone. Both these examples, together with several hitherto unknown Byzantine miniatures showing bowed instruments,[131] will be discussed fully elsewhere in this work.

Almost all the more recent studies on the history of our bowed instruments set great store by an illustration in the Utrecht Psalter of A. D. 860,[132] thought to be one of the earliest proofs of the use of the bow. Moser[133] describes this illustration as 'the first undoubted example' of a bowed instrument; while Behn[134] hails it as 'one of the most significant pieces of evidence in the whole history of instrument-making,' and adds: 'It is the first example of a bowed instrument in the field of European musical practice, and opens a new chapter in the history of music.' Sachs, in his *Handbuch der Musikinstrumentenkunde*,[135] also credited this illustration with some value, as being the first representation of a European bowed instrument – this despite the objections of Schlesinger,[136] who took the so-called bow to be a long sword. The authors of the article 'Fidel' in the encyclopedia *Die Musik in Geschichte und Gegenwart*,[137] and Struve in his recent work on the origins and evolution of bowed instruments,[138] refer to this same miniature.[139] A striking feature of this pen-and-ink drawing from the Utrecht Psalter is the inordinate length – in relation to the musician – of the line which runs obliquely across the long-necked, spade-shaped, stringed instrument, and which is interpreted as a bow. To avoid any doubt being cast on this thesis, every reproduction of this piece of pictorial evidence in the books mentioned shows only part of the complete illustration, cutting the alleged bow down to a third of its total length. It seems improbable that the instrument would be bowed in the position shown, quite apart from the fact that the musician is additionally burdened with a triangular harp, which would greatly hamper his bowing action.

from Manuscript Hh 58 in the *Biblioteca Nacional*, Madrid; cf. pp. 29 f. [130] Cf. p. 36, note 77. [131] These illustrations are fully discussed in Chapter II, pp. 35 ff. [132] University Library, Utrecht, Script. eccles. 484 (Latin Psalter Manuscript), fol. 63 v. The illustrations contained in this manuscript are available in a classic publication by E. T. de Wald, *The Illustrations of the Utrecht Psalter* (Princeton, 1932); cf. also A. Goldschmidt's earlier publication: 'Der Utrecht-Psalter', *Repertorium für Kunstwissenschaft*, Vol. XV (1892). [133] Op. cit., p. 1. [134] *Musikleben*, pp. 162 f. [135] 1st ed., p. 170. [136] Op. cit., p. 347. Galpin, *Textbook*, p. 138, also doubts whether it is in fact a bow. Andersson, in *The Bowed-Harp, A Study in the History of early Musical Instruments* (London, 1930), p. 26, considers the possibility that the man may be a blind musician, using the stick to feel his way along. [137] H. Hickmann, B. Dohme Siedersbeck, and H.-H. Dräger. The illustration (No. 4) bears the caption '9th-century musician with harp, fiddle and large bow, taken from the Utrecht Psalter (*c*. 860)'. [138] *Prozess formirovanija viol i skripok* (Moscow, 1959). [139] Cf. also the following quotations: D. J. Rittmeyer-Iselin, *Das Rebec*, p. 210: 'The earliest evidence of a western bowed instrument occurs in the so-called Utrecht Psalter'. P. Werland 'Musikinstrumente der spätromanischen Zeit', *ZfM* (1938), p. 1323: 'Probably the earliest illustration of a bow is that in the Utrecht Psalter.' See also Kinsky, *Geschichte der Musik in Bildern* (Leipzig,

Furthermore, the illustrator has drawn the 'bow' lying athwart the strings be-tween the tailpiece and the bridge. It should be said that this same long-necked stringed instrument appears in several other illustrations in the same manuscript,[140] when it is invariably held across the player's body and plucked, not bowed. What we have here, then, is clearly a type of plucked, long-necked lute. Since the illustrator of the Utrecht Psalter adheres very closely to the spirit of the text, and interprets the Psalms for the most part verse by verse, it seems advisable to examine the Psalter text in order to throw some light on this 'bowed instru-ment' drawing – a course of action hitherto nearly always neglected in organo-logical literature. The illustration in question refers to Psalm 108,[141] verse 8: 'Exsultabo et dividam sicimam et convallem tabernaculorum dimetiar.' Accor-dingly the man on the left-hand side of the drawing, identified as the Psalmist by his two musical instruments,[142] is in the process of measuring the surround-ings with a long measuring pole. The interpretation of this long object as a piece of measuring apparatus is further confirmed by the presence, on the right-hand side of the same illustration, of a second man handling a similar rod, which in this instance cannot possibly be mistaken for a bow, since he carries no stringed instrument. Thus the most frequently quoted piece of early medieval evidence for the use of the bow is revealed as a case of mistaken identity, arising from the fact that the illustration was explained and interpreted with reference only to itself.

A number of other illustrations allegedly representing bowed instruments must also be rejected, since a closer examination of the source material has shown that the 'bow' was really non-existent. Mistakes of this type have occurred primarily because almost every author engaged in instrumental research has had to be satisfied with poor quality reproductions or – even more often – with inaccurate sketches of the objects in question, which frequently distorted various details or omitted them altogether. One such example is an illustration from Albert Lavignac's *Encyclopédie de la Musique*,[143] representing a musician, and copied from an unfinished Hittite relief from Alaca Hüyük.[144] The drawing shows a man, holding in his left hand a long-necked, stringed instrument without pegs, while in his right he wields a bow. The curious position of the bow, under-neath or side-on to the instrument, is explained away[145] as 'un simple effet de la perspective orientale,' designed to avoid obscuring the instrument with the bow. However, a comparison of this copy with a good photograph of the original reveals that the illustrator not only changed and added to the picture in various ways,[146] but in addition totally misunderstood the instrument as represented. In reality the musician holds a plectrum in his right hand, secured to the instru-

1929), p. 32, illustration 2.   [140] See de Wald, op. cit.   [141] By Hebrew reckoning Psalm 108, in the Vulgate Psalm CVII.   [142] This refers to the psaltery and harp mentioned in Psalm 108, verse 3.   [143] *Première partie*, p. 52, Fig. 105.   [144] Various photographs of this illustration (dat-ing from the 15th or 14th century B. C.) have been published, for example, by Kinsky, op. cit., p. 1, illustration 5; Sachs, *Geist und Werden*, illustration 146; Behn, *Musikleben*, illustration 90; M. Wegner, article 'Hethitische Musik', in *MGG*, where further pictorial evidence is given. [145] Lavignac, op. cit., p. 53.   [146] For instance, the musician's head was completed by the illustra-

ment by a ribbon, as was the case with most of the ancient Egyptian spike-lutes.[147] Since the player is walking, the ribbons dangling from the neck of the instrument flutter out behind him, that is to say towards the right-hand side of the picture, as does the plectrum's retaining string.

Yet another example of an illustration misconstrued because of technically inadequate pictorial material is the Coptic fresco painting from the Egyptian monastery of Baouît (6th to 8th centuries), quoted by Kathleen Schlesinger[148] as 'the earliest representation of a bow'. She based her assertion on the very bad reproduction published by Clédat,[149] and interprets one of the lines on the clothing and the background as a bow. Subsequent investigations have proved beyond doubt that here, too, the instrument represented was clearly a plucked instrument.

The position today

The evaluation of ancient and medieval pictorial source material, the results of ethnomusicological research, and the considerations of early literary evidence and its philological interpretation, can today all be brought to bear on organo-logical problems.[150] This means that from now on research can stand on the broadest possible basis, and can take a real step forward. Nevertheless, almost all recent works on the subject hold to the common view that the origins of bowing are still totally obscure, and that, despite the numerous specialist studies devoted to the problem, Buhle's[151] outspoken comment at the Second Congress of the International Music Society in 1906 still holds good: 'the origin of bowed instruments remains an unsolved problem.' Thus in 1954 Behn wrote:[152] 'Few questions in musical history have stirred up such lively controversy as that of the true homeland of bowed instruments, or, more precisely, the origin of the bow . . . in all honesty we must allow that this most important problem is as yet unresolved, and will remain so if we continue to apply the same old methods to the material now available.' Matzke[153] and Farmer[154] share this view, as does Handschin:[155]

---

tor, and the shape of the instrument altered. [147] Illustrations in Hickmann, *Miscellanea musico-logica*, II. 'Sur l'accordage des instruments à cordes', *Extrait des Annales du Service des antiquités de l'Égypte*, Vol. XLVIII (Cairo, 1948), pp. 652 and 660, and *Miscellanea musicologica*, VI. 'Quelques précurseurs égyptiens du luth court et du luth échancré', *Extrait des Annales du Service des antiquités de l'Égypte*, Vol. XLIX (Cairo, 1949), p. 442; Kinsky, op. cit., p. 5, illustration 2. [148] Article on the bow in the *Encyclopaedia Britannica*. [149] J. Clédat, 'Le Monastère et la Nécropole de Baouît', *Mémoires de l'Institut français d'archéologie orientale du Caire*, Vol. XII (1904), Chapter 18, Plate LXIV (2). [150] Today we have the added resources of musical technology, which deals with the material and function of instruments. We also have historical research into the relationship between musical instruments and different social strata. [151] 'Über den Stand der Instrumentenkunde', p. 222. [152] *Musikleben*, p. 165. [153] H. Matzke, *Unser technisches Wissen*, p. 243: 'Even in professional circles uncertainty or ignorance still largely obscure not only the pre-history and early development of the violin, but also important aspects of its classical period and contemporary potentialities.' [154] 'Evidence for the time and place of the rise of the bow as a means of producing sound from strings is still as unreliable as it was in the 19th century'. *Grove's Dictionary*, 5th ed. (London, 1954), p. 854. [155] *Musikgeschichte im Überblick*, p. 198.

'The origin of bowing is still controversial, some locating it in the Orient, others supporting the "Nordic" theory.' 'The writer feels,' says Bessaraboff,[156] 'that it is too early to assign any definite chronology to the origin of the bow.' 'A mysterious darkness still obscures the origins of our bowed instruments' writes Nef,[157] a statement echoed by Schultz:[158] 'If we look back on the history of European bowed instruments, we lose the trail in the early Middle Ages, when a real darkness descends.' As Kinsky[159] puts it: 'Of all the problems posed by instrumental science, the early history of bowed instruments is one of the most controversial, and has by no means been finally settled.' Von Schlosser[160] stresses that 'the origins of those musical instruments that have so boldly assumed the leading rôle in our modern instrumental music – that is to say, the bowed instruments – still lie hidden in the mists of uncertainty, never fully dissipated. Their history is one of the most complex chapters in the history of organology.'

Postscript

This chapter summarizes the position at the time the original German edition of this book was published (1964). Several contributions to the subject have appeared since then and references to these have been inserted in the Bibliography. They deal with various topics, but do not I believe affect our view of the problem. In the course of my own research I have come across further illustrative material, mainly from the Byzantine area: details are given in the list of pictorial sources on pp. 164-8. This material too has confirmed rather than modified my previous conclusions.

[156] *Ancient European Musical Instruments*, note 552.   [157] K. Nef, *Geschichte unserer Musikinstrumente*, 2nd ed. (Basle, 1949), p. 68.   [158] H. Schultz, *Instrumentenkunde*, 2nd ed. (Leipzig, 1954), p. 106. [159] *Musikhistorisches Museum von Wilhelm Heyer*, Catalogue, Vol. II, p. 309; see also D. J. Rittmeyer-Iselin, *Das Rebec*, p. 210.   [160] J. v. Schlosser, *Unsere Musikinstrumente*, p. 14.

II

THE EARLIEST TRACES OF THE USE OF THE
BOW IN EUROPE AND THE EAST

ISLAM

The first evidence for the use of the bow

Scholars attempting to trace the development of the bow back to its origins find that the trail peters out early in the tenth century A. D. in the Near East. At that period Islamic civilization was at its height, under the rule of the Abbasids. In almost every sphere of science, technology, and art the East showed its superiority to the medieval West. Medieval Arabic sources reveal advances and discoveries in technology, as well as in medicine, chemistry, mathematics, astronomy, and optics. Arab geographers had acquired an astonishing knowledge of the world, journeying far and wide in the course of the tenth century. It was also the golden age of Arabic poetry, philosophy, and music, and it was this period which saw, along with the emergence of new musical instruments, the first use of the bow.[1]

As far as may be judged from the available sources, the area of distribution of bowing towards the end of the first millennium corresponded essentially to the area of the two great near-Eastern states, the Empire of Islam and the Empire of Byzantium, which were at the height of their powers around this time and united the most varied peoples, from Spain and North Africa to Transoxiana. From the beginning of the tenth century, isolated references in Arabic literature indicate with certainty that bowing was known during this period throughout the Arabic-speaking regions. This is, to date, the earliest known literary evidence that the bow was in use. Nearly all the references occur in the writings of men who were both competent musicians and outstanding scholars, so that the reliability of their assertions is beyond doubt, especially since the various sources complement and corroborate one another.

The first reference to bowing occurs in the *Kitāb al-mūsīqi al-kabīr* of al-Fārābī,[2] one of the most significant medieval works on musical theory. Among

[1] H. Ley, *Studie zur Geschichte des Materialismus im Mittelalter*, Berlin 1957, pp. 21 ff. (on the economic structure of Saracen feudalism); W. F. Semjonow, *Geschichte des Mittelalters*, Berlin 1952, pp. 103 ff.; G. E. Grunebaum, *Medieval Islam, A Study in Cultural Orientation*, 2nd ed. (Chicago, 1953). [2] Al-Fārābī lived roughly from 870 to 950. Cf. Farmer's article 'Al-Fārābī' in *MGG*. On the initial stages of bowed playing in Arabia, Farmer's valuable essay 'The origin of the Arabian lute and rebec', *JRAS* (1930), pp. 775 ff. is particularly informative. This essay is also included in *Studies in Oriental Musical Instruments* (London, 1931), pp. 91 ff. The different types of rabāb and their structural peculiarities are discussed in detail in the *Enzyklopaedie des*

other things, he classifies musical instruments according to their method of sound production.[3] He deals first with those chordophones the strings of which are caused to vibrate by plucking. Next he lists instruments where sound is produced by blowing; and last of all he tells of certain instruments 'the strings of which are made to sound by rubbing them with other strings (*autār*), or with some material resembling strings'.[4] This unmistakable proof of the bow's existence, dating from the first half of the tenth century, is confirmed by a reference in the *Kitāb al-Shifā'*, written by the famous scholar Ibn Sīnā,[5] who lived about A. D. 1000 and was known in Europe under the name of Avicenna. He, too, writes of instruments 'the strings of which are not struck [that is, plucked with a plectrum], but stroked'.[6] Ibn Sīnā cites the *rabāb* as an example of this kind, thus demonstrating beyond doubt that from the tenth century onwards it was a bowed instrument. In both these texts the verb *jarra*, meaning 'to glide' or 'to sweep lightly across' is used to describe the process of bowing, so that there can be very little doubt about their interpretation. Medieval European theorists, who based their work on al-Fārābī and took over his classification of musical instruments with its subdivision of the chordophones into plucked and bowed instruments, use the verb *tangere* or *trahere* to convey the action of bowing, and *pellere* for plucking.[7]

Another early reference to the use of the bow in the Arab-speaking world occurs in a treatise by Ibn Zaila,[8] a pupil of Ibn Sīnā. Here again musical instruments are sub-divided according to their sound; a distinction is made between

Islam (Leyden, Leipzig, 1936) in the article '*rabāb*'.   [3] E. A. Beichert, *Die Wissenschaft der Musik bei al Fārābī* (Dissertation, Freiburg im Breisgau, 1930, printed in Regensburg, 1931), pp. 34 and 35, reprinted in the *KmJb* (1932), summarizes the sharply-differentiating classification of musical instruments in al-Fārābī's writings.   [4] R. d'Erlanger, *La Musique Arabe*, Vol. I (Paris, 1930), p. 166, translates this passage as follows: 'Enfin certains instruments comportent des cordes que l'on frotte au moyen d'autres cordes ou de quelque chose de similaire.' Farmer renders it in English thus: '. . . upon whose strings are drawn other strings' (*JRAS*, 1930, p. 778).   [5] The classification of musical instruments by Ibn Sīnā is discussed in M. el Hefny's *Ibn Sīnā's Musiklehre* (Dissertation, Berlin, 1931), p. 43.   [6] This statement is translated by d'Erlanger, op. cit., II, p. 234: 'D'autres instruments sont à cordes et à touches, mais au lieu de les percuter, on traîne sur elles (un archet), tel est le cas du rebāb.' In the previous sentences Ibn Sīnā had been dealing with plucked instruments, which he classified according to morphological considerations, into instruments with or without a neck or fingerboard, and in the second category he makes a further distinction between instruments whose strings are attached to the belly of the resonator and those whose strings are stretched over a frame.   [7] Domenicus Gundissalinus, in his *De divisione philosophiae* (*c.* 1150), observes that sound is drawn from stringed instruments 'tactu et pulsu'. New edition by L. Baur in *Beiträge zur Geschichte der Philosophie des Mittelalters*, IV, 2.3, (Münster, 1903). According to Gerson, there were three ways of making the strings on chordophones sound: 'aut in rotatu, ut in symphonia; aut tractu aut retractu, sicut in viella aut rebella; sive cum impulso vel impulsivo quodam tractu cum unguibus vel plectro, cum virgula, ut in cithara et guiterna, liuto, psalterio . . .' Quoted in W. Sandys and S. A. Forster, op. cit., p. 25.   [8] Ibn Zaila died in 1048. The relevant passage in his treatise (BM. MS. Or. 2361, fol. 235 v), in which he discusses the classification of musical instruments, is translated by H. G. Farmer in *JRAS*

those in which the sound generated by striking or plucking ceases as soon as action ceases, and those in which the sound can be prolonged at will (*mumtadd*)[9] and joined together (*muttaṣil*). The lute and harp belong to the first group, while the second includes the *rabāb* and two wind instruments, the *nāy* and *surnāy*. Another passage in the same treatise[10] states that it was the bow which lengthened or connected separate notes played on the *rabāb*. Thus the author indicates that the *rabāb* was played by bowing its strings.

A similar distinction between instruments with 'detached' or 'connected' sound occurs in the Treatise of the Brothers of Purity, Ikhwān al-Ṣafā,[11] dating from the second half of the tenth century.[12] As examples of instruments producing detached sounds – 'between the strokes of which there is a perceptible silence' – plucked chordophones and idiophones are mentioned, while the second group again includes, among others, the *nāy* and the *rabāb*. The historian Ibn Khaldūn in his *Introduction to History*[13] comments on the different ways of playing the stringed instruments he mentions: *barbiton*, *rabāb*, and *qānūn*. 'The strings are set in motion either with a wooden plectrum, or with a string, made fast to each end of a bow, with which one strokes [the strings of the instrument] after rubbing it with pitch or resin. The sounds are accentuated by varying the pressure exerted by the bowing hand or by moving from one string to another.' We learn further that the strings of the instrument were stopped with the left hand, and hence that the right hand wielded the bow.

Summarizing this evidence we may with some certainty conclude that as early as the first half of the tenth century the region of Islamic culture was familiar with the use of the bow to prolong notes and connect them to each other on stringed instruments, in particular on the *rabāb*.

The rabāb and other instruments

The works mentioned make scant reference to the shape, construction, or tuning of the early Arabic bowed instruments. In this respect the most valuable single source of information is al-Fārābī's description of the *rabāb*,[14] given in his

---

(1930), p. 779.   [9] The participle *mumtadd* also means 'extended' or 'stretched'.   [10] Fol. 235 r.
[11] Quoted from the German translation of this essay in F. Dieterici, *Die Propädeutik der Araber im 10. Jahrhundert* (Berlin, 1865), p. 110. An important correction of this German edition is made by H. G. Farmer in *JRAS* (1930), p. 778, note 4. More recent works relating to this treatise include: A. Awa, *L'esprit critique des 'frères de la Pureté'* (Dissertation, Paris, 1946); E. L. Fackenheim, 'The Conception of Substance in the Philosophy of the Ikhwān aṣ-Ṣafā', *Medieval Studies*, V (Toronto, 1943), pp. 115–22; J. Karam, 'Las ideas filosóficas de los "Hermanos de la Pureza"', *Ciencia Tomista* (1937), pp. 398–412.   [12] M. Stern, 'The authorship of the epistles of the Ikhwān aṣ-Ṣafā', *Islamic Culture*, XX (1946), pp. 367 ff., and XXI, 1947, pp. 403 ff., concludes that this essay must have been written around the middle of the 10th century.   [13] F. Rosenthal provides an English translation in the Bollingen Series XLIII; *Ibn Khaldūn, The Muqaddimah, An Introduction to History*, Vol. II (New York, 1958), p. 397.   [14] R. d'Erlanger, op. cit., Vol. I, pp. 277 ff.

Kitāb al-mūsīqī al-kabīr. From this we learn that structurally the *rabāb* corresponded to the Khurāsān *tunbūr*, a narrow, plucked instrument with a long neck and pear-shaped body, originating in Central Asia. According to al-Fārābī's account, the strings on both instruments were attached to an end pin. In contrast to its plucked counterparts among the chordophones, the *rabāb* had no frets, so that performers on the bowed instruments presumably needed greater skill in fingering and a clearer conception of pitch. From what al-Fārābi says, it would seem that the *rabāb* was generally strung with one, or sometimes two, strings, but was only complete when it had four strings. In this final form the strings were arranged in courses, that is to say in pairs. Sometimes both strings in each pair were tuned in unison, so that the only difference from the two-stringed *rabāb* was the doubling of the strings.

In the early part of the tenth century the tuning of the *rabāb* was still carried out in very different ways. According to al-Fārābī[15] the augmented second was favoured as the interval between the two strings or pairs of strings, although tuning at the major third or diminished fifth (augmented fourth) is mentioned in the same source. These tunings, which appear so unusual to us, must clearly have sprung from the folk-musical practice of Central Asia, and corresponded to their tonal system and conception of consonance.[16] The plucked instruments of Central Asia – for instance the Khurāsān *tunbūr* – were tuned in a similar fashion in the tenth century. The Arabs, however, generally tuned their lutes in fourths. In order to facilitate playing of *rabāb* and *'ūd* (lute) in consort, al-Fārābī recommends tuning the *rabāb's* strings in perfect fourths or fifths[17] – a suggestion which, as later sources proved, was quickly adopted and widely used. For instance, Jerome of Moravia writes:[18] 'Est autem rubeba musicum instrumentum habens solum duas chordas sono distantes a se per diapente. Quod quidem, sicut et viella, cum arcu tangitur.'

Unfortunately, the Arabic literature of this period relating to music and musical instruments contains no information about how they were held or played, nor any more specific details regarding structural features of bowed instruments. Nor does Oriental pictorial art of the early Middle Ages offer help. It is only from the thirteenth century on that we find isolated illustrations of bowed instruments in the work of Islamic artists, as for instance on a thirteenth-century bronze bowl,[19] and on Turkestani, Persian, and Indian miniatures of the fifteenth and sixteenth centuries.[20]

Ibn Sīnā testifies that the rabāb was already a bowed instrument in the 10th century. [15] R. d'Erlanger, op. cit., Vol. I, p. 280. [16] These tunings were purely modal, and are in keeping with the medieval modal systems of Central Asia, in which augmented intervals were used. On the seven Central Asiatic modes and their origins cf. S. Kishibe in *Shigaku Zasshi* (1946), No. 9. [17] Al-Fārābī considers that a rabāb tuned in seconds or minor thirds is suitable only for accompanying the Khurāsān *tunbūr* (d'Erlanger, op. cit., Vol. I, p. 285). [18] S. M. Cserba, *Hieronymus de Moravia*, p. 289. [19] Farmer, 'Arabian Musical Instruments on a Thirteenth Century Bronze Bowl', in *Oriental Studies, Mainly Musical* (London, 1953). [20] Illustrations of Central Asiatic bowed instruments from the 15th to 17th centuries appear in the following publications: E. Kühnel, *Miniatur-*

The reason for the absence of musical scenes in early Islamic art[21] is that the tenets of Islam discouraged any form of illustration of actual objects or living things, in order to prevent Muslims from lapsing into idolatry.[22] By contrast, Mozarabic manuscripts dating from the ninth, tenth, and eleventh centuries in Spain not infrequently contain illuminations, sometimes including musical scenes.[23] These miniatures combine unmistakably romanesque and oriental stylistic elements,[24] and owe their development to the peculiar social and philosophical situation in which Spain found herself at the end of the tenth century, as a bridgehead of the Arab Empire in Europe. Although the population of Spain adopted Arabic during the centuries of Moorish domination and came under the influence of Islamic civilization, it clung obstinately to the Christian faith – especially in the north – and was not subject therefore to those Muslim precepts which sought to prevent the execution and the spread of illustrations such as these.

malerei im islamischen Orient (Berlin, 1922), pp. 39 and 94; Ph. W. Schulz, *Die persisch-islamische Miniaturmalerei* (Leipzig, 1914), Vol. II, Plates 65 and 80; A. K. Coomaraswamy, *Les Miniatures orientales* (Paris, 1929) (*Ars asiatica* XIII), Plates XXX and LXVI; A. Grohmann and Th. W. Arnold, *Denkmäler islamischer Buchkunst* (Munich, 1929), Plate 80; H. von Glasenapp, 'Die Literatur Indiens von ihren Anfängen bis zur Gegenwart', *Handbuch der Literaturwissenschaft*, ed. O. Watzel (Athenaion, 1929), Plate III; K. Holter, 'Die Galen-Handschrift und die Makamen des Hariri der Wiener Nationalbibliothek', *Jahrbuch der Kunsthistorischen Sammlungen in Wien*, New Series, Vol. XI (Vienna, 1937), Plate VI, 1; A. Sakkisian, *La miniature persane du 12ᵉ au 17ᵉ siècle* (Paris, 1929), Plate 144; E. de Lorey, 'Behzād', in *Ars islamica* 4 (1937), pp. 122ff., Fig. 3; Mehmet Aga-Oglu, 'Preliminary Notes on some Persian Illustrated Manuscripts', *Ars islamica* I (1934), pp. 183ff., Fig. 10b; R. H. Pinder-Wilson, 'Three illustrated manuscripts', *Ars orientalis* II (1957), Fig. 18 and Fig. 20; E. Blochet, *Les Peintures des Manuscrits orientaux de la Bibliothèque Nationale* (Paris, 1914–20), Plate LX; B. W. Robinson, *A Descriptive Catalogue of the Persian Paintings in the Bodleian Library* (Oxford, 1958), Plate XV; J. Strzygowski, *Asiatische Miniaturmalerei* (Klagenfurt, 1932), Plate 5 (15). [21] At the end of the 10th century Arab-Islamic art was limited to abstract ornamentation – what we usually describe as arabesques. 'Diverting the energies of painters and sculptors to the ancillary field of decorative art had one great advantage, namely that the distinction between "free" and "applied" art, which arose in the West, did not develop here. All art was, and remained, craft'. E. Kühnel, *Kunst und Kultur der arabischen Welt* (Heidelberg, Berlin, Magdeburg, 1943), p. 14. [22] Two works should be mentioned here: 'Alī al 'Inānī, *Das Bilderverbot im Islam* (Berlin, 1919); and Ahmed Mousa, *Zur Geschichte der islamischen Buchmalerei* (Cairo, 1931), pp. 15ff. On pp. 15 and 16 of the latter, the author quotes the following maxims, ascribed to Mahomet: 'Angels never enter a house that contains a dog or pictures', and 'On the day of resurrection, God's greatest punishment will fall on the pictorial artist'. The artist's task was to translate his impressions of nature into ornamentation, and thus give them new worth. On the other hand, the frescoes in the little castle of Qusair 'Amra, built in Umayyad times, and the murals of Samarra, show that the ban on pictorial art was by no means universally observed. [23] Mozarabic – that is to say 'Arabianized' – is the usual term applied to the culture of Christians of the Iberian Peninsula under Moorish rule. They were subjected to the influence of Islamic civilization, but were exempt from the Islamic veto on pictures. [24] These questions are dealt with in particular by M. Churruca, *Influjo oriental en los temas iconográficos de la miniatura española, siglos X al XII* (Madrid, 1939). Cf. also W. Neuss: *Die Apokalypse des hl. Johannes in*

A particularly valuable source for the early history of bowing is the Apocalypse manuscript Hh 58 in the Biblioteca Nacional, Madrid, with a commentary by a Spanish monk, Beatus of Liébana.[25] This manuscript was written and illustrated *c.* 920–30, in Spain, probably in the monastery of San Millán de Colloga, at a time when Moorish supremacy was at its peak, under the Caliph 'Abd al-Raḥmān III.[26] The strong Arabic influence that permeated the Iberian peninsula in the tenth century is firmly stamped on the miniatures of the manuscript.[27] Among them (fol. 127r) is a coloured drawing (Plate I) showing seven angels and four musicians with bowed instruments. This illustration refers to Chapter 15, verses 1–4 of the Apocalypse, where one of John's visions is described: 'and there appeared before him in the heavens seven angels with seven plagues, and holy ones "stantes super mare vitreum habentes citharas dei et cantantes canticum Moysi et agni".' Whereas the earliest illustrated Beatus manuscripts represent the *citharae dei* as plucked instruments, this copy, dating from the first part of the tenth century, shows for the first time bowed chordophones.[28] The instruments, which are represented as remarkably large, are played with an almost semi-circular bow. As far as we can tell from the drawing, the three strings are attached to sagittal pegs (that is, in the median, longitudinal, antero-posterior plane), protruding from a circular peg-disk. The flat rectangle at the lower end of the strings is probably a bridge or a tailpiece. The instrument's most striking features are its long, slender neck, sharply defined in relation to the body, the shape of the resonator, and the shape of the bow itself. Not only the style and technique of this miniature, but also the instrument represented, are Oriental in origin, for here, as in most early Mozarabic and Byzantine illustrations, we have a type of instrument which had barely established itself in Europe, and was probably not therefore a product of Western culture. The artist who painted the miniatures for this Spanish manuscript seems to have gone out of his way to draw attention to the process of bowing, as if representing something new and special in this musical scene, whereas the stopping of the strings is treated casually and with no attention to detail. The hand engaged in fingering is shown, not on

der altspanischen und altchristlichen Bibelillustration (Münster/Westphalia, 1931).   [25] The title of the manuscript is *S. Beati de liebana explanatio in apocalypsis S. Johannis*.   [26] This manuscript can be very accurately dated from palaeographic data. Cf. W. Neuss, *Die Apokalypse des hl. Johannes in der altspanischen und altchristlichen Bibelillustration* (Münster/Westphalia, 1931), text volume, p. 25 f.   [27] The Beatus manuscripts — among the most important sources of old Spanish illuminations — comprise a great number of transcripts of a commentary on the Revelation of St. John and the prophecy of Daniel. This commentary is the work of a Spanish monk, Beatus of Liébana, and dates from the second half of the 8th century (*c.* 776). Cf. Neuss, 'Probleme der christlichen Kunst im maurischen Spanien', *Neue Beiträge zur Kunstgeschichte des 1. Jahrtausends* (Baden-Baden, 1954), pp. 249 ff., esp. p. 254.   [28] Cf. H. A. Sander, 'Beatus of Liébana', *Apocalypsin* (Rome, 1930). A brief summary of the musical illustrations in Spanish-Mozarabic miniatures is given in E. Serrano Fatigati, *Instrumentos musicos en las miniaturas de los codices españoles, siglos X al XIII*, Discurso (Madrid, Academia de Belles Artes, 1901), Cf. also W. Giese, 'Maurische Musikinstrumente im mittelalterlichen Spanien', *Iberia, Zeitschrift für spanische und portugiesische Aus-*

the fingerboard, but beside it, and the sketchily drawn third string is simply left out on the fingerboard. Nevertheless this miniature shows clearly and unequivocally that by about A. D. 930 the bow was known and used in regions influenced by Arabic culture, to excite sound on stringed instruments. This bears out the statements of al-Fārābī reported above which also date from this time.

A more controversial illustration is a frequently reproduced miniature (Plate 2) from another Mozarabic Beatus manuscript, written in the Benedictine Abbey of Santo Domingo de Silos, near Burgos, between 1091 and 1109.[29] A minstrel, prancing along in high buskins, is here seen playing a somewhat more manageable type of bowed instrument, holding it in the typically Oriental position, that is to say vertically in front of his body. Again it has a slim neck, similar to that in the instruments previously described. In place of the round peg-disk, however, the five pegs are fixed in a cross-piece running at right angles to the neck.[30] For each peg a corresponding string – five in all – is shown running down the elliptical body, although only one is continued up the neck of the instrument. Judging by the stylized illustrations executed by Mozarabic copyists of the Beatus manuscripts, who frequently attempted to give a front and side view of objects simultaneously, it is probable that this cross-piece with its upright pegs is a cross-section of a round peg-disk with sagittal pegs jutting out in front, while the neck and body of the instrument are shown from the front.[31] If this were so, this fiddle would be in line with those just discussed, and with other, variously depicted stringed instruments found in Spanish miniatures of the thirteenth century.

In addition to these long-necked chordophones, old Spanish illustrations occasionally show the boat-shaped *rabāb*,[32] which was taken over from the Arabs. This instrument, usually known to Europeans as the *rebec*, has its peg-box bent sharply backwards at right angles, with laterally inserted pegs. This type of instrument was largely confined to the Western Islamic area, where it was played in the Eastern way, propped on the player's knee and bowed with a strongly arched bow. The evidence points to the presence of this instrument in Spain and Sicily, the two bridgeheads of the Arabic Empire in Europe, from about the

landskunde, Vol. III (1925), pp. 55 ff. [29] British Museum, MS. Add. 11695, fol. 86; cf. Meyer Schapiro, 'From Mozarabic to Romanesque in Silos', *The Art Bulletin* (December, 1939), Vol. XXI, No. 4, pp. 313 ff. [30] This type of instrument is often shown as a plucked instrument in tenth- and eleventh century Mozarabic miniatures. Cf. J. Dominguez Bordona, *Exposición de Códices Miniados Españoles*, Catalogue (Madrid, 1929), Plates 5, 15, and 18; also Neuss, *Die Apokalypse des hl. Johannes in der altspanischen und altchristlichen Bibelillustration* (Münster/Westphalia, 1931), Plates I, LXVI, CXI, CXLI, and M. Churruca, *Influjo oriental en los temas iconográficos de la miniatura española, siglos X al XII* (Madrid, 1939), Plate XIV, 2, 3, Plate XXII v, 3, Plate XXV v, 1, 2, 4. [31] On p. 274 of his *History*, Sachs also comes to the conclusion that the arrangement of the pegs as represented in these Mozarabic miniatures cannot have corresponded to reality. G. Schünemann: 'Die Musikinstrumente der 24 Alten', *AfMf* I, pp. 42 ff., has examined the structure of these instruments in greater detail. [32] For more detailed information relating to this instrument see Farmer's article '*rabāb*' (3) in the *Enzyklopaedie des Islam*, Vol. III (Leyden

tenth or eleventh century. Particularly clear illustrations of the *rabāb* played 'a gamba' may be seen in the frescoes of the Capella Palatina in Palermo,[33] where the whole range of Arabic instruments of that era are represented (Plate 21); and in the Aragonese reliquary triptych in the Academia de la Historia in Madrid.

From the eleventh century, pear-shaped and elliptical fiddles, supported at the shoulder, became increasingly numerous in Spain. Illustrations showing pear-shaped bowed instruments occur in the *Libro de los Reyes*, fol. 141, in the Biblioteca Provincial at Burgos, on eleventh-century Catalan miniatures,[34] and on early Spanish portal sculptures. The Beatus manuscript Sig. 33 in the Academia de la Historia in Madrid provides a particularly interesting link in the chain of pictorial evidence. It originated in the tenth century, in the Monastery of San Millán, and was probably illustrated in the first half of the eleventh century. The painting shows a mixture of Mozarabic and romanesque influences. The theme of the miniature from fol. 177 (Plate 3) is taken from the substance of Chapter 14 of the Apocalypse, John's vision of the Lamb of God on Mount Zion. The painter conveys the voice of Heaven, likened in the text to the sound of the *cithara*, by means of four haloed fiddlers. The short-necked instruments with their elliptical bodies, slightly waisted, are unique among the instruments of that time. Further, their position differs from that shown in illustrations so far cited. Here the fiddles are held in a variety of positions – though each permits an easy bowing action – against the upper part of the body. Some idea of the diversity of shapes and sizes of the instruments used in medieval Spain may be obtained from a poem composed by the Archpriest of Hita, Juan Ruiz,[35] in which he mentions three different bowed instruments (*rabé morisco, rabé gritador* and *vihuela de arco*); and from the lavishly illustrated manuscript of the *Cantigas de Santa Maria*, dating from the second half of the thirteenth century.[36] This Codex contains six miniatures showing various types of bowed instruments.

Instruments of the Kamanja type

Although they made no perceptible impression on the development of Western musical instruments, Oriental bowed instruments of the *kamanja* type (Persian *kamāncha*)[37] were widely used in the Islamic Empire. If the editor[38] of Abū Bakr Ibn al-Faqīh's geography book is right in his emendation of the Arabic

and Leipzig, 1936).   [33] This mural was executed early in the 12th century.   [34] Bibliothèque Nationale, Paris, Ms. lat. 11550, fol. 7 v.   [35] See C. Engel, *Researches*, pp. 85 and 121, and G. Reese, *Music in the Middle Ages* (New York, 1940), p. 385.   [36] Madrid, Escorial Library, MS. T-i-I; illustrations in J. Ribera, *La Musica de las Cantigas* (Madrid, 1922).   [37] These bowed instruments, which belong to the genus of the spike lute, have a long, slender neck, a spike (on which to prop up the instrument) and a small, round resonator, made from half a coconut, or of bronze, the opening of which is covered with snakeskin. For further details see Sachs, *History*, pp. 217 and 255.   [38] M. J. de Goeje. This passage in the work of the Arab geographer is referred to by A. Hammerich, *Zur Frage nach dem Ursprung der Saiteninstrumente*, p. 229. Cf. also article 'Bow' in

text to contain a reference to the *kamanja*, then this instrument would appear to be present in both Egypt and Sind, a province on the Lower Indus, at the beginning of the tenth century.[39] (Al-Faqīh says that the Copts had mastered the art of performing on the *kamanja* to a far greater degree than the people of Sind.) The advance of the Seljuks into Asia Minor[40] brought the *kamanja* to Byzantium also in the eleventh or twelfth century. This is proved by a poem written during the Seljuk occupation of Anatolia,[41] in which the *kāmancı*, *ıklık*, and *kopuz* are all mentioned, as well as by a miniature illustrating a thirteenth-century Byzantine Psalter manuscript,[42] where a *kamanja* is depicted, complete with bow, together with other musical instruments originating in Inner Asia.[43] The twelfth-century Persian poet Nizāmī, who came from Gandsha, includes the *kamāncha* in a list of more than thirty musical instruments. The same instrument appears on a bronze bowl[44] made in the Near East during the thirteenth century, and in an illustration from the Persian treatise *Kanz al-tuhaf*,[45] written in the mid-fourteenth century. The latter source describes the instrument as a *ghishek*, and pictures it with an unusually flat bow. It has two gut strings, attached to lateral pegs, a long neck, a bowl-shaped resonator covered with stretched skin, and a supporting spike.[46] The *shishak* and *ghichak*, mentioned respectively in a Pahlavi text[47] and in Dervish Ali's treatise on music,[48] are probably instruments of the same type. Exact structural details are given in the Turkish treatise by Aḥmed-oghlu Shükrullāh,[49] written between 1402 and 1404.[50] According to his description, the neck of the instrument should be made from the wood of the almond or walnut tree, or even ebony, and the body cast in bronze. The spike, to which the horsehair strings were secured, must be one and a half hand-spans in length, and the two strings should be tuned a fifth apart. The Turkish term *iqliq*, used to describe the instrument, is found in various other forms (*ıglık*, *ıklık*, *yıklıj*) in Turkish sources from the thirteenth and fourteenth centuries.[51] Further examples of bowed instruments similar to the spike lute are illustrated in fifteenth and six-

Grove's Dictionary, 5th edition (London, 1954). [39] The date of this Arabic source is 902 or 903. [40] Around 1100 the Seljuk empire stretched from Kashgar, across Persia and Mesopotamia as far as the Caucasus and Asia Minor. [41] Quoted in M. R. Gazimihâl, *Asya ve Anadolu kaynaklarında Iklığ* (Ankara, 1958), p. 23. [42] Berlin, Kupferstichkabinett, Hamilton MS, 119, fol. 41 v. [43] This miniature shows among other things cymbals, kettledrum, bagpipe, long trumpets, horn, transverse flute, organ, trapezoidal psaltery, angular harps, including the Indo-Persian vertical angular hooked harp, and *kamanja*. [44] Illustrated in Farmer, 'Arabian Musikal Instruments on a Thirteenth Century Bronze Bowl', *Oriental Studies, Mainly Musical* (London, 1953). [45] British Museum, Oriental MS. 2361, fol. 262. [46] W. Friedrich, *Die älteste türkische Beschreibung von Musikinstrumenten aus dem Anfang des 15. Jahrhunderts* (Dissertation, Breslau, 1944). [47] J. M. Unvala, *The Pahlavi Text 'King Husrav and his boy'* (Paris, 1921) p. 27. [48] A. A. Semenov, *Sredneaziatskij traktat pro musyke dervisha Ali* (Tashkent, 1946), p. 19. [49] A German translation of this description is given by W. Friedrich, *Die älteste türkische Beschreibung von Musikinstrumenten*, p. 65 ff. [50] The contents of the Turkish musical treatise are largely based on the Persian treatise *Kanz al-tuhaf*, mentioned above. [51] In a poem from the Seljuk period, in the writing of Ebu-Hayyan Telefi (1312) and in Ibni Mühenna Lūgatī (1387). Cf. M. R. Gazimihâl, *Asya ve Anadolu*

teenth-century Persian/Turkestani miniatures,[52] while the fifteenth-century essay on music *Kashf al-humūm* (Cairo MS.) contains both a drawing and a detailed description of the *kamanja*.

A special form of this bowed spike lute is mentioned by Ibn Ghaibī.[53] In this, the resonator, covered back and front with stretched hide, was tile-shaped, that is to say, rectangular, and strung with a horsehair string. This instrument is variously portrayed in Persian miniatures[54] and corresponds to the Mongolian *morin chur*,[55] still played today.

These then are the most important of the bowed instruments that emerged in the Islamic Empire during the Middle Ages. Their names occur sporadically in Arab manuscripts from the end of the eighth century: al-Khalīl (d. 796) speaks of the *r'bāb*;[56] the *kopuz* appears in a Central Asiatic source dating from the eighth/ninth century;[57] the *shishak* (*ghichak*) and *kapīk* (*kabak*), in a Pahlavi text.[58] Abū Bakr Ibn al-Faqīh[59] mentions the *kamanja*, and Maḥmūd Kashgarli's *Divan* has a reference to the *ekeme*.[60] However, there is as yet no clear proof that these instruments were at this stage played with the bow. Not until early in the tenth century do Arabic literary and artistic sources point conclusively to its use.

BYZANTIUM

In the Byzantine Empire too bowing can be traced as far back as the tenth century, more or less simultaneously with the first references to the bow in Arabic sources. In those days the Byzantine Empire was ruled by Macedonian emperors and was all the zenith of its greatness, stretching out across South-Eastern Europe – the Balkan Peninsula, Southern Italy, and Crete – and into Asia Minor as far as Armenia and Northern Syria, including parts of the Crimea. These latter Oriental components of the Byzantine domain left their mark on every aspect of Byzantine culture.[61] Just as many details of Byzantine painting may be traced

---

kaynaklarında Iklīğ (Ankara, 1958), pp. 12 and 23.   [52] A number of works containing illustrations of the *kamanja* in Islamic art are listed on p. 27, note 20. Cf. also M. R. Gazimihāl, *Asya ve Anadolu kaynaklarında Iklīğ* (Ankara, 1958), pp. 10, 30, and 37.   [53] Cf. Farmer, *JRAS* (1930), p. 781. [54] Cf. among others A. Sakisian, *La miniature persane du 12ᵉ au 13ᵉ siècle* (Paris, 1929). Plate 144; E. de Lorey, 'Behzād', *Ars Islamica* 4 (1937), pp. 122ff., Fig. 3 ; W. Friedrich, *Die älteste türkische Beschreibung*, Plate 12.   [55] Illustrated in A. Buchner, *Musikinstrumente im Wandel der Zeiten* (Prague, 1956), plate 320. Cf. E. Emsheimer, 'Preliminary Remarks on Mongolian Music and Instruments', in *The Music of the Mongols, Part I, Eastern Mongolia* (Stockholm, 1943), pp. 82ff.   [56] Cf. *Islamic Culture* XVIII (1944), p. 202, and *Grove's Dictionary*, 5th edition (London, 1954) article 'Bow'. The quotation runs as follows: 'The ancient Arabs sang their songs to its [the rebab's] sound'. Since vowels are omitted from the name of the instrument here, no distinction can be made between *rabāb* and *rubāb*.   [57] N. Dmitriev, *Ataiskij epos kogutej* (published by the Academy of Sciences of the USSR, 1953), p. 77.   [58] J. M. Unvala, op. cit., p. 27.   [59] Cf. p. 31, note 38. [60] M. R. Gazimihāl, op. cit., p. 13 ff.   [61] Oriental influences on Byzantine civilization are examined by E. Wellesz, *A History of Byzantine Music and Hymnography* (Oxford, 1949), pp. 21 ff.

back to Oriental sources, in particular to the monuments at Palmyra,[62] and do not stem from Hellenistic traditions, so, too, Byzantine music is 'entirely divorced from ancient Greek music, having been brought to Constantinople, the Imperial capital, from Asia Minor, Syria, and Armenia.'[63]

The heritage from antiquity

The range of Byzantine musical instruments also reveals a marked Oriental influence, along with a striking change as compared with the Greek instruments of classical antiquity. Few of the latter were still in use in the Middle Ages.[64] The ancient double *aulos*, for instance, had been almost entirely ousted by the transverse flute. Apart from a Greek illustration of a transverse flute dating from the fourth century B. C., there is no prior evidence that it was in use among the Greeks; whereas it was one of the most popular instruments in Eastern Asia[65] in ancient times, and even more so in the early Middle Ages. Likewise the small frame drum, the Greek *tympanon*, was superseded by the Eastern cylindrical drum. Among stringed instruments, the lyre, ubiquitous in hellenistic musical illustrations, became significantly less popular in the Byzantine period, and in its stead we find new instruments of the lute and fiddle types, plucked or bowed, as well as strikingly slender triangular harps, the existence of which in antiquity has yet to be proved.

Greek antiquity did, however, bequeath the organ to posterity, together with the names of several instruments of Ancient Greece, names later applied to new instruments. Thus in medieval times the term *lyra* usually no longer denotes a lyre with a yoke-like bar to which the strings were attached, but an instrument of the fiddle type. There is evidence that this change of meaning had already taken place in Byzantium by the end of the ninth century. In an address to the Caliph al-Mu'tamid (d. 893) the Persian-born Ibn Khurdādhbih[66] observed that the Byzantines had a five-stringed wooden instrument called a *lūrā* (λύρα) which was identical with the *rabāb* of the Arabs.[67] This interesting piece of information

[62] J. H. Breasted came to this conclusion in his study of the *Oriental Forerunners of Byzantine Painting*. [63] Quoted from E. Wellesz, 'Die orientalische Musik im Rahmen der musikgeschichtlichen Forschung', *Festschrift für Hermann Kretschmar* (Leipzig, 1918), p. 173. [64] There is as yet no pictorial evidence available of the complete series of instruments used by the Byzantines, and scholars have perforce had to rely on a few lists and descriptions of instruments in Byzantine literary sources, for example, Wellesz, *A History of Byzantine Music and Hymnography* (Oxford, 1949), pp. 63 and 80ff.; O. Gombosi, 'Studien zur Tonartenlehre des frühen Mittelalters (III)', *AMl* 12 (1940), pp. 43ff. and 48; Farmer, 'Byzantine Musical Instruments in the ninth Century, *JRAS* (1925), p. 299ff.; E. Wiedemann and F. Hauser, 'Byzantinische und arabische akustische Instrumente', *Archiv für die Geschichte der Naturwissenschaften und der Technik* (1918), p. 155. [65] Hickmann, article 'Flöteninstrumente (C)' in *MGG* and 'The antique Cross-Flute', *AMl* XXIV (1952). [66] The transcription of the name is given as Ibn Horradādbeh by C. Brockelmann in *Geschichte der arabischen Literatur*, Vol. I, 2nd ed. (Leyden, 1943), p. 258. [67] H. G. Far-

is confirmed by an eleventh-century Latin-Arabic glossary,[68] where the Arabic word *rabāb* is translated as *lyra dicta a varietate*. Two annotations to twelfth/ thirteenth-century European miniatures also describe pearshaped bowed instruments as *lyra* or *lira*.[69] The name survives into the sixteenth century in *lira da braccio* and *lira da gamba*, and to this day fiddle-type folk instruments in the Balkans are called *lyra* or *lijerica*.[70]

There is no indication, however, that the five-stringed Byzantine instrument described by Ibn Khurdādhbih at the end of the ninth century was played with the bow, since he does not discuss the technique involved. But a few decades later we find irrefutable pictorial evidence that the bow had by that time come into use in the Byzantine Empire. There is even proof from a Chinese source – the Annals of the Sung Dynasty (970–1270)[71] – that, apart from the harp and the single-skinned drum, the *hu-ch'in* was at that time in current use in Asia Minor. This *hu-ch'in* is clearly described as a bowed instrument in the fourteenth-century *Yüan Shih*.[72]

It has still not been positively determined whether or not the Bulgars, who ruled over large areas of the Balkans in the first half of the tenth century, were then in possession of bowed instruments. We gather, from the sermon preached by the priest Kosma (tenth century) against the Bogomils,[73] that the lower reaches of Bulgarian society were given to playing the *gusla* and singing demonic songs; but it cannot be shown that the *gusla* was already a bowed instrument, as it is throughout the Balkans today.

Pictorial evidence

By contrast with the cultural sphere of Islam, Christian Byzantium offers a rich harvest of pictorial sources, particularly subsequent to the lifting of the ban on pictorial representation by the Council of Constantinople in 843. This material

mer, 'Ibn Khurdādhbih on musical instruments', *JRAS* (1928), p. 509ff. A somewhat different definition of the Byzantine lyra is given by al-Khwārizmī (10th century) in his encyclopaedic work *Mafātīḥ al'ulūm*. He writes: 'To the Greeks, *al lūr* is *al ṣang* (harp)'. In addition, according to this source, Byzantine musical instruments included the organ, the *schaljāq* – a stringed instrument resembling the *gunk* – and the *qītāra*, which was rather like the *ṭunbūr*. E. Wiedemann gives a translation of this Arabic source in *Sitzungsberichte der physikalisch-medizinischen Sozietät in Erlangen* (1922), pp. 7ff. esp. p. 9.   [68] Quoted by Farmer in the article 'Rabāb' (3) in *Encyclopaedia of Islam*.   [69] In the *Hortus deliciarum*, by the Abbess Herrad von Landsperg (illustration in H. Besseler, 'Die Musik des Mittelalters und der Renaissance', *Handbuch der Musikwissenschaft*, ed. E. Bücken (Potsdam, 1931-4), p. 92), and in a copy of a miniature from a manuscript (since destroyed by fire) in the library at St Blasien (Gerbert, *De Cantu*, Vol. II, Plate XXXII, 18).   [70] M. Gavazzi, 'Jadranska "lira-lirica"', *Narodna starina* IX (Agram, 1930).   [71] Cf. W. Eberhard, 'Die Kultur der alten zentral- und westasiatischen Völker nach chinesischen Quellen', *Zeitschrift für Ethnologie* 73 (1941), p. 241.   [72] Yüan-shih, Book 71, Chapter 22, p. 5.   [73] I. Kačulev, 'Gdulkite v B'lgaria', *Izvestija na instituta za muzika*, No. 5 (1959), p. 132.

3*

includes, among other things, a number of illustrations of bowed instruments. Most of the Byzantine evidence is still either unknown or has not been properly evaluated, so that it is necessary to describe the most important sources in chronological order.

Among the earliest illustrations of a bow is a miniature in the eleventh-century Graeco-Byzantine psalter now in the Vatican Library (MS. graec. 752, fol. 23 v) showing King David carrying a scroll, accompanied by musicians playing a transverse flute and a bowed stringed instrument.[74] Obviously the Psalmist is making cheironomic signs to the two minstrels with his left hand (Plate 4). The opening pages of this Byzantine manuscript, fol. 3 r (Plate 5), fol. 5 r, and fol. 7 v, contain three more miniatures representing King David with a bowed instrument, which he plays propped against his shoulder, drawing a remarkably long bow across its strings. In general he appears surrounded by dancers and musicians. Yet another miniature from the same eleventh-century manuscript, fol. 449 v, shows eight minstrels, identified as Asaph, Yeman, Ethan, Jeduthun, singers, and *boukolios*, within a circle of dancing girls (Plate 7). Kathi Meyer[75] interprets this as a pictorial realization of the eight ecclesiastical modes; according to her theory Jeduthun, seen third from the left in the upper row playing a bowed instrument, symbolizes the seventh mode. The text encircling the dancers derives from a fourth-century commentary on the Psalms, written by the Pseudo-Chrysostomos,[76] which mentions a number of instruments. It is interesting to note that the artist applies old Greek names to illustrations of new Byzantine instruments, such as the transverse flute, the bowed instrument, the cylindrical drum, and the slender triangular harp. Unfortunately most of the miniatures in this psalter manuscript are in a very poor state of preservation, so that it is hardly possible to identify details.

By contrast, a very clear illustration of a bowed instrument (Plate 9) may be seen on a richly carved Byzantine ivory casket in the Museo Nazionale in Florence (Coll. Carrand, No. 26), dating from the tenth or eleventh century.[77] On the right-hand end of the casket is a carving of a boy seated on an acanthus leaf and playing a bowed instrument propped on his left knee. This bas-relief has frequently been reproduced or described in works relating to organology.[78]

Another source is a Byzantine fresco in the North Tower of the Cathedral of St. Sophia in Kiev,[79] showing a minstrel playing a bowed instrument (Plate 8).

[74] On the dating and interpretation of this illustration cf. E. T. de Wald, *The Illustrations in the Manuscripts of the Septuagint*, III, *Psalms and Odes*, Part 2 (Princeton, 1942). [75] K. Meyer, 'The eight Gregorian Modes on the Cluny Capitals', *The Art Bulletin* (June, 1952), Vol. XXXIV, No. 2, p. 75 ff. [76] Published in J. P. Migne's *Patrologia graeca* LV, col. 534. [77] The difficult problem of the date of this ivory casket is discussed in great detail by A. Goldschmidt and K. Weitzmann in *Die byzantinischen Elfenbeinskulpturen des 10.–13. Jahrhunderts*, Vol. 2 (Berlin, 1930), p. 87. [78] For example, Buhle, *Die musikalischen Instrumente*, p. 4, note 3; Behn, 'Die Laute im Altertum und frühen Mittelalter', *ZfMw* I, p. 106, and *Musikleben im Altertum und frühen Mittelalter*, Plate 213. [79] For more detailed information relating to this illustration see A. N. Grabar, 'Les fresques des escaliers à Sainte Sophie de Kiev et l'iconographie impériale byzantine', *Seminarium*

This mural dates from around 1050, and its theme is continued elsewhere in the church with further illustrations of Byzantine musicians and tumblers[80] – evidence that a close relationship existed in the eleventh century between the Rus of Kiev and the city of Byzantium. Early documents do in fact show that from the ninth century wandering musicians from Byzantium were active at the court of Kiev.[81]

The next source, a Byzantine psalter manuscript in the British Museum, London (Add. MS 19352, fol. 191) contains a marginal illustration showing three women playing musical instruments – a bowed instrument (Plate 11), a cylindrical drum, and a triangular harp.[82] This manuscript was written at the Monastery of St. Basil in Caesarea by the Archpriest Theodoros, for the Abbot of the Studion Monastery in Constantinople.

Also of great organological value are two miniatures from the Pseudo-Nonnus Manuscript in the Patriarchal Library at Jerusalem (Codex Taphou 14), dating from the second half of the eleventh century.[83] The first of these (Plate 10) represents the birth of Zeus. Music is provided by a group of corybants – priests of Cybele, Asia Minor's Goddess of Plenty, or of Rhea, Mother of the Gods – who frame this scene from Greek mythology while performing on the cross flute, cylindrical drum, bowed instrument, and cymbals.[84] The second miniature of the Byzantine Pseudo-Nonnus manuscript[85] shows in the background three statues of the Muses (Plate 6). Here for the first time a bowed instrument features in an illustration representing the Muses. Later such an instrument occasionally appears as an attribute of Musica personified, in the context of *artes liberales*.[86]

As in the illustration of the birth of Zeus, a number of corybants are once again seen dancing and playing in a miniature from the Codex graecus 1947, fol. 146r, in the Vatican Library (Plate 12). As before, the bowed instrument takes its place alongside transverse flute, cylindrical drum, and a second wind instrument.

Finally we come to a Byzantine ivory relief, dating from the first half of the twelfth century,[87] which adorns the binding of the manuscript psalter Codex Egerton 1139 in the British Museum (Plate 55). Within a circle sits King David with four musicians, two holding bowed instruments and two harps. Stylistic elements from Western Europe here mingle with those of Byzantine art, so that the instruments shown cannot with any certainty be classified as belonging exclusively to Byzantine civilization.

Kondakovianum, Recueil d'études VII (Prague, 1935), pp. 103 ff.   [80] Illustrated in H. Besseler, *Die Musik des Mittelalters*, p. 73.   [81] W. Salmen, *Der fahrende Musiker*, p. 80.   [82] The representation of the bowed instrument is discussed and described by Schlesinger, op. cit., Vol. II, p. 448; and by E. S. J. van der Straeten in *History*, p. 15.   [83] K. Weitzmann, *Greek Mythology in Byzantine Art* (Princeton, 1951), Plate XII, 36 and Plate XXIII, 77.   [84] The use of musical instruments in the cult of Cybele is treated in J. Quasten, *Musik und Gesang*, p. 52 ff.   [85] Cod. Taphou 14, fol. 100r.   [86] Bachmann, *Bilddarstellungen der Musik im Rahmen der artes liberales* p. 49.   [87] A clue to the date of this illustration is the fact that this psalter manuscript was written for Mélisande,

Byzantine bowed instruments

From this wide range of comparative material we can form a clear picture of the outward appearance of Byzantine bowed instruments, and how they were used. Most of the Byzantine miniatures have unfortunately suffered considerable damage in the course of time, and frequently it is impossible to recognize any details. Nevertheless, definite types of bowed instruments emerge, differing appreciably one from another. In all this pictorial material the hallmarks of the lute are unmistakably evident – the frontal stringholder to which the strings were attached and the lateral pegs.[88] Not one Byzantine illustration gives a clear picture of tailpiece or bridge, or of the sagittal (rear or frontal) pegs, so typical of early Western bowed instruments.

Morphological differences between plucked and bowed instruments in Byzantium cannot as yet be confirmed. This differentiation most likely did not come about until later, probably in Europe. That all were originally plucked instruments is suggested by the fact that they seem designed specifically to be played with the plectrum – they exhibit constructional details and stringing which are rendered pointless if a bow is used. This is specially true of the fan-shaped arrangement of the strings recognizable in some of the illustrations:[89] the strings spread out near the stringholder, which takes up almost the full width of the body. They are widely spaced in this way so that each separate string can be played with the plectrum without touching adjacent strings. In bowing, however, the fan shape was meaningless, not to say disadvantageous, particularly since strings secured to a frontal stringholder all lie in the same plane.[90]

If we classify these Byzantine bowed instruments according to the shape of their resonator and neck, they fall into two groups. In the first, the body of the instrument is waisted (in this resembling our guitar) and has a narrow, clearly-defined neck, with a peg-box, traversed from side to side by the pegs,[91] bent slightly backwards. Instruments belonging to the second group have a pear-shaped body, gradually tapering off into a short neck.[92] For the first type, the incurving sides of the sound-box were once looked on as a criterion for the use of the bow, since this shape allegedly gave the necessary freedom for the musician to play each string separately. Hickmann and Schaeffner[93] have demon-

daughter of the King of Jerusalem, Baldwin II (1118–31). [88] Clearly discernible in Plates 4, 6, 8, 10, and 11. [89] See Plates 4, 8, and 11. [90] This problem is discussed in all its aspects by K. Geiringer in *Die Flankenwirbelinstrumente in der bildenden Kunst der Zeit zwischen 1300 und 1500* (Dissertation, Vienna, 1923), pp. 16 and 48, Note 1. [91] Plates 4, 6, 10, and 11. This type of instrument appears on a painted Fatimid-Egyptian earthenware plate (12th century) in the Egyptian Museum, Cairo. The painting on this plate is clearly based on Byzantine models. Illustrated in A. Lane, *Early Islamic Pottery* (New York, 1948), Plate 27 B. [92] Plates 7, 8, 9, and 55. [93] H. Hickmann, 'Ein unbekanntes Saiteninstrument aus koptischer Zeit', *Mf* III (1950), pp. 8 ff.; by the same author, 'Un instrument à cordes inconnu de l'époque copte', *Extrait du Bulletin de la Société d'Archaeologie copte*, XII (1946-7), pp. 63 ff.; also 'Quelques précurseurs', *Extrait des Annales du Service des antiquités de l'Egypte*, XLIX (Cairo, 1949); A. Schaeffner, *Origine*, p. 214.

strated the untenability of this theory, and our Byzantine illustrations also dis-
prove it, for only rarely is the bow drawn across the strings at the narrowest
part of the body. Furthermore, this inward curve in the resonator occurs in plucked
instruments of antiquity, when there could have been no question of bowing.
Thus we find the lines of this Byzantine instrument in an illustration from Asia
Minor, dating from the fifteenth century B.C., showing an instrument of which
the long neck tilts backwards a little at its upper end, and the long sides of the
elliptical body are slightly waisted.[94] In this Hittite relief from Alaca Hüyük the
instrument shown is certainly a spike lute, widely used throughout the East in
ancient times.[95] It would, however, be premature to try to bring these ancient
long-necked Oriental lutes and the Byzantine bowed instruments into a direct
genetic line of descent, since the connecting links in the chain of development
– those which would show us when the lateral pegs and frontal string-holder
were introduced – are still missing.[96]

This type of 'bowed guitar with lateral pegs', which first appeared in the course
of the tenth century, survived in Byzantium for centuries almost unchanged.
A fourteenth-century miniature[97] shows that it retained its very narrow neck and
lateral pegs, while its four strings were still attached to a frontal string-holder.

The picture of bowed instruments in the Byzantine Empire, which we have
derived from the available iconographic material, is completed by a description
of this type of instrument in a Turkish manuscript[98] dating from the early fifteenth
century. We are told that the *rebab* was 'double-bellied', that is to say it had a
figure-of-eight shape, or was like a guitar, from 28 to 30 cm. wide, with an overall
length of 38 to 40 cm. and about 12 cm. deep, the length of the neck being about
65 cm. These details coincide with the dimensions of Byzantine fiddles in illustrations, the size of which may be estimated approximately from the relationship
between the size of the instrument and that of the player.[99] According to the Tur-

---

[94] Cf. p. 21, Note 144.   [95] A reproduction of a similar ancient Egyptian waisted lute on the
ostracon C. 63805 (Cairo, Museum), from the 18th dynasty, is published by Hickmann in *Mf*
III (1950), Plate 4.   [96] A stringed instrument with a guitar-like body, that is, with incurved
sides, and a frontal string-holder to which the four strings are attached, is shown on the Airtam
frieze (1st century A. D.), discovered near Termez in Uzbekistan, south of Samarkand. This valuable
monument of pre-Islamic art in Central Asia is now in the Hermitage in Leningrad. The neck
of the stringed instrument, which was plucked with a plectrum, has unfortunately been broken
off. Elsewhere on the frieze, female musicians are depicted playing cylindrical drum and harp.
The relief is illustrated and described in M. Prynne, 'Angelic Musicians from Central Asia',
Galpin Society Journal VII (1954), p. 54, and VIII, Plate VIII.   [97] Illustrated in S. der Nersessian,
L'Illustration du roman de Barlaam et Joasaph (Paris, 1937), Plate XC, 360.   [98] A treatise in old
Osmanli by Ahmed-oghlu Shükrullāh between 1402 and 1404. A German translation of this
passage is given by W. Friedrich in *Die älteste türkische Beschreibung*, p. 68 f. The details relating
to the structure of the *rabāb* correspond in every way to the bowed instrument shown in Byzantine illustration. The fact that no mention is made of the bow in the description of the *rabāb* in
no way implies that around 1400 the Turkish *rabāb* was a plucked instrument.   [99] In Plate 11
the total length of the bowed instrument is approximately 95 cm., the body being 40–45 cm.

kish account, the body and neck were made of apricot wood or walnut. The upper part of the wooden sounding-board – the part nearest the fingerboard – generally had a circular sound hole, sometimes covered with a membrane. Frequently, only the underside of the body was made of wood, whereas the upper half was covered with stretched skin. The stringholder to which the strings were anchored must, the writer says, be about 8 cm. from the lower rim of the sounding board. He goes on to state that these instruments had six strings, arranged and tuned in three double courses. Ibn Khurdādhbih's[100] description of the Byzantine bowed instruments, written almost five hundred years earlier, speaks of only five strings. Illustrations of guitar-shaped Byzantine bowed instruments usually show four or five strings.

The second type of bowed instrument used in the Byzantine Empire, characterized by its pear-shaped body, present a significantly less uniform picture. Here the number of strings ranges from two to six,[101] the position of the pegs is variable,[102] the peg-box mostly lies in line with the neck – that is to say it is not inclined – and to anchor the strings an end-pin appears as well as a frontal stringholder.[103] Neck and body are a continuation of one another, with no clear dividing line between the two. Even the position of the instrument is not constant. While the guitar-shaped Byzantine bowed instruments were always supported against the player's chest (contrary to normal Oriental practice[104]), the *a gamba* position is occasionally found among the pear-shaped instruments.[105] Exceptionally, the second type of instrument was also held horizontally,[106] whereas Byzantine bowed instruments were otherwise always held sloped or propped nearly vertically against the player's chest, with the neck pointing obliquely downwards.

A striking feature of most Byzantine representations of bowed instruments is the inordinate length of the bow,[107] which is nearly always held in the reverse position, in an underhand grip. In order to use it right to its point, the player was therefore obliged to extend his bowing arm – the right arm – sideways. This uncomfortable position is reproduced in a number of Byzantine illustrations.[108] The varying degrees of curvature in the bow also seem strange. From pictorial sources it is clear that the shaft of the bow, with one exception – a very flat bow with no grip[109] – extends well beyond the end of the horsehair, thus forming a handle.[110] At this point it would be superfluous to elaborate on the details of structure and technique, since these will be fully discussed in the following chapter.

long, if we take the player's height as 1.70 m. These Byzantine instruments would therefore have been even bigger than modern violas. [100] Cf. p. 34, Note 67. [101] Plate 9 clearly shows two strings, whereas the bowed instrument on Plate 8 obviously has six. [102] There is no evidence of lateral pegs on any of the Byzantine pear-shaped instruments. The method of attaching the strings in Plates 5, 7, 8, 9, and 12 is not very clear. [103] Plate 8 offers an example of strings attached to a frontal string-holder, while Plate 9 clearly shows an end-pin fastening. [104] In the East, bowed instruments were stood upright on the player's knee or on the floor. The various positions of the instrument are discussed in detail in Chapter III. [105] Plate 9. [106] Plate 8. [107] Judging by the relative sizes of player and instrument, the majority of Byzantine illustrations show bows from 1–1.30 m. in length. [108] Especially clear in Plate 12. [109] Plate 8. [110] Plates

Where did bowing originate?

To summarize the preceding pages: in the period up to the end of the tenth century the spread of the bow was confined to the area encompassed by the Arabic and Byzantine Empires.[111] There is as yet no evidence[112] that it was known in Europe[113] at this time, and in the East the spread of bowing ended at the borders of Islamic territory.[114] It was not until appreciably later that this style of playing came to be practised in countries of Eastern Asia, China, and India, or even in Eastern Turkestan, the gateway to the Far East.

When it comes to establishing more specifically just where the bow originated and developed, we are faced with serious problems. These arise primarily from the fact that very few Near-Eastern peoples have bequeathed us an even approximately complete picture of their civilization. Further, the unification of so many of the peoples of Western and Central Asia into massive power structures (the Empires of Islam and Byzantium) meant that within these vast territories new achievements spread swiftly and freely, resulting in a certain uniformity in patterns of thought and behaviour. This makes it all the more difficult to determine the intellectual achievements of individual Oriental peoples, or to determine their share in general cultural development.

The assimilation of different stylistic elements is also revealed in the music of these countries. From the notes on the songs in the *Kitāb al-Aghānī* of Iṣfahānī,[115] a voluminous tenth-century song collection, it is clear that Arab musicians borrowed and adapted musical forms and techniques from the various peoples of the Islamic culture area. Certain songs in this collection derive from songs sung by Syrian muleteers and the folk-songs of Persian artisans; others are inspired or influenced by Byzantine folk music.[116] 'Persian song made an early début among the Arabs; Persian singers, both male and female, soon found their way – initially from Hīra – to Damascus and then to Baghdad, and Persian skill in song and pageantry was soon paramount at the Caliph's court.'[117]

4, 5, 7, 9, 10, 11, and 12. [111] P. 24. [112] Mozarabic Spain and the Byzantine Peninsula stood outside the limits of European, as opposed to Eastern, civilization during the 10th century. [113] Cf. p. 20. There is as yet no proof that bowed instruments were used in the Slav cultural area during the 10th century. Whereas the anonymous Arabic source Ḥudūd al-ʿālam (translated by V. Minorsky, London, 1937, p. 158) says only that stringed instruments unknown to the Arabs were played in the Slav countries, the Arab writer, Ibn Dasta, gives a more detailed description of Slav musical instruments: 'They [the Slavs] have divers lutes, guslas, and shawms. These shawms are instruments, two ells long, and the lutes have eight strings' (quoted from N. S. Derzavin, 'Die Slawen im Altertum', *Arbeiten aus dem Gebiet der Slawistik in Übersetzung*, Part I (Weimar, 1948), p. 154). The details given in these 10th century Arabic sources are borne out by various art finds and archaeological evidence. [114] Cf. special studies quoted on p. 18 of this book. [115] To supplement the article on al-Iṣfahānī in *MGG* there is also Farmer's 'The Song Captions in the Kitāb al-aghānī', *Transactions of the Glasgow University Oriental Society* XV (1955). [116] J. Fück, '"Arabische" Musikkultur und Islam', *Orientalistische Literaturzeitung* 48th Year (1953), Cols. 24 and 25. [117] B. Spuler, *Iran in früh-islamischer Zeit* (Wiesbaden, 1952),

Musical instruments also were exchanged and gradually lost their regional characteristics.[118] It is reported that in A. D. 743 the Caliphs caused various instruments native to Khurāsān to be brought from thence to Baghdad, in order to complete the court orchestra.[119]

This continuous exchange makes it well-nigh impossible to establish when and where bowing was first developed and the bow emerged. The first real evidence we have of its use, dating from the tenth century,[120] shows that it appeared almost simultaneously at different places within the two great Mediterranean empires – in Byzantium as in Islam – in Spain, Egypt, Arabia, and Persia, and in Central Asia on both banks of the Oxus.

Faced with the striking coincidence in time of the earliest Byzantine and Arabic evidence, it is tempting to suppose that the bow was transferred directly from one Mediterranean power to the other. Although a religious gulf separated Byzantine Christian culture from that of Islam, such a supposition does not seem out of place, since there was a perceptible increase, around the end of the first millennium, in the flow of ideas between the two relating to the arts, the sciences, and to culture in general. However, a comparative analysis of the earliest available pictorial evidence for the use of the bow reveals, in the Byzantine miniatures, so many peculiarities and variations among the instruments and in the shape of the bow, and so many styles of holding and bowing, that it is impossible to prove any directly dependent relationship on pictorial grounds when these are set against the corresponding Mozarabic illustrations.[121]

p. 290. [118] Curt Sachs refers to this in his *History*, p. 246. Despite this continuous traffic in instruments, certain ethnological ties subsisted. Thus Ibn Khurdādhbih in the 9th century (*JRAS* (1928), pp. 511 ff.) and Muhammad b. Yūsuf al-Khwārizmī in the 10th century (*Sitzungsbericht der physikalisch-medizinischen Sozietät in Erlangen*, 54th Year (1922), pp. 7 ff.) list the instruments characteristic of the different Oriental peoples at that time, discussing the Oriental instrumentarium in the light of ethnography and geography. In music, too, national traits were largely preserved, in spite of constant interchange. In the Ikhwān al-Ṣafā essay (F. Dieterici, *Die Propädeutik der Araber*, p. 111 f.) we are told 'that one tribe may find airs and melodies to their taste, and take great delight in them, which others neither appreciate nor can take pleasure from. Witness the singing of . . . the Turks, the Arabs, the Armenians . . . These peoples have different tongues, natures, characters, and customs.' [119] B. Spuler, *Iran in früh-islamischer Zeit* (Wiesbaden, 1952), p. 270. [120] We know from pictorial sources that the bow was used in the 10th century in Spain and in the Byzantine Empire. The essay of the Order of the Brothers of Purity (whose headquarters were in Basra) confirms that bowing was also known in Mesopotamia and Syria at that time. A 10th-century Arab scribe (cf. Farmer, *JRAS* (1930), p. 775) observes that the rabāb was played in Persia and Khurāsān. In this connection it is not without interest that the two Arab scholars, al-Fārābī and Ibn Sīnā, who refer to bowing in the 10th century, hail from Transoxiana. [121] Byzantine bowed instruments are principally characterized by lateral pegs and frontal stringholder: they are played on the shoulder and bowed with a remarkably long bow. As against this, the bowed instruments known to have existed in the Islamic empire in medieval times usually had their strings attached to an end-pin (inferior stringholder or button) and sagittal pegs. When played, these instruments stood upright on the floor

CENTRAL ASIA

For this reason the hypothesis of a common origin in Central Asia, and two separate lines of development, one in the Arab world and the other in the Byzantine, is more attractive. As yet, however, this suggestion has not been backed by any positive evidence as to what instruments were then used by the nomadic races of Inner Asia – the peoples of the mountains and the steppes, or the tribes of horsemen – or for that matter by the peoples of high culture on both sides of the Oxus.[122] The cultural achievements of these Central Asian[123] nations – in particular any literary or iconographic sources – were largely destroyed, by the conquering Arabs in the eighth century[124] or during the period of Mongol rule in the thirteenth and fourteenth centuries, as well as in the course of their subsequent chequered history.[125] In music, too, the individuality of the different racial groups was obscured by the Muslim conquest, relics of the past being ruthlessly destroyed and valuable records of songs or of musical theory burned. Any information we have relating to the peoples and countries of Central Asia derives in the first instance, therefore, from occasional references to musical instruments in contemporary reports by Arab, Persian, Turco-Uigurian, Byzantine, and Chinese writers; and there are a few representations of Central Asian instruments which by some fortunate chance have survived. This material will help us to see how far the hypothesis[126] that bowing originated in Central Asia is supported by the sources.

or on the player's knee. The bow was curved, and had no handle. [122] The Oxus, now the Amu Darya, was known to the Arabs as Raihun. [123] 'Central Asia' here implies the Turkestan Basin, that is to say, the area between the Caspian Sea, the Aral Sea and the high plateau of the Pamirs. Its area corresponds roughly to what today are the Kazakh and Turkmen Republics, the Karakalpak Republic, and the Uzbek, Kirghiz, and Tadzhik Republics. [124] The scholar Abū Raihān al-Bīrunī – a native of Khwārizm – writing during the 10th century, already comments on the lack of sources in tracing the history, culture and science of the peoples of Inner Asia: 'Qutaiba [an 8th-century Arab general] did his utmost to ruin and destroy anyone who could read and write the script of Khwārizm who was familiar with the country's traditions or had studied its literature and science. As a result, these things are now so shrouded in darkness, that it is impossible to trace the true history of the country since the coming of Islam' (quoted from S. P. Tolstow, *Auf den Spuren der altchoresmischen Kultur* (Berlin, 1953), 14th supplement, 'Sowjetwissenschaft', p. 9). [125] Some idea of the valuable work by Soviet archaeologists and orientalists on early civilizations of Central Asia may be obtained from the following works. S. P. Tolstow, op. cit.; W. A. Schischkin, *Archaeological work carried out in 1937 in the Western part of the Bokhara Oasis* (Tashkent, 1940) (Russian); H. Field and E. Prostov, 'Archaeological Investigations in Central Asia, 1917–1937', *Ars islamica* V (1938) and 'Excavations at Khwarazm, 1937–1938', *Ars islamica* VI (1939), pp. 158 ff.; 'Trudy sredneasiatskogo gosudarstv. Universiteta', *Archeologija srednei Asii*, New series (Tashkent, 1950, 1953, 1958); B. Denike, *Iskusstvo srednei Asii* (Moscow, 1927); B. V. Veimarn, *Iskusstvo srednei Asii* (Moscow/Leningrad, 1940); Abdul Kadir Inan, 'Archaeological Finds in Central Asia' (Russian), *Westnik Drevnoi Historija, 1942* (Istanbul, 1948); cf. also the bibliographical sections of the dissertations by O. Pritsak, *Studien zur Geschichte der Verfassung der Turk-Völker Zentralasiens* (Göttingen, 1948) and F. Kussmaul, *Zur Frühgeschichte des innerasiatischen Reiternomadentums* (Tübingen, 1953). [126] See

The cultural background

We have only recently come to appreciate the full significance of these peoples of Central Asia, conquered by the Arabs, for cultural development within the confines of the Islamic Empire. Previous research into the history and archaeology of the East concentrated more on the peoples on the borders of Asia; Central Asia was considered solely in connection with the theory of migration, under the misapprehension that these territories were backward and unprogressive. Recent archaeological research in the Republics of Turkmenistan and Uzbekistan, Kirghizia, and Tadzhikstan has revealed that even in antiquity, but more especially during the Middle Ages, the peoples of Central Asia had their own individual and highly-developed civilization. Their struggles for independence, accompanied by violent national revolts, led in the tenth century to the formation of virtually autonomous states. In the Mawerannahr, between the rivers Amu-Darya and Syr-Darya, the realm of the Samanids was established, with its capital at Bokhara, while to the south lay the territory of the Ghaznavids, the capital of which was Ghazni. During the ninth and tenth centuries these Central Asiatic regions progressed rapidly, both economically and culturally, and developed an early type of feudalism. By all accounts it was a time of unprecedented wealth. The number of towns multiplied,[127] urban trade developed, intensive irrigation created conditions for abundant crops, and widespread trade-connections raised the standard of living of the population. According to the Arab geographer al-Iṣṭakhrī,[128] Khwārizm in the tenth century was a fertile area 'rich in fruit and other foodstuffs ... Many articles made from cotton and wool are exported to distant places. The inhabitants are noted above all for their wealth and for their desire to prove their courage ... The greatest wealth derives from trade with the Turks and from stock raising.' The anonymous Persian author of the *Ḥudūd al-ʿālam* (tenth century) also refers to the boundless wealth of this region and to flourishing trade with peoples of Eastern and Western Asia.[129] Qazwīnī[130] describes Sogdia as an earthly paradise, and reports that the route from Bokhara to Samarkand wound for eight days through an unbroken landscape of fertile gardens. The widely-travelled Arab geographer Jāqūt[131] (tenth century) doubts 'the existence anywhere in the world of more extensive or more densely-populated lands than those of Khwārizm,' or that 'any capital city on earth can compare with its chief city, in either wealth or size.' The works of famous scholars from Khwārizm or Transoxiana – men such as Muḥammad ibn Mūsā al-Khwārizmī, al-Bīrūni, al-Fārābī, and Ibn Sīnā (Avicenna) testify to

above. [127] 'The majority of the Khwārizm settlements are towns that have markets, food supplies and shops' report the Arab geographer Jāqūt (quoted from Tolstow, op. cit., p. 298). [128] Cf. Tolstow, op. cit., p. 260. [129] Tolstow, loc. cit. [130] Qazwīnī's geography book exists in an English translation, by G. Le Strange, *The Geographical Part of the Nuzhat-al-Qulūb composed by Hamd-Allāh Mustawfī of Qazwin* (Leyden, 1919) (E. J. W. Gibb Memorial Series XXIII, 2), p. 255. [131] Tolstow, op. cit., p. 298.

the country's high standard of scholarship and education, which were also spoken of in glowing terms by the geographer Muḥammad ibn Aḥmad al-Maqdisī[132] during the tenth century.

The musical background

Describing the Merv region in his book of geography,[133] the Arab geographer al-Iṣṭakhrī writes: 'In the time of the Persians the scholars of Iranshahr sur-passed all others in the arts and sciences ... just so did the musician Barbud outshine all other musicians of his day.' Several more musicians of note, among them Pahlpat, who lived at the court of the Sassanid Emperor Khosrav II, and Abū-'Abdallah Ja'far Rūdakī, born towards the middle of the ninth century, hailed from the region of Samarkand and Bokhara. Treatises on music by Central Asian scholars – al-Fārābī, Ibn Sīnā, Ṣafī al-Dīn, 'Abdarraḥmān al-Jāmī, and the Dervish Ali[134] – bear witness to a highly developed theory of music. Espe-cially towards the end of the first millennium, the musicians of Central Asia enjoyed high esteem. We learn from a Chinese manuscript of the T'ang period[135] that Turkish tribes of Central Asia (Ku-t'u) sent female musicians abroad as a tribute. Music-making was largely a female affair. The Chinese travel book Pei-shih Chi (c. 1200) records that women of Central Asia 'do nothing but sing and dance etc. . . . Sewing and embroidery (and other work) are carried out by men.'[136] Already in the eighth century the Caliphs summoned musicians of both sexes from the Eastern provinces of the Arab Empire, especially from Khurāsān, to Damascus to complete the court orchestra.[137] When a census of professional singing girls in Baghdad was taken in 918, it was found that, with a few excep-tions, all of them were slaves of Central Asian origin.[138] The autobiography of Chodscha Aḥrār[139] mentions that many minstrels, as well as male and female singers, were engaged from Samarkand to take part in festivities in Tashkent.

[132] The relevant excerpt has been published (in Russian) in the sourcebook *Materiali po istorii Turkmen i Turkmenii*, Vol. I (Moscow/Leningrad, 1939), p. 187.   [133] Quoted from *Das Buch der Länder von Schech Ebu Ishak el Farsi el Isztachri*, translated from the Arabic by A. D. Mordtmann (Hamburg, 1845), p. 171.   [134] R. d'Erlanger, *La Musique Arabe*, Vols. I–III; A. A. Semenov, *A Middle Asiatic Treatise on Music of Dervish Ali* (Tashkent, 1946), *Abdurachman Dǧami*; *Traktat o mu-zyke*, ed. V. M. Bel'aev (Tashkent, 1960). In Tashkent, Professor Radǧabov is at present engaged in translating others of these Central Asian treatises on music.   [135] W. Eberhard, 'Die Kultur der alten zentral- und westasiatischen Völker nach chinesischen Quellen', *Zeitschrift für Ethnologie* 73 (1941), p. 243.   [136] E. Bretschneider, *Medieval Researches from Eastern Asiatic Sources*, Vol. I (London, 1910), p. 31 f.   [137] Cf. B. Spuler, *Iran in früh-islamischer Zeit* (Wiesbaden, 1952), p. 290.   [138] Cf. A. Mez, *Die Renaissance des Islam* (Heidelberg, 1922), p. 154. – Singing-girls cost approxi-mately twenty times as much as an ordinary slave girl. Thus in 912 a famous singing-girl was sold for 13,000 dinars, and the trader received an additional 1,000 dinars.   [139] Cf. W. Barthold, 'Ulug Beg und seine Zeit', *Abhandlungen für die Kunde des Morgenlandes* XXI, I (1935), p. 142 f.

At the Chinese court also were orchestras of Western 'barbarians', that is, of peoples from Central Asia. The so-called 'music of the Nine Divisions', *Chiu-puyüeh*, which the T'ang Dynasty took over from the beginning from the Sui Dynasty, included the music of Chiu-tzu (Kuchā), the Province of An (Bokhara), Shu-lei (Kashgar), and the Province of K'ang (Samarkand).[140] The following comment, from a Chinese source of the Sui period (589–618) highlights the great love of music displayed by the inhabitants of Samarkand: 'They love music and wine, and they dance in the streets.'[141] Muḥammad ibn Aḥmad al-Maqdisī (tenth century) discussing Khwārizm in his geographical treatise, says: 'They have beautiful melodies, which they perform superbly.'[142] Various old laments, and songs on historical themes, are mentioned in Narshakhi's *History of Bokhara* (tenth century),[143] and the Damascus-born historiographer, Ibn 'Arabshāh, who spent a number of years in Samarkand, praises the music of Khwārizm in his monumental work on the life of Tamburlaine.[144]

References to exorcism by music, and to Shamanism, occur frequently in early accounts of journeys in Central Asia. The Byzantine historian Menander Protector (sixth century) describes exorcism rites witnessed among Turkish tribes of Central Asia: 'Next they kindled a fire with twigs of incense (galbanum?), muttered a few barbaric words in the Scythian tongue, and while they kept up a din with bell and drum over the baggage, they carried round the twigs of burning incense, still crackling, and seemed to be warding off evil spirits with their frantic gesticulations.'[145] Gardīzī (eleventh century) likewise tells of certain Central Asiatic tribes who foregathered every year with their musicians to partake of a festive banquet. While the musicians played, the Shamans worked themselves into a frenzy and finally fell to the ground in a coma. On regaining consciousness, they acted as soothsayers, and foretold the future.[146] Al-Bīrūnī[147] (tenth century) describes many gala occasions – often protracted – which formed the climaxes of the varied musical life of Central Asia. Chinese sources also tell of special celebrations in a musical setting; for example, an exorcism ceremony among the Yen-chi, living south of the Altai Mountains, where the music went on for four successive days.[148] In Samarkand, in the early Middle Ages, the Festival of Inviting the Cold took place in the eleventh month. To the accompaniment of music and dancing, people repeatedly drenched themselves with water in the

[140] Quoted from Liu Mau-Tsai, *Die chinesischen Nachrichten zur Geschichte der Ost-Türken* (Wiesbaden, 1958), p. 466. [141] W. Eberhard, 'Die Kultur der alten zentral- und westasiatischen Völker nach chinesischen Quellen', *Zeitschrift für Ethnologie* 73 (1941), p. 236. [142] *Materiali po istorii Turmen i Turkmenii*, Vol. I (Moscow/Leningrad, 1939), p. 187. [143] R. N. Frye, *The History of Bukhara* (Cambridge (Mass.), 1954), pp. 17, 23, 40, and 122 (Notes 111 and 113). [144] Cf. B. Spuler, *Die goldene Horde* (Leipzig, 1943), p. 437. [145] K. Dietrich, *Byzantinische Quellen zur Länder- und Völkerkunde, Quellen und Forschungen zur Erd- und Kulturkunde*, Vol. V, Part II (Leipzig, 1912), p. 17. [146] V. Vinogradov, *Kirgizskaja narodnaja muzyka* (Frunze, 1958), p. 33. [147] *The Chronology of Ancient Nations, an English version of the Arabic text of the Athār-al-Bākiya of Albīrūni*, translated by C. Edward Sachau (London, 1879). [148] W. Eberhard, 'Die Kultur der alten zentral- und westasiatischen Völker nach chinesischen Quellen', *Zeitschrift für Ethnologie* 73 (1941, Berlin, 1942),

course of this festival.[149] Music also played a major rôle in the traditional New Year celebrations in Khwārizm.

Further evidence of a highly developed musical culture among the peoples of Inner Asia is the existence of a form of tablature in Khwārizm in medieval times.[150] The earliest surviving example of this Khwārizmic tablature dates from c. 1200. In Central Asia the art of instrument-making had also been developed to a high level during the ninth and tenth centuries. We learn of improvements to certain instruments and also that entirely new sound-producing devices emerged at this time. In the year 913, according to Arab sources,[151] a certain Ibn al-Aḥwas, a native of the Samarkand region, invented a stringed instrument of unusually wide compass known as the *shārūd*.[152] Whereas among the Arabs musical instruments were used almost exclusively as an accompaniment to song, Turkestan, Transoxiana, Khwārizm, and Khurāsān witnessed, in the tenth century, the emergence of independent instrumental music,[153] in which definite suite-like forms of a purely instrumental nature were developed, and new expressive techniques were tried out and adopted. The wide range of musical instruments in use already in the early Middle Ages is noteworthy, as is the fact that some of them certainly originated there, or were modified and further developed.

This enumeration of facts and reports relating to the history of music in Central Asia at the end of the tenth century could be substantially expanded with the help of material at present available. It points to the existence among these peoples of a high level of musical culture, which has so far received regrettably scant attention from writers on the history of music.[154] We are thus justified in thinking that Central Asia is a region in which bowing could have originated.

The first use of the bow

This theory is strengthened by a number of additional facts. First of all it is significant that the authors whose works first refer to the existence of bowed instruments of the *rabāb* type are natives of Central Asia. Al-Fārābī was born in Wasij (Transoxiana) and pursued his studies in Khurāsān, while Ibn Sīnā came from Afshana, near Bokhara, and grew up in Bokhara.[155] Another scholar, Muḥammad ibn Aḥmad al-Khwārizmī,[156] who hailed from Khwārizm, discusses

---

p. 224. [149] W. Eberhard, op. cit., p. 236. [150] Cf. V. Bel'aev, 'Khoresmian Notation', *The Sackbut* (1924). [151] The following sources are particularly important: al-Fārābī's treatise on music (R. d'Erlanger: *La Musique Arabe*, Vol. I, pp. 42 ff.); al-Istachrī's *Buch der Länder* (translated by A. D. Mordtmann, Hamburg, 1845, p. 117); *Mafātiḥ al-ʿulūm* by al-Khwārizmī (E. Wiedemann in *Sitzungsberichte der phys.-med. Sozietät in Erlangen*, 54th Year (1922), p. 9). [152] No details regarding the morphology of this instrument are available; cf. R. d'Erlanger, op. cit., Vol. I, p. 311 f., p. 43, Note 5. [153] Farmer, 'The Music of Islam', in *The New Oxford History of Music*, Vol. I (London, 1957), pp. 442 and 452. [154] Various scholars are at present working on early musical sources from Central Asia in the Institute of Aesthetics and in the Oriental Institute in Tashkent. [155] For proof of Ibn Sīnā's Turkish extraction see A. Süheyl Ünver, 'İslâm tababetinde Türk hekimlerinin mevkii ve Ibn Sina'nın Türklüğü', *Belleten* 2 (Ankara, 1937). [156] Trans-

the *rabāb* in his encyclopedic work *Mafātīḥ al-ʿulūm*, observing that this instrument was also known in Fars (Persia) and Khurāsān. About the beginning of the tenth century, the *rabāb* was also known in Ghazna, which roughly corresponds to present-day Afghanistan.[157]

The much-travelled Persian writer, Ibn Khurdādhbih[158] who, like al-Khwā-rizmī, enumerates the musical instruments played in different Eastern countries, tells of a two-stringed folk instrument (*watār*) played so enchantingly by a herdlad from Bokhara that the Naiads enticed him away. He, too, remarks on the special manner of performance, which also excited some comment from al-Maqdisī[159] when writing about Khwārizm. This suggests that it must have been unfamiliar, and therefore particularly noteworthy, to the Arab writers – and may well imply the use of a bow. The two-stringed instrument noted by Ibn Khurdādhbih is obviously the *qobuz*, to which there are frequent references in Central Asian, and more specifically in Uigur, sources from the ninth century onward, and which still survives among the Uzbeks and Sarts (valley Tadzhiks) in the Chardzhou and Ferghana regions, and is found in Central Syr-Darya (*kobuz*, *kavuz*, *qāʾūs*, *qūbūz*) among the Kirghiz (*komuz* or *kyjak*), the Kazaks (*kobys*), the Mari (*kovysh*) and Mongolian tribes (*khuʾur*) as a bowed instrument. Early sources describe the *qobuz* as both a bowed and plucked instrument.[160] The earliest reference, dating from the ninth and tenth centuries,[161] unfortunately gives no information relating to technique, and so contributes nothing to the search for the origins of bowing. Not until after the year 1000 do we find positive proof that the *qobuz* was played as a bowed instrument. The term *iklik* (*iqlïq*, *iklij*, *yiklij*) – supposedly a contraction of *oklu qobuz* (= a bowed *qobuz*)[162] – has been used to describe bowed instruments by the Turkish peoples of Central Asia and the Near Eastern Turks from the fifteenth century to the present day. There are various types of Central Asiatic *iklij*, differing from one another in certain details – the *ikili* from the Altai, the *igilʾ* of Tuva, the Khakasskayan *y y ch* – but all are bowed. As a rule they have a remarkably long neck, an elliptical body with a stretched skin resonating surface, and two horsehair strings, attached to frontal pegs and an end pin, and played with a horsehair bow. Usually the melody was played only on the first string, the other providing a drone accompaniment.

A wealth of information relating to the question of the origins of bowing is contained in a musical treatise from Central Asia by the Dervish Ali.[163] This work, dating from the early seventeenth century, comments on the entire range of instruments known and played in Central Asia. In the chapter on bowed instruments (*ghichak*, Persian *ghishek*) the author observes that these were 'invented' during

lated by E. Wiedemann, op. cit., p. 9.   [157] Cf. B. Spuler, *Iran in früh-islamischer Zeit* (Wiesbaden, 1952), p. 270.   [158] Translated by H. G. Farmer in *JRAS* (1928), p. 518.   [159] Published in Russian translation in *Material po istorii Turkmen i Turkmenii*, Vol. I (Moscow/Leningrad, 1939), p. 187.
[160] P. Pelliot, 'Le k'ong-heou et le qobuz', *Natio Hakushi Kwanseki Shukuga Shinagaku Ronso* (Kyoto, 1926).   [161] Cf. N. Dmitriev, *Atasikij epos kogutej* (published by the Academy of Sciences of the UdSSR, 1925), p. 77.   [162] M. R. Gazimihāl, *Asya ve Anadolu kaynaklarīnda Iklīğ* (Ankara, 1958), pp. 6ff.   [163] A. A. Semenov, *A Middle Asiatic Treatise on Music of Dervish Ali*, (Tashkent,

the reign of the Sultan Mahmud Ghasnavi (998–1030) in Central Asia, then ruled over by the Ghasnavids. He stresses the fact that his assertions are based on popular legends and old tales which he had often heard repeated in his own country. He suggests Nasir-i-Khusrau[164] as a possible 'inventor' of bowed instruments, together with that famous scholar from the Bokhara district, Ibn Sīnā, who was one of the first to write on bowed instruments as a species, in his *Kitāb al-Shifā*.[165] This is an interesting example of how oral traditions dating back centuries may be corroborated by historical research.

The construction of the earliest authenticated examples of bowed instruments also points to a Central Asian origin. Morphologically they correspond to the *ṭunbūr*, native to Transoxiana or Khurāsān: a long-necked, pear-shaped, plucked instrument with two strings or pairs of strings attached to an end pin; or to the Central Asian *qobuz*. Al-Fārābī drew attention to the similarity between the *rabāb* and the Khurasan *ṭunbūr* in his *Kitāb al-mūsīqī al-kabīr*.[166] The *Yüanshih*[167] reveals that the earliest Chinese bowed instruments (*hu-ch'in*) corresponded to the *qobuz* (*huo-pu-szu*), and Dervish Ali[168] indicates the common roots of *rabāb* and *qobuz*.

Valuable evidence in support of the theory that bowing originated in Central Asia is contained in al-Fārābī's comments on the tuning of the *rabāb*,[169] the strings of which were usually tuned an augmented second apart. This type of tuning was uncommon in Arab and Persian countries, and the only other instrument known to have been similarly tuned is the Central Asiatic *ṭunbūr*. Al-Fārābī calls it 'Bokhara tuning'.[170] Thus in the early part of the tenth century Oriental bowed instruments[171] were tuned after the fashion of Central Asia.[172]

Chinese sources are extremely helpful in this quest. The origins of Chinese musical instruments can often be determined with great accuracy, not only from references in contemporary treatises on music, but from etymological study of the names of instruments. In almost every Chinese term denoting a bowed instrument (*hu-ch'in, êrh-hu, hsi-hu, pan-hu, yeh-hu, ching-hu, hu-hu*) we find the component 'hu'. This is the equivalent of 'barbarian', and is used by the Chinese to describe the Turco-Mongolian tribes of Central Asia. According to recent research,[173] this word 'hu' was used from about the end of the sixth century to refer to the Iranians in Central Asia, and more specifically to the Sogdians, in contrast to T'u-chüeh (Eastern Turks). The Sogdians inhabited the region between Amu-Darya and Syr-Darya, especially the territory around Bokhara and Samarkand. There is evidence that extensive Sogdian colonies also existed at that time in

1946). [164] Nasir-i-Khusrau, a contemporary of Ibn Sīnā, came from Khurāsān and gained fame primarily through his travel books. [165] Translated into French in R. d'Erlanger's *La Musique Arabe*, Vol. II, p. 234. [166] Translated into French in d'Erlanger, op. cit., Vol. I, p. 277. [167] *Yüan Shih*, Book 71, Chapter 22, p. 5. [168] A. A. Semenov, *A Middle Asiatic Treatise on Music of Dervish Ali* (Tashkent, 1946). [169] D'Erlanger, op. cit., Vol. I, p. 280. [170] D'Erlanger, op. cit., Vol. I, p. 253. [171] At the end of the 10th century there is evidence, particularly in Arab sources, that the *rabāb* was used as a bowed instrument. [172] Tuning bowed instruments in seconds is known to be practised today both in Central Asia and in the Balkans. [173] E. G. Pulley-

Eastern Turkestan and Mongolia. Thus the *hu-ch'in*, which appears in Chinese texts from the ninth century onwards, and is positively described in the *Yüanshih*[174] as a bowed instrument 'the two strings of which were made to sound by means of a horsehair bow', was imported into China from Central Asia. There is also the *hsi-ch'in*, mentioned in Ch'en Yang's *Yüeh Shu*[175] (1101) as a friction instrument the two strings of which were rubbed by introducing a slip of bamboo between them. It is listed in this source, together with the *hu-ch'in*, in the category of 'hu' instruments. The *Yüeh Shu* tells us that it was a favourite instrument of the Hsi, a tribe of the Tung-hu with an old-Mongolian culture. Its popularity spread, until at length it found its way into China as a folk instrument. This would support the assumption that the bow was first used in Central Asia, probably in Sogdian Transoxiana, to excite the strings of instruments in common use there.

Another point of some significance is that Khwārizm and Transoxiana were the centre for the manufacture of hunting bows. A number of Arab writers are loud in their praises of the population of these regions because of their skill in making hunting bows.[176] Al-Maqdisī,[177] enumerating the various articles exported from Khwārizm to the countries of the Caliphate, notes among other things 'bows that only strong men may string'; while the unknown author of the *Ḥudūd al-'ālam* says of Urgench: 'its inhabitants are renowned for their skill and dexterity in archery.'[178] In the Orient, the bow was the chief weapon, both in war and in the hunt; but medieval Chinese sources[179] report that about the year 1000 certain tribes living in Central Asia were trying out its musical possibilities. Among the Hsi-hsia, for instance, the twang of the bowstring was regarded as the voice of the oracle. It thus seems highly probable that the bow was used in this region at an early stage to excite strings.

Pictorial evidence

Although all the signs point to the conclusion that bowing originated in Central Asia, in the North-Eastern border provinces of the Islamic Empire, in Khwārizm and Transoxiana, and *not* in the Arab lands themselves, this theory can in the last analysis only be confirmed by iconographical proof. For this reason we must take full account of every available illustration showing musical instruments of the first millenium the origin of which can be traced to Central Asia.

Of all the Central Asiatic illustrations that have survived from this period, only a few have any bearing on the problem. The greater part of the available

blank, 'A Sogdian Colony in Inner Mongolia', *T'oung Pao* 42 (1952), pp. 318 ff.   [174] *Yüan Shih*, Book 71, Chapter 22, p. 5,   [175] This source, which contains descriptions of the Chinese musical instruments, was first printed in 1195.   [176] J. Hein, *Bogenhandwerk und Bogensport bei den Osmanen* (Dissertation, Hamburg, 1925). — There is no proof of any connection between the development of the hunting bow and that of the musical bow.   [177] S. P. Tolstow, *Auf den Spuren der altchoresmischen Kultur* (Berlin, 1953), p. 260.   [178] Tolstow, op. cit., p. 263.   [179] W. Eberhard 'Die Kultur der alten zentral- und westasiatischen Völker nach chinesischen Quellen', *Zeit-*

pictorial evidence shows the usual run-of-the-mill instruments – various types of harp and lute, transverse flute, shawm and double shawm, syrinx, cylindrical drum, and cymbals – all of which are listed in the *Annals* of the T'ang Dynasty in an account of the music of An-Kuo (Bokhara).[180] There is a notable abundance of chordophones, especially of necked instruments, but only some three or four of these can be classified as bowed instruments.

The musical illustrations on the Airtam frieze,[181] excavated near Termez in Uzbekistan, south of Samarkand, date from pre-Islamic times. Most of the female musicians represented are so badly damaged that their instruments are beyond recognition, and only the harp, lute (guitar), double shawm, and cylindrical drum are distinguishable. Nevertheless this important archaeological discovery has a contribution to make to our research. The guitar-shaped instrument held by one of the female musicians shown on the frieze (Plate 14) bears a striking resemblance, morphologically speaking, to early Byzantine bowed instruments dating from the tenth and eleventh centuries. The instrument's resonator has incurving sides and four C-shaped sound-holes. Its four strings are attached to a frontal string-holder on the sound-board of the body, and are plucked with a plectrum. In fact, this find goes some way towards justifying the hypothesis that the birthplace of the first bowed instruments shown on Byzantine miniatures should be sought in Turkestan,[182] especially since there is no evidence that this type of instrument existed in the Near East or in Europe prior to the tenth century,[183] while it is depicted in various forms in Central Asia.[184]

Further illustrations of Central Asian musical instruments appear in the frescoes of Pendshikent and Topraq-Qal'a,[185] although only fragments of these important relics have survived. One of the mural paintings of Topraq-Qal'a shows a hand holding the neck of a two-stringed musical instrument. It is, however, impossible to determine whether the instrument is a *rabāb*, and therefore bowed, or a *ṭunbūr*.

The outer rim of a silver vessel dating from the post-Sassanid era[186] and found in Central Asia shows *inter alia* two musicians and a dancing girl. One of the musi-

---

schrift für Ethnologie 73 (1942), p. 219. [180] M. Courant, 'Chine et Corée', *Encyclopédie de la musique*, ed. A. Lavignac (Paris, 1912), p. 193. [181] Illustration and description in M. Prynne, 'Angelic Musicians from Central Asia', *GSJ* VII (April, 1954), p. 54, and *GSJ* VIII, Plate VIII; cf. also M. E. Masson, 'Skul'ptura Airtama', *Iskusstvo* (1935), 2. [182] The other early medieval instruments of West Turkestan also appear in the Byzantine Empire from the 10th century onwards. [183] Lateral pegs, so typical of the early Byzantine fiddles, predominate also on Central Asian chordophones of the period. The well-preserved neck of a Central Asiatic stringed instrument, complete with peg-box and four lateral pegs, has been excavated in Eastern Turkestan. Cf. M. A. Stein, *Ancient Khotan* (Oxford, 1907), Vol. II, Plate LXXIII (N. XII, 2). On the spread of instruments with lateral pegs see K. Geiringer in *ZfMw* X (1927/28), pp. 560ff. [184] For example, on a terracotta figure from Afrasiab, dating from the beginning of the Christian era, now in the Hermitage in Leningrad, Central Asian section. [185] Cf. description of the frescoes of Topraq-Qal'a in Tolstow, op. cit., p. 193. The Pendshikent frescoes (*c.* 700) show a girl playing a harp; cf. *Shivopis' drevnego Pjandshikenta* (Moscow, 1954), Plate XXXIV. [186] Illustrated in O. M. Dalton,

cians is blowing a long, slightly curved trumpet-like instrument. The second is obviously playing on a stringed instrument, unfortunately badly damaged, so that its function and construction are no longer recognizable. It may be a bowed instrument of the fiddle type, with a bent back neck held in the player's right hand so that the resonator rests against his chest, while his left hand clutches a long bow in the inverted grip and bows an oblique up-stroke. The instrument shown in the left hand of a musician who appears on the remains of an earthenware vessel from Central Asia (Plate 15) may also be of the bowed type.[187] Unfortunately the figure has lost its head, the upper part of its body, and its right arm, which would normally carry the bow. We are left with the vague indication of the almost vertical *a-gamba* position in which the small pearshaped instrument is held, generally encountered only where the instrument is bowed, and not usually relevant to plucked chordophones. More useful to our enquiry is a painting originating in Central Asia [188] and dating from the ninth or tenth century A. D. This painting, representing a hunting scene, decorates the sounding-board of a valuable lute (p'i-p'a)[189] preserved in the Shōsōin, the treasure-house at Nara.[190] In the central part,[191] the artist has portrayed a banquet (Plate 13). Between two musicians, squatting on the floor, sits the host, to whom a servant is offering food, and in the right foreground is his guest. One of the two musicians holds a large lute, the strings of which he plucks with a plectrum. The second, as far as one can judge, is playing a slender, long-necked, bowed instrument, propped up on the floor. This bowed instrument answers the descriptions of the *rabāb* in al-Fārābī's treatise on music,[192] which specifically mentions the great similarity in construction between the *rabāb* and the long-necked lute of Central Asia – the Khurāsān *ṭunbūr*.[193] Unfortunately, the evidence of this illustration is by no means incontrovertible. Even from the special enlargement in my possession it is impossible to determine whether or not the object is in fact a musical instrument at all. Whereas the artist responsible for this lacquer painting has reproduced the details of the *p'i-p'a* with considerable accuracy, the object interpreted as a bowed

The Treasure of the Oxus (London, 1905), Plate XXV. [187] This fragment is in the Central Asian section of the Hermitage in Leningrad, Petrovski Collection. [188] Reproductions of this painting are to be found in the following works: O. Sirén, *Chinese Painting*, Part I, Vol. III (Plates) (London, 1956), Plate 49; J. Harada, *English Catalogue of the Imperial Repository Shōsōin* (Tokyo, 1932), Plate LXXVII; O. Fischer, *Die Kunst Indiens, Chinas und Japans* (Berlin, 1928) (*Propyläen der Kunstgeschichte*, Vol. IV), Plate 408; *Tōyei Shukō* I, 50. [189] The painting lies under the spot where the plectrum touches the strings, and is therefore scratched in several places. [190] The Treasure-house of Nara, Residence of the Japanese Emperors in the 8th century, is the oldest and best maintained museum in the world. The 'Chinese Collection' in the Treasure-house, which in addition to the painted lute contains many other Chinese musical instruments of the T'ang period, was presented to the Shōsōin in 756 by the widow of the Japanese Emperor Somu. Since then the objects in the collection have remained just as they were. According to recent research, this *p'i-p'a* is one of the items subsequently added to the Imperial collection. [191] A slightly inaccurate drawing of this appears in *The Museum of Far Eastern Antiquities, Bulletin 29* (Stockholm, 1957), Fig. 73b. [192] D'Erlanger, op. cit., Vol. I, p. 277. [193] The painting suggests that the object may be a two-stringed instrument, the strings being attached to an

instrument is treated somewhat casually. Did he wish to imply by this that the instrument in question was a crude, imperfect folk instrument, or did he have no really clear idea of how it looked, having seen it only briefly? Or is it, perhaps, not a musical instrument after all? No source material has yet been found which might give a definite answer to these questions; and we must therefore content ourselves with the hypothesis that this painting may represent one of the earliest illustrations of a bowed instrument. One thing is, however, certain, namely that the illustration originated in Central Asia;[194] and the position in which the instrument is played is illuminating, since it corroborates evidence gleaned from other medieval Eastern sources, and applies to folk instruments widely used today in Turkestan and Uzbekistan.[195] All the various types of bowed instruments native to Central Asia are played in the same position – *a gamba* – as for instance the aforesaid Chinese lute from the T'ang period (Plate 13). Apart from the *ghichak (gydjak)*, which resembles the Arab *kamanja*, the bowed chordophones of the Central Asian states of today are outwardly similar to the narrow, long-necked fiddle shown in this early illustration. In view of the unchanging, age-old traditions of this region, the agreement between historical sources and ethnological material is of special interest.[196] When the construction and performing technique of these modern Central Asian bowed instruments are studied, it is easier to interpret and understand the earliest known pictorial representations of bowed chordophones, and valuable conclusions follow regarding the origins of bowing.

The evidence of Central Asian instruments today

The following results of ethnomusicological research are of special note:

1. Structurally there appear to be no basic differences between the bowed and plucked instruments of Central Asia. The Altai *ikili* and *topschur* are identical in every respect, though the former is played with a horsehair bow and the latter plucked. Most of the two-stringed fiddles used by the Kirghiz (*komuz* and *kyjak*), the Kazaks (*kobyz*), the Sarts and Uzbeks (*kobuz, kavus, qā'ūs*), and the Mari, are

end-pin. [194] O. Sirén, 'Central Asian Influences in Chinese Paintings of the T'ang Period' *Arts asiatiques* III (1956), pp. 3 ff., in particular p. 20 f. [195] Descriptions of Central Asian musical instruments are contained in the following works, *inter alia*: V. Vinogradov, *Kirgizkaja narodnaja muzyka*, (Frunze, 1958); V. Bel'aev, *Muzykal'nye instrumenty Uzbekistana* (Moscow, 1933); V. Uspenskij and V. Bel'aev, *Turkmenskaja muzyka* (Moscow, 1928); A. Petrosjanz, *Instrumentovedenie, Uzbekskij orkestr rekonstruirovannych narodnych instrumentov* (Tashkent, 1951); Ja. Pekker, 'Ob Uzbekskom orkestre narodnych instrumentov', *Sovjetskaja Muzyka* 11 (1946), pp. 41 ff.; P. M. Sykes, 'Notes on Musical Instruments in Khorasan', *Man* IX (1909), pp. 161 ff.; M. G. Capus, 'La musique chez les Kirghizes et les Sartes de l'Asie centrale', *Revue d'Ethnographie* 3 (1885), p. 97. [196] This section of the present investigation, dealing with early bowing in Central Asia and including the present-day practice of folk music in the Uzbek and Turkmen Republics, is primarily based on archaeological and ethnological publications. An exhaustive study of the archaeological material – for the most part still unpublished – in museums of the Soviet Union, and a detailed survey of bowing techniques used by the peoples of Central Asia at the present

used both as bowed and plucked instruments. The same is true of the Tadzhik-Uzbek *setar* (*satō*), while the three-stringed *ṭunbūr*, the main Central Asian plucked instrument, frequently appears in the role of a bowed instrument.

2. The methods of tuning and playing present-day folk instruments of Central Asia largely correspond to medieval practice. The two-stringed fiddles of the Sarts and Kirghiz are often tuned in the same way as were the *rabāb* and *ṭunbūr* at the time of al-Fārābī. Central Asian three-stringed instruments are frequently tuned thus: key-note, fifth, octave; and Jerome of Moravia tells us that bowed instruments were similarly tuned in medieval Europe.

3. An essential feature of fiddling in Central Asia is the use of the drone. Melodies are played on the top string only; it is the only string to be stopped, while the other strings maintain a constant drone. Here, too, we have a close correspondence with the testimony of early historical sources in Europe relating to fiddling.

4. One of the chief characteristics of Turkmen, Uzbek, and Kirghiz folk music is the practice of doubling the melodic line at the fourth. This improvised form of multi-part music is widespread in both vocal and instrumental music, and performers on bowed instruments native to this region frequently resort to stopping two strings with the same finger. The resulting sound resembles early medieval parallel organum, as recorded in the ninth-century *Musica enchiriadis*.

5. Again in the folk music of Central Asia there is no clear division between plucked and bowed playing, and there are various transitional stages between the two techniques. By varying the technique of sound-production performers can obtain a wide range of sound effects. This gives a correspondingly wide range of expression in the delivery of a melody. For instance, the Kirghiz musician playing his *komus* as a plucked instrument (that is to say without the bow) does not limit himself to tremolo and pizzicato, but occasionally rubs the strings with the flat of his hand and so, by friction, keeps them in a state of continuous vibration.

6. Sart (valley Tadzhik) and Kirghiz folk musicians use either a symmetrically arched bow, strung with horsehair, or a flat friction-stick, on which the horsehair, instead of being taut, hangs loosely from each end of the stick. The player may tighten the hair at will, by flexing the fingers of the hand holding the stick. Frequently, he rubs the wooden shaft itself over the strings. This type of sound production clearly represents a transitional stage between friction-stick and bow.

The bowed instrument represented in the Central Asian painting from the ninth/tenth century already discussed[197] (Plate 13) was apparently played with a friction stick. The rod-like object held in an overhand grip by the squatting musician can hardly be interpreted as a curved bow. Medieval Chinese sources also point to the friction stick as the fore-runner of the bow proper. Ma Tuan-lin's encyclopedia, compiled *c.* 1300,[198] as well as the *Yüeh Shu* (1101) contain references to

time, are tasks that remain to be undertaken. [197] P. 52. [198] A. C. Moule, 'A List of the Musical and

stringed instruments similar to the tube-fiddle (*hsi-ch'in*), the strings of which were rubbed with a slip of bamboo. The East Asian board-zither (*ya-cheng*) was also played in this fashion up to the tenth century,[199] and to this day there exists, in the Chinese province of Hopei, a stringed instrument of much the same type,[200] played by rubbing the strings with a *kao-liang* stalk.[201]

Summary of the evidence

Briefly, then, on the evidence of the sources, Central Asia may be regarded as the birthplace of bowing; the use of the friction stick in this region before the tenth century can be demonstrated with a high degree of probability; and the first mention of a horsehair bow, early in the tenth century, also refers to Central Asia.[202] We may assume from al-Fārābī's description that in the tenth century 'other similar implements' apart from the bow were employed to excite the strings of Central Asian chordophones.[203]

In their early stages bowed instruments were evidently folk instruments, and it is not until relatively late in their development, and then only sporadically, that we find evidence of their participation in the ceremonial and court music of Asia's ancient civilizations.[204] Cultivated Muslim musicians and theorists were unimpressed by the bowed instrument's thin, unattractive tone, and regarded it as a most imperfect instrument, to be included in their writings solely for the sake of completeness. Thus al-Fārābī writes in his *Kitāb al-mūsīqī al-kabīr*:[205] 'owing to its construction, the sound of the rebab is not as strong as that of certain other instruments. From this point of view, the rebab is inferior to most others.' In addition, al-Fārābī regards the absence of frets as a defect in bowed instruments, since this makes it difficult to pitch notes or scales accurately.[206] The Arabic manuscript Berlin We 1233, fol. 47v also reveals that the *rabāb* was not very highly thought of by the Arabs in medieval times.[207] Likewise the *ya-cheng* and *hsi-ch'in*, the early Chinese friction instruments noted and described in the

other Sound-producing Instruments of the Chinese', *JNChBRAS* XXXIX (1908), p. 149. [199] There is a description of the technique used in playing the *ya-chêng* in Book 29 of the *Chiu T'ang Shu.* [200] *Muzykal'nye instrumenty kitaja* (Moscow, 1958), p. 22 f. (Russian translation from the Chinese). [201] Kao-liang is *Andropogon sorghum*, Brot. var. *vulgaris* often referred to as 'Chinese millet'. [202] Up to the present, horsehair strings have chiefly been used on chordophones, in Central Asia. When al-Fārābī observes that the strings of bowed instruments were rubbed with similar strings, this indicates the use of horsehair strings. [203] Al-Fārābī says, literally, that the strings of bowed instruments were rubbed by means of other strings (autār) 'or with something similar' (D'Erlanger, op. cit., Vol. I, p. 166). [204] Cf. T. Norlind, 'Beiträge zur chinesischen Instrumentengeschichte', *STMf* 15, p. 75. [205] D'Erlanger, op. cit., Vol. I, p. 285. [206] D'Erlanger, loc. cit. As a point in favour of bowed instruments, al-Fārābī cites their capacity for differentiated performance: 'To compensate for this, the *rabāb* has other good features that are peculiarly its own. The musician can play loudly and softly at the same time'. [207] H.G. Farmer, *Historical Facts*, p. 265, Note 1.

Yüeh Shu (1101), were numbered by the author among the instruments of 'the common people'.[208]

Thus bowing evolved in the world of simple folk music, and had no initial contact with that of art music. It soon came to be the most typical means of expression among the people.[209] Its musical potential was perhaps best suited to the nature of Oriental music, based as it was on vocal monody, highly developed improvisatory skill and flowing, richly ornamented line, 'the intervals of which are highly labile and often reduced to sequences of "shades" by ornaments any slurs'.[210] In Eastern instrumental playing, too, the 'lyrical element', the freeld flowing melody, is always paramount,[211] and this is best expressed on bowed instruments, since the bow makes it possible to prolong and connect the notes. The player strives to follow the voice through all the intricacies of its melodic line. While wind instruments are restricted to fixed notes or scales by the harmonic series or the spacing of fingerholes, harps and zithers by the tuning of their strings, and lutes by the distance between their frets, on bowed instruments the player can produce portamenti and slurs, as well as every conceivable intermediate pitch value within the scale. Whereas most instruments are forced to simplify certain parts of the melodic line, so that when the instrument plays with the voice there are heterophonic discrepancies between the two, every detail of the melodic line can be reproduced on bowed instruments. The structure of Oriental bowed instruments, above all the absence of a finger-board, greatly facilitates the achievement of a high degree of musical flexibility.[212] The strings of Western fiddlers are pressed against the fingerboard, to produce individual notes of fixed pitch; but those on Oriental bowed instruments stand well away from the neck and are merely stopped with the fingers, using varying degrees of downward pressure. In this way pitch and melodic movement can be modified in finest detail. Thus the bowed chordophones of the East successfully meet the demands of Oriental melody, 'a play of arabesques, of vine-like endlessly extending melismata and flowing coloratura at rest in itself,'[213] which only cheironomic gestures and neumes can represent – not our Western notation.[214] Furthermore, the bowed

---

[208] Pp. 68 ff.   [209] This would explain why, to begin with, bowed instruments so rarely figure in literary sources and in illustrations, since medieval scholars and artists were scarcely concerned with the affairs of the common people.   [210] A. Berner, *Studien zur arabischen Musik auf Grund gegenwärtiger Theorie und Praxis in Ägypten* (Dissertation, Leipzig 1937), p. 31.   [211] According to al-Fārābi, Eastern instrumental music was closely related to vocal music, imitated the singing voice, varied and ornamented its line, accompanied it, all the time following the shape of the melody in all its refinements (as far as was technically possible or confined itself to providing brief preludes and interludes to allow the singer to rest). Cf. d'Erlanger, op. cit., Vol. I, pp. 17, 21 and 23.   [212] The morphological characteristics of Oriental bowed instruments are discussed in H. H. Dräger, *Prinzip einer Systematik der Musikinstrumente* (Casel and Basle, 1948), p. 10: on the other hand, the instruments of the *Kamanja-rabāb* family are capable of great melodic freedom, for the absence for a fingerboard makes it possible to achieve a much more finely wrought melodic line than on European bowed instruments. We see from this last example how what outwardly appears to be a technical defect can in actual fact be a source of great riches'.   [213] H. Besseler, *Die Musik des Mittelalters*, p. 40.   [214] With regard to the actual sound, the rough, nasal, often

instrument provides the drone accompaniment so indispensable to eastern peoples.[215] Bowed chordophones are better adapted than other musical instruments to sustain single notes indefinitely, thus providing sustained support for the vocal line; or to play melody and drone simultaneously, in which case an open string is bowed throughout alongside the stopped string. These special possibilities of sound production and technique strengthen the theory that bowing developed in an area where drone accompaniment formed an integral part of music-making.[216]

The motivation for the invention and early development of bowing can thus be explained by the attitude towards music of the peoples of Western and Central Asia. Their ideal musical sound was the long-unbroken melodic line. Arab writers of the time[217] expressed the view that the human voice was incapable of affording the listener unalloyed pleasure, since breathing constantly introduces caesuras into the melodic line. It was necessary, they said, to invent and employ musical instruments which could sustain and join notes as required in an uninterrupted line.[218] This requirement was met by the musical automata capable of producing a continuous flow of sound[219] and often mentioned in Arabic sources, as well as by the hurdy-gurdy, the bagpipe, the organ, and the various types of bowed instrument.[220]

pinched tone of primitive bowed instruments came nearer to Eastern conceptions of ideal sonority as exemplified in the singing style, than did the clear-cut single notes obtainable on plucked strings. [215] A. H. Fox Strangways, *The Music of Hindostan* (Oxford, 1914), p. 46, relates a significant remark made by an Indian, that for him, playing music without a drone was like being a ship without a rudder. Examples of extra-European drone polyphony are given by Curt Sachs in *The Rise of Music*, pp. 181 and 289; by Marius Schneider in *Geschichte der Mehrstimmigkeit*, Vol. I (Berlin, 1934); by E. von Hornbostel, 'Über Mehrstimmigkeit in der außereuropäischen Musik', Vienna Congress of the *IMG* (Vienna, 1909), p. 300 f.; by R. Lachmann, 'Zur außereuropäischen Mehrstimmigkeit' *Beethoven zentenarfeier* (Vienna, 1927), pp. 321 ff.; and by L. Propper, *Der Basso ostinato als technisches und formbildendes Prinzip* (Dissertation, Berlin, 1926), p. 7. [216] In his essay 'Ist die vokale Mehrstimmigkeit eine Schöpfung der Altrassen?' Marius Schneider has outlined the area affected by the spread of drone-singing (*AMl* 23 (1951), p. 42 f.). The presence of a drone in instrumental music was already so widespread among ancient civilizations that any attempt to localize the practice is impossible. [217] Particularly informative is the exposition of these principles of musical aesthetics by al-Akfānī al-Sakhāwī (died 1348); cf. E. Wiedemann, 'Zur Geschichte der Musik', Sitzungsberichte der phys.-med. Sozietät in Erlangen, 54th Year (1922), p. 9. [218] The relevant passage in al-Akfānī al-Sakhāwī's dissertation on music runs as follows: 'Instruments were invented primarily to satisfy a need, but also to provide an advantage. The need arose in the following way. The sound of the human voice [that is the singing voice] affects the soul, captivates it etc. But this sound is interrupted by pauses, so that one's pleasure is disturbed. The advantage derives from the fact that certain instruments are capable of producing sounds that are not to be found in nature (that is, in the human voice). To deny one's self these is inadmissible.' [219] Al-Jazarī refers to everlasting flutes as being mechanical musical instruments (E. Wiedemann and F. Hauser, 'Byzantinische und arabische akustische Instrumente', *Archiv für die Geschichte der Naturwissenschaft* 8 (1917), p. 142). Another of the Arab musical automata is described as follows: 'Al-Hannāna, the endless moaners, are man-made instruments which moan on one note, like the sound of the Mi'zaf, Mizmār.' [220] These instruments are probably of Oriental

EUROPE

Having discussed the beginnings of bowing in the Orient, we turn now to the European cultural zone, where the bow did not appear until after A. D. 1000. Continual conflicts between East and West led to lively cultural exchanges at that time,[221] in the course of which the highly-developed arts and sciences of both Islam and Byzantium strongly influenced the intellectual progress of the Western world.[222]

By the eleventh century, the feudal organization of the European states, and their economic and social structure, had reached a point where one may justifiably speak of the beginning of a new phase in medieval history.[223] In the arts, too, this period is a decisive turning-point, marking the inauguration of a separate 'Western' culture. A new genre of vernacular poetry took its place beside the Latin literature of the scholars. In the plastic arts the breakaway from antique models was carried still further; and a specifically European musical language was in the process of emerging.[224]

This era of growth in Western music, which led ultimately to a permanent schism with Oriental music, is marked by the creation of a European system of musical notation in which the progress of a melody is recorded visually and spatially using a system of intervals set out on lines and spaces, by exactly pitched notes, and by modal theory. In music itself the most important advance was the growth of polyphony.[225] The various types of improvised multi-part music, such as drones, parallel organum, and heterophony,[226] which had played a significant rôle in ancient times,[227] provided a basis for medieval organum, which was closely related to the instrumental techniques of the time, as John Cotton testifies.[228] We shall see that the growth of polyphony was stimulated not only by the organ, but by the advent of bowing in Europe.

provenance. [221] R. Grousset, *Orient und Okzident im geistigen Austausch* (Stuttgart, 1955); G. Jacob, *Der Einfluß des Morgenlandes auf das Abendland vornehmlich während des Mittelalters* (Hannover, 1924); P. H. Feist, 'Untersuchungen zur Bedeutung orientalischer Einflüsse für die Kunst des frühen Mittelalters', *Wissenschaftliche Zeitschrift der Martin-Luther-Universität Halle/ Wittenberg*, IInd Year (1952/53), No. 2, pp. 27ff.; H. Ley, *Studien zur Geschichte des Materialismus im Mittelalter* (Berlin, 1957). [222] P. Wagner, 'Morgen- und Abendland in der Musikgeschichte', *Stimmen der Zeit*, 58th Year, Vol. 114, 2 (1927) p. 142. [223] L. Stern, 'Zur Periodisierung der Geschichte Deutschlands im Feudalismus', *Zeitschrift für Geschichtswissenschaft* 5 (1957), pp. 61ff. [224] H. Besseler, *Die Musik des Mittelalters*, pp. 82 and 83. [225] E. Jammers, 'Anfänge der abendländischen Musik', *Sammlungen musikwissenschaftlicher Abhandlungen*, Vol. 31 (Strasbourg, 1955), p. 7; H. P. Lang, *Die Musik im Abendland*, Vol. I (Augsburg, 1947), p. 152. [226] G. D. Sasse, *Die Mehrstimmigkeit der ars antiqua in Theorie und Praxis* (Dissertation, Berlin, 1940), p. 16: 'In parallelism and the drone-technique we have the two cornerstones of the polyphony fostered in Europe's *Ars antiqua*'; cf. also E. L. Waeltner, *Das Organum bis zur Mitte des 11. Jahrhunderts* (Dissertation, Heidelberg, 1955); and B. L. Spiess, *Polyphony in theory and Practice from the 9th Century* (Dissertation, Harvard University, 1948). [227] The question of polyphony in ancient times is treated in greater detail in the following works. C. Sachs, 'Zweiklänge im Altertum', *Festschrift für Johannes Wolf* (Berlin, 1929), H. Hickmann, *La musique polyphonique dans l'Egypte ancienne* (Cairo, 1952); J. Quasten, *Musik und Gesang*, p. 91. [228] 'Qui canendi modus (diaphonia) vulgariter

Instruments and plectra before the introduction of the bow

The different types of bowed instrument shown in Western illustrations after the tenth century were certainly present in Europe centuries earlier, identical in form and structure but played as plucked instruments.[229] This is as true of fiddle-type chordophones, with their sagittal pegs and end-pins, as it is of lyres. Thus what was taken over from the East was not, as so often suggested, bowed instruments, but merely the bow itself, which was applied to instruments already present. Whereas in early medieval times the strings of these antecedents of our bowed instruments were generally plucked with the fingers, after the tenth century illustrations show a marked preference for the plectrum, which only began gradually to die out with the change to polyphonic playing in the fifteenth and sixteenth centuries.[230] Around A. D. 1000 long, rod-like plectra were commonly used, the precise function of which is not always easy to determine. Occasionally there appears to be no real difference between the rods used for plucking, striking, or rubbing. This is supported by the use of the word *uiedelstaf* (fiddle-stick) to translate *plectrum* in the Old High German glosses of the Oxford manuscript Junius 83.[231] In a later Middle English source[232] *fydylstyk* appears as a translation of *arculus*.

From the mass of iconographical evidence a few examples may be selected showing these long, rod-like plectra in use. A glossed psalter manuscript in the library at Amiens, dating from the tenth century, contains a miniature (Plate 18) showing St. Asaph[233] playing on a pear-shaped fiddle supported on his left knee, using a stick 30 to 40 cm. in length. From the same period there is a similar illustration in the Psalterium of Ivrea (Plate 17). Here again the artist has drawn a stringed instrument of the fiddle type being played with a remarkably long plectrum. The length and position of the rod rule out the theory that the strings were plucked separately, as in mandoline playing today. It is clear that the point of the plectrum, which appears in some illustrations to be bent back, scrapes across all the strings. A miniature from the Stuttgart Psalter[234] (Plate 16) shows

organum dicitur; eoquod vox humana apte dissonans similitudinem exprimat instrumenti, quod organum vocatur', *GS* II, p. 263. For the relationship of organum to medieval instrumental music, see W. Apel, 'Early History of the Organ', *Seculum*, XXIII (1948), p. 210; cf. also Dom Anselm Hughes, *Early medieval Music up to 1300, New Oxford History of Music*, Vol. II (Oxford, 1954), p. 275 f.   [229] A survey of the main types of early medieval chordophone, insofar as these may be regarded as the forerunners of the bowed instruments, is given by D. Droysen in *Die Saiteninstrumente des frühen und hohen Mittelalters (Halsinstrumente)* (Dissertation, Hamburg, 1961). [230] K. Geiringer, *Die Flankenwirbelinstrumente in der bildenden Kunst der Zeit zwischen 1300 und 1500* (Dissertation, Vienna, 1923), p. 29; cf. also *ZfMw* 10, p. 582.   [231] *Althochdeutsche Glossen*, Vol.3, p. 383, line 7.   [232] H. Kurath, *Middle English Dictionary* (Ann Arbor, 1956 ff.), S. V. 'fidel stik'. [233] Asaph, a Levite credited with the authorship of several Psalms, was a poet and mastersinger under King David, and founder of a school of female singers. A footnote describes the instrument as a 'cythara'. In the psalter manuscript fol. 23 in the Württembergische Landesbibliothek in Stuttgart, the word 'cythara', which appears in the text, is represented in the illustration by an elongated plucked instrument with an end-pin, frontal pegs and a bridge.   [234] Württembergische Landes-

an S-shaped plectrum, by which the strings would presumably have been rubbed rather than plucked.

The beater also crops up frequently during the Middle Ages, especially in connection with the psaltery and the stringed *tambourin*. The ivory cover of the Codex Egerton 1139 (London, British Museum), dating from the early part of the twelfth century, has a bas-relief on which King David is shown striking the strings of a trapezoidal psaltery with two long rods (Plate 55). 'Dulcimer' illustrations of this type are not uncommon in the Middle Ages. It is worth noting also the stringed *tambourin*, often illustrated and described in medieval times,[235] which consisted of a long, rectangular sound-box and several strings tuned to fundamental key-note and fifth. It invariably appears in conjunction with the one-handed flute. The player holds the wind instrument with one hand, while with the other he strikes the strings of the suspended *tambourin* with a stick, to produce a fixed drone accompaniment.[236]

In this context it is useful to consider the plucked instruments in general use in Asia during the ninth and tenth centuries, and their playing technique. The various forms of plectrum referred to in Sanskrit texts[237] (*koṇa, śarika, parivāda*) indicate a certain diversity both in shape and purpose, while Chinese sources confirm that at that time the ideal was to achieve a richly varied touch in chordophone playing.[238] This also applied to instruments whose strings were plucked with the fingers, as for instance the board-zither, *ch'in*. The usual medieval form of notation for this instrument distinguishes between various types of pizzicato, and also calls for the 'soft touch', where the string is rubbed with the fingers.[239] The *Chiu T'ang Shu* (c. 920–45)[240] records that the ancient Chinese lute (*p'i-p'a*) was played with a wooden plectrum, whereas ever since the ninth century – supposedly since the time of Ziryāb (d. 809) – the strings of the Arab lute ('ūd) were plucked with a quill.[241] It is interesting to examine the shape of the wooden plectrum that appears repeatedly in tenth-century illustrations from Central and Eastern Asia (Plate 20), though it is also recognizable in early Byzantine representations (Plate 19). In striking contrast to the pointed plectra of ancient times, here the end touching the strings splays out in a fan-shape, like the segment of a circle. This alteration in the shape of the plectrum would seem to imply a change in its function, and illustrates clearly the transition from plucking to friction. It was hardly feasible to pluck the strings individually using this wooden

bibliothek, Stuttgart, Cod. bibl. folio 23, fol. 125r. (10th century); cf. E. T. Dewald, *The Stuttgart Psalter* (Princeton, 1931). [235] Several illustrations are given in T. Norlind, *Systematik der Saiteninstrumente*, Part I, 'Geschichte der Zither' (Stockholm, 1936) pp. 166ff. Gerson (end of the 14th century) cites and describes this instrument, which he defines as a 'chorus'. [236] This instrument still has its place in French folk music. The 'tambourin de Béarn' is generally used in association with the *galoubet*. [237] A list of Sanskrit sources on music is given by A. Ramaswami in *JRAS* (1941), pp. 233ff. [238] *Muzykal'nye instrumenty kitaja* (Moscow, 1958). [239] H. Trefzger, 'Über das k'in', *Schweizerische Musikzeitung* 88 (1948), pp. 81ff. [240] L. Picken, 'The Origin of the Short Lute', *GSJ* VIII (1955), pp. 32ff. [241] H. G. Farmer, *JRAS* (1930), pp. 775ff.

segment, but easy to sweep across all the strings simultaneously with the broad, slightly curving, forward edge.·

This diversity in the shapes and functions of plectra, so strikingly evident during the tenth century, indicates the efforts that were being made to create new performing techniques and achieve a greater variety of expression than was obtainable simply by plucking the strings. Before the end of the first millennium these efforts had prepared the ground, both in Europe and in Asia, for the coming of bowing.

Nowadays, medieval Western civilization is generally regarded as a homogeneous whole, and many people overlook the differences that existed in the thinking, as well as in the art and music, of individual peoples.[242] In fact specific regional types had evolved throughout the whole range of musical instruments – not only bowed instruments. This is particularly obvious in the case of the medieval fiddles used in Spain and the Balkan Peninsula (both enclaves of Oriental culture in Europe) which contrast markedly with those of the rest of Europe. Even within the bounds of Western culture, however, there are striking differences in the structure of the various bowed instruments. For example, the Western European fiddle, slender and pear-shaped, is quite unlike both the spade-shaped fiddle of Southern Europe and the Central European fiddle with its almost circular body. Further proof of this divergence crops up from time to time in medieval literature. Middle High German texts refer to the *welsche fidel* and the *Behemer fedeler*; while Old French manuscripts speak of the *gigeours d'Alemaigne*. The fiddle was played in two ways, the *welhischer* or the *franzoiser wîse*, and comparisons were drawn between instrumental types peculiar to different countries.[243]

The first evidence of bowing in Europe

From the available pictorial evidence it would seem that by the beginning of the eleventh century playing with the bow had passed beyond the frontiers of Islamic and Byzantine civilization, and gradually spread into Europe. After the tenth century we find bowed instruments featuring for the first time in illuminations from Northern Spain and Catalonia, where artists had largely succeeded in resisting Oriental influences, so that outwardly their work was predominantly Western in style. A Catalan Bible manuscript written in the Monastery of Santa Maria at Ripoll early in the eleventh century contains an illustration showing a sizeable three-stringed instrument (Plate 22) supported on the player's knee and played with a bow which has a handle. At its upper end, towards the neck, the elongated body of the instrument is rectangular, while the lower end is rounded. The neck is remarkably short and squat. We find a similar, though somewhat smaller and narrower spade-shaped bowed instrument illustrated in

[242] The rôles of the various nations in the history of medieval music are discussed by J. Handschin in an essay in the *Schweizerisches Jahrbuch der Musikwissenschaft*, Vol. V (Aatau, 1931), pp. 1 ff.
[243] W. Salmen, *Der fahrende Musiker im europäischen Mittelalter* (Kassel, 1960), pp. 177, 187, and 215.

a fragmentary Catalan psalter manuscript[244] of the late eleventh century. A dancing musician (Plate 24) in King David's retinue supports his three-stringed fiddle against his chest, while he draws a slightly arched bow across the strings. Spade-shaped instruments of this type may also be seen on a Spanish mural in the Church of St. Michael at Fenouilla,[245] and in twelfth-century miniatures from Northern Italy. Typical examples are shown in a psalter manuscript from Lombardy,[246] dating from the early part of the twelfth century and written in the Abbey of San Benedetto di Polirone (Plate 26). Once again the subject of the illustrations is King David with some of his musicians;[247] and the bowed instruments are played resting against the upper part of the body. In Italy, as in Catalonia, we can prove that the bow was already in use at the beginning of the eleventh century. Among the earliest of the Italian sources is a fresco, dating from *c.* 1011, in the Crypt of San Urbano alla Caffarello, near Rome.[248] The painting represents the bringing of the Christmas message to the shepherds in the fields (Plate 28). One of the shepherds, clearly in a dancing pose, is playing a fiddle, held propped against his chest. The characteristics of the spade-shaped fiddle are not as distinctly reproduced here as in the twelfth-century Lombardy miniatures previously noted. This illustration shows a small, dainty instrument with lateral pegs. A particularly interesting source is a miniature dating from *c.* 1100, illustrating a psalter manuscript from Northern Italy[249] (Plate 23), for it supplies the hitherto missing link in the chain of development leading from the yoked lyre, through the fingerboard lyre, to the fiddle. At different time since the eighth or ninth centuries the simple yoked lyre adopted the principles of the neck and finger-board,[250] thus depriving the arms of the yoke of their function as string-carriers, and making them redundant. Nevertheless this anomaly persisted for more than a thousand years, as is shown by the plucked lyres with fingerboards which are encountered in the early Middle Ages, the French bowed rote (twelfth-thirteenth centuries),[251] and the Welsh crwth. In the Northern Italian illustrations mentioned above, one of the yoke's arms has evidently been abandoned. Thus at the finger-board end the body assumes the rectangular shape which is so typical of the spade-shaped bowed instruments. It is tempting, on the basis of the pictorial evidence, to try and trace the structure of the spade-shaped fiddles of Southern

[244] The manuscript is in the Museo Diocesaro, Barcelona (Ms. 8011). [245] Illustrated in P. Guinard and J. Baticle, *Histoire de la Peinture Espagnole du XIIe au XIXe siècle* (Paris, 1950), p. 16. [246] Biblioteca Civile, Mantua, Ms. C. III, 20, fol. 1 r. [247] Another miniature from the same manuscript (King David with musicians, among them a fiddler) is published in H. Besseler, *Die Musik des Mittelalters*, p. 75. [248] For more specific details regarding the date of the painting, see G. Ladner, 'Die italienische Malerei im 11. Jahrhundert', *Jahrbuch der kunsthistorischen Sammlung in Wien*, New Series 5 (Vienna, 1932). [249] This *Brunonis Psalterium*, which originated in Italy, once belonged to Petrarch and has marginal notes in his handwriting. It is now in the Bibliothèque Nationale, Paris, Ms. lat. 2508, fol. II r. [250] Miniature from Charles the Bald's Bible; Paris, Bibliothèque Nationale, Ms. lat. 1, fol. 215 v (published in H. Besseler, *Die Musik des Mittelalters*, Plate II). Miniature from the Bible of San Paolo fuori le mura, Rome (illustrated in A. Boinet, *La miniature Carolingienne* (Paris, 1913), Plate CXXIV). [251] The medieval bowed rote is

Europe back to the fingerboard lyre which had lost both arms of its yoke.[252] This hypothesis is partly borne out by the semi-circular shape of the peg-board, the width of which is the same as that of the resonator. It would be a simple matter to add the arms of the yoke and thereby transform the fiddle into a lyre.[253]

Side by side with the spade-shaped fiddle, we find the narrow, pear-shaped version appearing in illuminations executed in Northern Spain and Catalonia from early in the eleventh century onwards. This instrument, usually three-stringed, is nearly always shown lying against the player's shoulder. A Catalan psalter miniature – the manuscript is in the Bibliothèque Nationale in Paris (MS. lat. 11550, fol. 7v) – dating from around the middle of the eleventh century, represents a group of instrumentalists in the process of tuning up. The musician with the fiddle, who is depicted holding his bow in his right hand, is plucking at one of the strings to verify that it is properly tuned and to give the note to the other players (Plate 25). This same type of narrow instrument occurs repeatedly in other Spanish and French illustrations of this period, for example in miniatures from the Beatus Manuscript of San Millán (Plate 3, eleventh century);[254] in a Psalterium written in the latter half of the eleventh century at Soignes in Hainault (Plate 30); and in another eleventh-century illumination (Plate 27) from a manuscript in the Bibliothèque Nationale in Paris.[255] This last illustration shows a dancing fiddler and a horn-player, and the artist has added diastematic (or heighted) neumes and the caption *Consonancia – cuncta musica*. From the second half of the eleventh century comes a further illustration of a bowed instrument (Codex 2777 in the Gräflich Schonbornsche Bibliothek at Pommersfelden) (Plate 29). This manuscript was written and illustrated in the Rhineland *c.* 1070. Anglo-Saxon miniatures dating from *c.* 1050 also reveal bowed instruments of a similar type (Plate 31). Around 1100, pear-shaped fiddles with sagittal pegs and an end-pin for securing their strings were widely used throughout Western Europe. Illustrations of such instruments dating from the twelfth century, the region of origin of which is known precisely, are from Canterbury (Plate 32), from Shaftesbury Abbey,[256] from Northern Italy,[257] from Languedoc in Southern France (Plate 33), Marchiennes (Plate 35), the Toulouse region (Plates 38 and 41), Paris,[258] the Augustine Monastery at Marbach in Upper Alsace (Plate 36), Burgos,[259] Santiago de Compostela,[260] Estany,[261] Foussais,[262] Toulouse (Plate 40),

fully discussed in Chapter III, pp. 111 ff.   [252] While there was undoubtedly a connection between the two instruments there is no evidence to support the evolutionary theory that the fiddle derives from the fingerboard-lyre. Cf. A. W. Ambros, *Geschichte der Musik*, 3rd, ed., Vol. II, p. 36; also H. Riemann, *Musiklexikon*, article 'Chrotta' and 'Streichinstrumente'.   [253] The connection between the fingerboard-lyre and the spade-shaped fiddle is confirmed by other miniatures. [254] Description of the illustration on p. 31 f.   [255] Published in *Larousse de la musique*, Vol. I (Paris, 1957), p. 285.   [256] British Museum, MS. Landsdowne 383, fol. 15 v.   [257] Deutsche Staatsbibliothek, Berlin, MS. theol. lat. fol. 561, p. 77.   [258] Bibliothèque Nationale, Paris, MS. lat. 11565, fol. 63.   [259] Biblioteca Provincial, Burgos, *Libro de los Reyes*, fol. 141.   [260] Illustrated in A. Kingsley Porter, *Romanesque Sculpture of the Pilgrimage Roads*, Vol. VI (Boston, 1923), A. 687.   [261]Illustrated in J. Gudiol Ricart, *Arte de España Cataluna* (Barcelona, 1955), Fig. 8.   [262] Bildarchiv Foto

Meillers (Plate 42), Ripoll,[263] and Moissac (Plate 43). On the whole the spade-shaped fiddle was confined to Southern Europe, that is to Spain and Italy, during the eleventh and twelfth centuries,[264] while in Central Europe bowed instruments with a broad, almost circular body and a curiously thick-set appearance were used in the twelfth and thirteenth centuries (Plates 47–50 and 52).[265] The evidence suggests that the so-called figure-of-eight fiddle, with its indented body, became firmly established in England and Northern France (Plates 51, 53, 54, 56, 60, 62). German illustrations of medieval fiddles show a preponderance of elliptical resonators or, at the most, only slightly undulating sides.[266]

We have thus traced the development of bowing in Central Asia and the Near East, and subsequently in Europe, up to the twelfth century. Now we must turn to the bowed instruments of Eastern and South-Eastern Asia, which found their way there from Central Asia in the latter part of the Middle Ages.

EASTERN ASIA

The first clear proof of the existence of bowing in Eastern Asia dates from the Yüan Dynasty (1271–1368).[267] During this period, when China was ruled by the Mongols, the bowed instrument known as the *hu-ch'in* took its place in the Chinese Court orchestra and was therefore mentioned and described in some detail in court records written at the behest of the Mongolian ruling house. In the *Yüan Shih*, the Annals of the Yüan Dynasty, completed not later than 1370 by a group of official chroniclers under the leadership of Sung Lien, the following description is to be found (Book 71, Chapter 22): 'The *Hu-ch'in* is constructed like a *ho-pi-szu* (*kobuz*) with a curled neck, a dragon's head, and two strings. It is thrummed with a bow. The string of the bow is from a horse-tail.'[268] The name *hu-ch'in* indicates beyond all doubt that this stringed instrument came from foreign parts. *Hu* signifies 'barbarian', and was used to describe the tribes of Central Asia, in particular the Iranian Sogdians,[269] while *ch'in* was employed as a general term embracing all chordophones.[270] The names of the more modern Chinese bowed instruments also generally include the word *hu*.[271]

Marburg, No. 39389. [263] A. Kingsley Porter, op. cit., Vol. V, Plate 562. [264] Cf. above, p. 61f. [265] Cf. also Staatsbibliothek, Munich, Cod. germ. 51, fol. 37v; also Oesterreichische Nationalbibliothek, Vienna, Cod. 1879, fol. 104. [266] Cf. the fiddles illustrated in the *Manessische Liederhandschrift* (e. g. in H. Besseler, *Die Musik des Mittelalters*, Plate VII), also Staatliche Bibliothek Bamberg, MS. bibl. 48, fol. 101; cf. also J. Klein, *Die romanische Steinplastik des Niederrheins* (Strasbourg, 1916), Plate XXXI, left. [267] The early Chinese sources containing descriptions of bowed instruments have recently been translated, dated, and interpreted by Laurence Picken. The author has very kindly given me access to his manuscript, since published in the *Galpin Society Journal* under the title 'Early Chinese Friction Chordophones' (see *GSJ* XVIII, 1965, p. 82). [268] Cf. also *Hsü wên-hsien t'ung-k'ao* 110, 5a; also *Yü-chih-t'ang-t'an-wei*, by Hsü Ying-ch'iu, 33, 1a. [269] This view is supported by E. G. Pulleyblank in 'A Sogdian Colony in Inner Mongolia', *T'oung Pao* XLI (1952), p. 318. [270] This name was applied specifically to the narrow board-zither; cf. R. H. van Gulik in *Monumenta Nipponica*, 1st–3rd Years (1938–40). [271] The follow-

The resemblance between *hu-ch'in* and *kobuz*, commented upon in the *Yüan Shih*, provides further evidence of the Central Asian provenance of China's bowed instruments. Up to the end of the tenth century, the *kobuz* was almost entirely confined to Central Asia, where its name occurs repeatedly in Uigur texts dating from the ninth and tenth centuries.[272] But these early sources offer no clue to the technique of playing the instrument.

The Uigur word *qobuz* or *qubur* corresponds to the Mongolian *khu'ur* found in Old Mongolian texts from the thirteenth century onwards. Here again the question whether the Mongolian instrument *morin khuur*, played with a horse-hair bow, was also bowed as early as the thirteenth century, remains unanswered. All we can gather from these early Mongolian texts is that the said instrument was employed in funeral sacrifices, and as an accompaniment to what were pro-bably epic songs sung by rhapsodists before the beginning of a battle.[273] The Chinese *hu-lei* is identical with the *hu-ch'in*, and both terms were used at different times throughout the T'ang period (618–907) to denote the same instrument.

References in the *Yüan Shih* to the *hu-ch'in* are elaborated and corroborated by evidence from other sources. Particularly informative are instruments of the *hu-ch'in* type, dating from the T'ang period, and preserved in the Treasure House at Nara and the Palace Museum in Peking, since their ergological features coincide with the description given in the *Yüan Shih*.[274] Invariably the instruments concerned have two strings only. The body, an elliptical or sometimes oval wooden bowl, its opening covered with snakeskin, merges directly into an elongated neck, ending in a peg-box carved in the shape of a dragon's head. The strings, supported on a bridge, spread out above the skin sounding-board, being attached to the body of the instrument at the lower end, and to lateral pegs at the top.

Even in the early T'ang period we find references to the *hu-ch'in*, not in the official accounts contained in the Annals of the various dynasties, which are mostly concerned with court music, but mainly in literature devoted to curiosities or strange, foreign objects. The first of these references to the *hu-ch'in* occurs in the *Ling-i Chi* ('Chronicle of Curiosities'), an account written in the sixth or seventh century by an unknown author.[275] He tells how certain Shamans regarded

---

ing Chinese names of bowed instruments are compounded with the syllable '*hu*': *êrh-hu, sê-hu, yeh-hu, pan-hu, ching-hu, hui-hu* and *hu-ch'in*. [272] N. Dmitriev, *Altaiskij epos Kogutej*, published by the Academy of Sciences of the USSR, 1935, p. 77, This Central Asian source, which contains the earliest reference I have found to the *kobuz*, probably dates from the 9th century. In the Uigur version of the story of Kalyânamkara and Pâpamkara (translated by P. Pelliot in *T'oung Pao* (1941), pp. 258 ff.), the blinded Prince Kalyânakamra plays on a musical instrument described as a *qobuz*. Cf. also P. Pelliot, 'Le k'ong-heou et le qobuz', *Naitô Hakushi Kwanseki Shukuga Shinagaku Ronso* (*Mélanges Naitô*) (Kyoto, 1926). [273] A musicological assessment of medieval literary sources relating to the Mongols has recently been undertaken by E. Emsheimer. Cf. article 'Mon-golische Musik' in *MGG*. [274] Pictures of these instruments are to be found in the following publications: *Shōsōin Gomotsu Zuroku* (Tokyo, 1932) and *Muzykal'nye instrumenty kitaja* (Moscow, 1958). [275] Quoted in the *T'ai-p'ing-kuang-chi*, by Li Fang, Chapter 283. This 10th century encyclopedia is a collection of ancient source material relating to folklore and popular beliefs.

the *hu-ch'in* as their oracle, using the twang of the strings to help them in foretelling the future.[276] From the descriptions of Arab, Byzantine, and Chinese writers we know that Shamanism was indeed practised at this time, especially among the tribes of Central Asia, a fact which ties up with the etymological significance of the word *hu-ch'in*, an instrument of the *hu* 'barbarians'. Lu Shi's *I-shih*,[277] a Chinese source of the T'ang period, tells of a man who interpreted the future, using the strings of the *hu'ch-in* as his oracle. Li K'ang, a ninth-century author, writes in his *Tu-i Chi* ('Concerning certain rarities')[278] that the *hu-ch'in* was uncommon enough to cause a sensation in China. The reference in Li K'ang's book is to the poet Ch'ên Tzû-ang (653–95) who, on his first visit to the capital, was still completely unknown. On his way he stopped in a market-place, where for the remarkably large sum of 1000 strings of cash he purchased a *hu-ch'in* from a folk musician, and subsequently passed himself off as a famous performer on this instrument, his purpose being to attract a large audience. In the middle of his musical performance, he smashed the *hu-ch'in* to fragments before the eyes of the astounded onlookers, and began distributing his poems among them. In this way he achieved fame in a very short space of time.

Later, in the eighth century, eminent people in China commissioned instruments to be made which were modelled on this Central Asiatic folk instrument used by the Shamans. There is for example a reference in the *Nan-pu hsin-shu* of Ch'ien I (*c*. 1010) to the fact that Han Huan (723–87) a well-known dignitary of the T'ang Dynasty, commanded a master craftsman to make him large and small *hu-ch'in*, also known, according to the author, as *hu-lei*.

The instrument found its way into Chinese court music as early as the ninth century. The important musical treatise known as the *Yüeh-fu tsa-lu*, by Tuan An-chieh,[279] written between 894 and 897, says that in the reign of the Emperor Wen-tsung (827–40) there lived in the palace a serving-woman of the house of Chêng, who was an accomplished performer on the *hu-ch'in*, and that two types of *p'i-p'a*, that is to say the large and small *hu-lei*, were used within the palace. Tuan An-chieh records how on one occasion the servant-girl Chêng was performing on the large *hu-lei* when suddenly one of the strings broke. This instrument was sent for repair to the Chao family, who lived in the southern part of the Ch'ung-jên ward. In Ch'ên Yang's *Yüeh Shu*, a treatise on music written in 1101,[280] a certain Shih Ts'ung is named (along with the slave-woman of the house of Chêng) as a notable performer on the *hu-ch'in*. He lived towards the end of the reign-period of Cha Tsung (*c*. 900).

[276] A source from the Sung period describes the following Shaman custom, as practised among the Hsi-hsia, who lived to the North of the Chinese: 'Or else they hearken to the sound of the string on the bow (that is, as to an oracle)'. W. Eberhard, 'Die Kultur der alten zentral- und westasiatischen Völker nach chinesischen Quellen', *Zeitschrift für Ethnologie* 73 (1941), p. 219. [277] *T'ai-p'ing-kuang-chi*, by Li Fang, Chapter 307. [278] *T'ai-p'ing-kuang-chi*, Chapter 179. [279] For further details relating to the *Yüeh-fu-tsa-lu* and its author see E. D. Edwards, *Chinese Prose Literature of the T'ang-Period* (London, 1937), Vol. I, p. 200f. [280] This treatise was printed for the first time in 1195. The section devoted to the *hu-ch'in* is translated by L. Picken in: 'Early

Textual sources from the T'ang and Sung periods unfortunately shed no light whatever on either the construction or structure of the instrument. All that is mentioned is that *hu-ch'in* and *ch'in* – the Chinese board-zither – have very little in common from the ergological point of view.[281] In the *Yüeh Shu* Ch'ên Yang writes: 'It is a kind of *ch'in* indeed, but has a special place of its own. Among the differences between Turco-Mongol and Chinese *ch'in*, however, the difference in structure is particularly marked.'[282]

Until recently we were at a loss to know how the *hu-ch'in* was played prior to the fourteenth century. A recent study by Picken[280] sheds light on the matter: 'a line from a poem by Po Chü-i leaves no doubt that it was a lute plucked with the fingers. The poem is entitled: "On the ninth day (of the ninth month of 825), at a festive gathering, written while drunk in the Prefectural Tower; also shown to Secretaries Chou and Yin." The line in question may be translated as: "The *Hu-ch'in* tinkles as the fingers strum." The binome *chêng-tsung*, translated as "tinkles", consists of two lexigraphs with the metal determinative and strongly suggests a metallic sound; *chêng* by itself is also used for a gong. "Strum" is the usual translation for the binome *po-la*, the components of which mean "to pluck" and "to slash" and thus the forward and backward movement of the hand in playing a lute. Furthermore, in a quatrain entitled "*P'i-pa*", written not later than 824, Po Chü-i refers to the sound of the *p'i-pa* in almost exactly the same terms:

"The strings' clear twang goes 'tinkle tinkle'." "Twang" is *po-la*, as in the previous line, and "tinkle tinkle" is the *chêng* of the previous line repeated. In the light of these descriptive passages, it seems quite certain that the *Hu-ch'in* known to T'ang authors was a lute plucked with the fingers. The use of terms suitable for metallic sounds may mean that both *Hu-ch'in* and *p'i-pa* were strung at this time with metal strings.' The very fact that in instrumental treatises of the T'ang period the *hu-ch'in* is included in the chapter on the *p'i-p'a*[283] is a clear indication that, at least until the end of the tenth century, it was played as a plucked instrument.

Once this has been established we are faced with new problems. From what date was the *hu-ch'in* played with a bow? When did bowing become an accepted feature of Chinese musical practice? Did the Mongols import the bow into China during the Yüan period or was it already known there? This group of questions draws our attention to the *hsi-ch'in*, a folk instrument discussed in the *Yüeh Shu* in the same context as the *hu-ch'in*, the two being clearly very closely related, if

---

Chinese Friction Chordophones', *GSJ* XVIII (1965), p. 82. [281] Sociologically, too, a deep gulf separates *ch'in* and *hu-ch'in*. According to medieval Chinese sources, the '*hu*'-barbarians were forbidden to listen to the *ch'in*. Cf. *Ch'in-ching*, Chapter 8: 'The *ch'in* is essentially an instrument, through the music of which China's wise men and high-ranking dignitaries ennoble their existence and refine their character. Such a thing is unknown in the lands of the *Hu*, and for this reason it [the playing of the *ch'in* in the presence of 'barbarians'] is not permitted'. [282] The same rather vague description of the *hu-ch'in* is given c. 1300 in Ma Tuan-lin's *Wên-hsien t'ung-k'ao*: '*Ch'in* are the same thing indeed, but there are differences between Turco-Mongol and Chinese ones.' [283] E. g. in the *Yüeh-fu tsa-lu* by Tuan An-chieh.

not actually identical. This treatise, printed in 1195, contains the following definition: 'The *Hsi-ch'in* was originally a foreign [that is, Turco-Mongol] instrument. It arose from a strung rattle-drum, and its shape also resembled the same. It was an instrument beloved of the Hsi tribe. Now concerning its structure: the two strings are made to creak (*ya*) by a slip of bamboo between them. Up to the present it is in use among the common people.'

This is a source of the utmost significance for any research into the origins of bowing in East Asia, and deserves more detailed consideration.

(a) 'The *hsi-ch'in* was originally a foreign instrument.' This indicates the region of origin. It was a foreign instrument, derived from the 'Hu' – 'Barbarians' – China's neighbours to the west or north. Thus *hsi-ch'in* and *hu-ch'in* spring from a common source.

(b) 'It arose from a strung rattle-drum, and its shape also resembled the same.' It would seem, then, that the *hsi-ch'in* had a rounded body, the resonating surface of which, and possibly the rear surface also, was made of stretched animal skin, as with Chinese bowed instruments of the present day.[284]

(c) 'It was an instrument beloved of the Hsi tribe.' With this information, Ch'ên Yang indicates precisely its place of origin. The Hsi belonged to the Tung-hu, the proto-Mongolian Shi-wei tribes, who from the T'ang period inhabited the Wu-han mountains in Outer Mongolia north of the Great Wall, and were in close contact with Turkic peoples of Central Asia. In the *Hsin T'ang Shu* (219) the Hsi are described as follows: 'they are a nomadic race, dwelling in felt tents protected by a surrounding fortress of waggons. They live by hunting and cultivate a type of millet. Their mortars are of wood and their tripods of clay. They have good horses and black sheep.'[285] It was from this Turco-Mongolian tribe of nomadic horsemen then that the Chinese learned the art of bowing.

(d) The instrument had two strings, played by inserting a slip of bamboo between them. In the number of strings, therefore, it corresponded to the *hu-ch'in*. The technique involved in playing it shows a marked similarity to the Chinese method of bowing used today. At the present time the horsehair of the bow is drawn between the strings, one string (or pair of strings) being bowed from below, the other from above. Ch'ên Yang's account describes a similar operation, where the friction stick is pushed between the *hsi-ch'in*'s two strings, which are then set in vibration by moving the bamboo shoot backwards and forwards.

(e) 'Up to the present it is in use among the common peoples.' This means that by the eleventh century at the latest, bowed instruments of the *hsi-ch'in* type were known in China. To begin with, however, the *hsi-ch'in* – still rather undeve-

---

[284] The *Wên-hsin t'ung-k'ao*, an encyclopedia compiled *c.* 1300 by Ma Tuan-lin, contains this same quotation from the *Yüan Shih*, with the following alteration: in place of 'strung rattle-drum', we find 'Hsi rattle-drum'. A translation of the instrumental section of this encyclopedia is given by Moule in *JNChBRAS* XXXIX (1908).   [285] Translation given by W. Eberhard, 'Kultur und Siedlung

loped – was not admitted to the court music. Ch'ên Yang expressly places the *hsi-ch'in* in the category of folk instruments. In its early stages, bowing remained confined to the lowest social strata, in China as in Central Asia.

Later the technique of *hsi-ch'in* playing became the same as that for *hu-ch'in* and the remaining Chinese bowed instruments; the strings were bowed with a horse-hair bow. As shown by an illustration in a Chinese publication dated 1759,[286] this 'bow' corresponds to that currently used in Central Asia. The bow represented is a shaft to the two ends of which a skein of horsehair is attached. The hair hangs loosely, and is tightened by the player's hand.

If we summarize the results of our analysis of the above text, the main fact that emerges is that during the eleventh century there is evidence of the use of the friction stick in Eastern Asia, a first step towards bowing. This musical practice can be traced back in China at least to the tenth century. In descriptions of the *ya-chêng*, we again encounter the bamboo friction stick. This instrument emerged towards the end of the T'ang period, and is mentioned in Chapter 29 of the *Chiu T'ang-shu*, the earlier T'ang chronicles completed around the middle of the tenth century. The scribe records that 'The *ya-chêng* is made to creak (*ya*) with a slip of bamboo, moistened at its tip.'

The syllable *ya* is used to convey the creaking of wheels or of door hinges, and clearly indicates the sound of friction. *Chêng* is the term for the elongated board-zither, which during the T'ang period had twelve or thirteen strings.[287] The sole difference between the *chêng* and the *ya-chêng* was one of technique. The strings of the *chêng* were plucked with the fingers, while the *ya-chêng* was bowed with a moistened bamboo shoot.

All enquiries into the origin of the *ya-chêng* lead to the same region as that from whence the *hsi-ch'in* found its way into China: the territory of the Northern Turco-Mongols. For example, the *Chiu T'ang-shu*[288] notes the presence of the *ya-chêng* in a Mongolian orchestra playing at the court of the Chinese Emperor. The instrument reappears time and again in later sources, together with *hu-ch'in* and *hsi-ch'in*, also in accounts of Mongolian orchestras.

In a four-line poem, the T'ang poet Tu Mu[289] (803–52) compares the sound of the *ya-chêng* to that of the cicada. The poem runs as follows: 'A beautiful bird-call – I mistake it for a stroke on the lithophone. The sound of a cicada on the wind – I take it to be the friction-zither (*ya-chêng*).' As we know from Ch'en Yang's *Yüeh Shu* (1101) the instrument's name conveys the friction sound it made when played. 'In the T'ang Dynasty there was a *ya-chêng*. It was made to creak (*ya*) with a slip of bamboo moistened at its tip. From this the name (*ya-chêng*) was taken.' Ch'ên Yang divides musical instruments not only into the eight sound categories, but into three genera: ritual instruments, folk instruments and foreign

der Randvölker Chinas', *T'oung Pao* XXXVI, Suppl. (Leyden, 1942), p. 44. [286] M. Courant publi-shed a copy of this illustration in 'Chine et Corée', in A. Lavignac, *Encyclopédie de la musique, première partie* (Paris, 1913), p. 181. [287] Cf. W. Bachmann, *Die chinesischen Musikinstrumente der T'ang-Zeit* (in preparation). [288] Chapter 28. [289] This reference was obtained from the concordance, *P'ei-wên*

instruments; and he classifies the *ya-chêng* under the heading of folk (*su*) instruments.[290]

The rather limited textual sources are supplemented by the results of folk-music research. The *ya-chêng*, also known as *la-ch'in*, has remained in use up to the present day as a folk instrument in Wu-an, in the Northern Chinese Province of Hopei. Here it is still played by stroking the strings with a kao-liang stalk – kao-liang being a kind of millet – rubbed with rosin.[291] This archaic practice has remained alive in this district for more than a thousand years. As we have shown, in the tenth and eleventh centuries the Northern frontier peoples of China used chordophones played by rubbing the strings with a slip of bamboo.

Having digressed at some length, we now return to our point of departure, namely the description of the *hu-ch'in* in the *Annals* of the Yüan Dynasty. In this fourteenth-century text we find the first evidence of a horsehair-bow being used in China. What we are not told is whether the bow was imported into China by the Mongols during the Yüan Dynasty or whether it was perhaps already familiar to the Chinese. But the source definitely proves that bowed instruments were first allowed to take part in Chinese court and ritual music during the period of Mongol supremacy, which accounts for their inclusion in the *Annals*. In the *Yüan Shih* the *hu-ch'in* features in the section devoted to instruments used at palace banquets.

A reorganization of China's ritual music had already been planned by Kublai Khan, a descendant of Genghis Khan and founder of the Yüan Dynasty. Even before he succeeded to the throne he had turned his attention to these problems. In 1264 he caused musical instruments of all the provinces to be collected, and these were found to be very numerous. In 1256 he granted certain privileges to musicians, sometimes inherited by their children. In 1282 he summoned to his service[292] all the remaining musicians of the court orchestra of the Sung Dynasty, and proceeded to augment the orchestra with new chime-lithophones, cast bells, and sundry newly made instruments. From this time onwards, bowed instruments of the *hu-ch'in* type became a permanent feature of the Chinese court orchestra. In Chapter 1357 of the *Kêng-shên Wai-shih*,[293] a source for the late Mongol period, the orchestra that played for the Emperor's pleasure is described in detail. 'The instruments on which they played were dragon flutes, headed flutes, drums, harps, lutes, bowed instruments (*hu-ch'in*), clappers, and beaters. They were led by the Eunuch Ch'ang-an Buqa.' The *hu-ch'in* is also mentioned in other sources of the Yüan period, and according to the *Cho-kêng Lu*,[294] was regarded as a specifically Mongol musical instrument.

yün-fu. [290] In the *T'ung-chih*, by Chêng Chiao (1108–66), Chapter 50, the *ya-chêng* is mentioned in parenthesis in the course of a description of the *chêng*. [291] *Muzykal'nye instrumenty kitaja* (Moscow, 1958), p. 23. [292] The sources quoted here contradict the widely-held belief that the Mongolian emperors were unmusical or hostile to any form of art. [293] H. Schulte-Uffelage, *Das Kêng-shên Wai-shih, eine Quelle zur späten Mongolenzeit* (Dissertation, Munich, 1955), p. 117. [294] *Cho-kêng-lu* 28: *Ts'ung-shu chi-ch'êng* 430.

III

EUROPEAN BOWED INSTRUMENTS IN THE ELEVENTH AND TWELFTH CENTURIES

THE FIDEL AND RELATED CHORDOPHONES

As early as the tenth century Arab scholars[1] recognized the craft of instrument-making as a scientific discipline, and treated it as such in their musical treatises;[2] but in the Latin literature of the early Middle Ages we look in vain for definite information on the structure of instruments. Not until the thirteenth century did the principles of *compositio instrumentorum* find a place in the treatises of European musical theorists. Albertus Magnus,[3] for instance, in his *Ethica* treats bowing under three headings. The first includes the structure of the instrument, and the nature and arrangement of the strings ('viellae constructio et chordarum'); the second discusses the tuning and fingering of the strings; and the third deals with the musical sounds produced by bowing. In his *Opus maius*,[4] Roger Bacon also refers *inter alia* to the making of musical instruments. In these treatises, however, questions of mathematics and acoustics were always uppermost in the writers' minds, together with details of the dimensions of pipes and the division of strings, whereas constructional problems were scarcely ever discussed.

The body

The craft of instrument-making, which in the Middle Ages was the exclusive province of the players themselves,[5] was based primarily on oral tradition. This accounts for the diversity of shapes and styles among the instruments represented in medieval illustrations. The structure of an instrument was left to the individual taste of its maker, and was thus determined by his capabilities as a craftsman, his awareness of the acoustical problems involved, and his skill in handling the material at his disposal.[6]

---

[1] Knowledge of how musical instruments were made already formed part of Avicenna's (Ibn Sīnā's) system of instruction; cf. G. Pietzsch 'Die Klassifikation der Musik von Boethius bis Ugolino von Orvieto', *Studien zur Geschichte der Musiktheorie im Mittelalter* I (Halle, 1929), p. 92.
[2] The majority of the Arabian treatises on music contain information relating to the making of instruments. This aspect of their writings is discussed in particular by H. G. Farmer, *Studies in Oriental Musical Instruments* (London, Glasgow, 1931–9). [3] Albertus Magnus, *Ethics* (ed. Borgnet, Vol. VII), 6, 1, 6, p. 404b. [4] Ed. by J. H. Bridges (Oxford, 1897), Part IV a, p. 238.
[5] One of the main skills expected of a minstrel was the ability not only to master the techniques of various instruments, but to make and repair them, if necessary. [6] It was not until a separate

Methods of construction and materials

In certain rural areas of Europe, as in Asia and North Africa, there exist to this day fiddle-type folk instruments corresponding to the fiddles of medieval times, made as they were eight or nine centuries ago and with similar primitive tools.[7] Here, too, the same man usually both plays and makes the instrument. From a suitable block of wood the shape of the instrument – body, neck and peg-board, all in one – is sawn out. The body is hollowed out from the upper surface and covered over with a wooden sound-board. This procedure can be observed in every surviving medieval fiddle and lyre yet unearthed,[8] and medieval literary sources[9] refer only to a body consisting of two parts: *pauch* and *poden* (belly and back).[10] Whether the resonating chamber had straight or slanting side walls and a flat bottom, like a box, or was carved in the shape of a rounded bowl, giving the body a bellied shape, is of secondary importance. Many attempts have been made to distinguish, among medieval fiddles, between those with sides (ribs) and those without;[11] but to no purpose, since there is no evidence to show that either the bellied lute as we know it today, or glued sides, existed.

The material most commonly mentioned as used in making bowed instruments in the Middle Ages is wood. In the East, apricot, walnut, and almond wood, and occasionally ebony – the last especially for the fingerboard – were used.[12] In fourteenth-century Europe, craftsmen already preferred spruce or fir wood for the sound-board. 'Dâ von wirt daz gedoen süez' ('it sweetens the sound of the music') writes Master Konrad von Megenberg,[13] describing the fir-wood

guild of instrument-makers was established that uniform instrumental types emerged. [7] For further details regarding the making of folk bowed instruments cf., for example, the following works. O. Dincsér, 'Zwei Musikinstrumente aus dem Komitate Csik', *A Néprajzi Múzeum Füzetei* 7 (Budapest, 1943); J. Žak, 'Die Bauernfiedeln der Iglauer Sprachinsel', *ZföV* VI (Vienna, 1900), p. 105 ff.; L. Kunz, 'Skřipky', *Acta Musei Moraviae* XXXV (1950), pp. 1 ff. [8] Among the few existing examples from the Middle Ages are an Egyptian fiddle or lute from the Coptic period, and the lyres from Oberflacht and Cologne; cf. H. Hickmann, 'Ein unbekanntes Saiteninstrument aus koptischer Zeit', *Mf* III (1950); F. Behn, *Musikleben*, pp. 151 ff.; J. Werner, 'Leier und Harfe im germanischen Frühmittelalter, Aus Verfassungs- und Landesgeschichte', *Festschrift für Theodor Mayer* I (Constance, 1954); E. Emsheimer, 'Die Streichleier von Danczk', *STMf* 43 (1961), pp. 109 ff. [9] Further details are given by Meister Konrad von Megenberg in his *Buch der Natur* (14th century), ed. F. Pfeiffer (Stuttgart, 1861), p. 314, line 20. [10] The part of the instrument designated in medieval times as 'poden' thus corresponds to the 'belly' or 'soundboard' of our stringed instruments. [11] J. Rühlmann, *Die Geschichte der Bogeninstrumente*, p. 38, regards ribs as 'characteristic of the Occidental nature' of this type of instrument. He writes: 'At a very early date we find bowed instruments which have special sidepieces inserted between belly and back, a negation of the principle of a two-part violin structure, since the resonator is basically made in three sections'. L. Grillet, in *Les Ancêtres*, pp. 30, 37 ff., 45, also distinguishes between instruments with or without ribs; but this system of classifying medieval bowed instruments is rejected by Curt Sachs in his *Handbuch*, 1st ed., p. 173. [12] W. Friedrich, *Die älteste türkische Beschreibung*, p. 67 f. [13] *Das Buch der Natur von Konrad von Megenberg*, ed. F. Pfeiffer (Stuttgart, 1861), p. 314, lines 20 ff.: 'Fir wood is unsuitable for the back of a stringed instrument,

sounding-board ('aus tänneim holz') – though he considers this type of wood unsuitable for the rest of the body, as it is too porous, and therefore incapable of holding the air from which the sound comes ('es halte den luft nicht vast, dâ von der dôn kümt'). In constructing the body, the craftsman made his task lighter and the wood more pliable by seething it for a time in boiling milk.[14] Only then was the work of hollowing out the resonator begun. The upper surface of the instrument was carefully smoothed and polished, since experience had proved that a rough fiddle – 'ain rauheu videl' – spoke less well than one that was well polished ('ain wol palierteu fidel').[15] Finally the wood was stained ('gebrûnieret'), and exceptionally valuable instruments might be inlaid 'with gold and jewels, and precious ivory' ('gezieret mit golde und mit gesteine, von edelem helfenbeine').[16] To improve the tone, the resonator of bowed instruments was sometimes given a coat of varnish, made of powdered glass and glue.[17] Apart from wood, other materials occasionally used included metal, gourds, and animal skins. The cauldron-shaped body of the Turkish *ıqlıq*, for example, was made of bronze, and its opening covered with stretched skin.[18] There are frequent references to the use of skin for the soundboard on bowed instruments with wooden resonators.[19]

Shapes

If we attempt to classify – on construction grounds – the various representations of musical instruments, we can choose as criteria either the shape of the instrument, or the method by which its strings are attached.[20] If we take the shape of these instruments, the available material divides into two main groups. In instruments of the first group, neck and body merge into one another, whereas in the instruments of the second group there is a sharp dividing line between the two.

either fiddles, lyres or anything else, since wood of this sort lets the air through' and is very porous. 'And therefore it does not hold the air, from which the sound comes; but fir wood makes a good belly for such an instrument, for, when the air has pushed against the strong strings into the belly of the thing, it filters slowly through the soft top, making the sound sweeter.' [14] This is mentioned in the account given by the Turkish author Aḥmed-oghlu Shükrullāh; but it does not occur in any European sources; cf. W. Friedrich, *Die älteste türkische Beschreibung*, p. 68. [15] These details are from Konrad von Megenberg's *Buch der Natur*, ed. F. Pfeiffer (Stuttgart, 1861), p. 16, line 9. The much-quoted Turkish treatise from the early 15th century also stresses that the body of the *rabāb* should be cut as thin and smooth as possible; cf. W. Friedrich, op. cit., p. 68. [16] F. H. von der Hagen, *Gesammtabenteuer*, Vol. I (Stuttgart and Tübingen, 1850), p. 348: 'he then ordered a fiddle to be made, with silken strings, fit for a prince, its wood varnished, the cappellon inlaid with gold and jewels and precious ivory.' [17] The account of fiddle-varnish and how it was made is from the oldest-known Turkish treatise on music, c. 1400[18]. Cf. W. Friedrich, op. cit., pp. 65 ff. [19] Bowed instruments covered with stretched animal skin were largely confined to the East. In medieval times the belly of the *rabab* was sometimes half-wood, half-skin; cf. W. Friedrich, op. cit., p. 69 [20] The various possible methods of classifying chordo-

The first category includes narrow, club-shaped instruments (Plates 25, 27, 30, 36, 37), pear-shaped instruments (Plates 31–35 and 38–44), and nearly circular instruments (Plates 47–50 and 52). Scholars have often tried to relate the names of bowed instruments which recur in medieval texts – *rubebe*, *rebec*, *giga*, *lira*, *fidula* and *viella* – to definite types,[21] speaking of 'the slender *rubebe*', the 'ham-shaped *gige*' or the 'bellied *lira*'. This has little value in the earliest period of bowing, for we have incontrovertible evidence[22] that the same

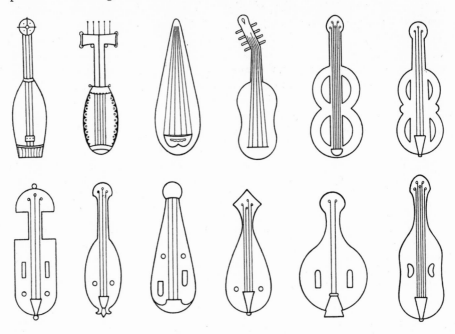

name was often given to several instrumental types, provided they resembled each other in their function and method of performance.[23] The reverse was also true, and there are instances when a number of different terms are used to describe one and the same instrument. A notable example of this is found in the

phones are discussed in detail in Chapter V. [21] This happens in nearly every 19th-century work on the history of musical instruments dealing primarily with the medieval bowed instruments. [22] Sundry authors have pointed out the change in meaning or ambiguity of medieval instrument names, for example, F. Behn, 'Mittelalterliche Terminologie von Musikinstrumenten, Miszellen zur Musikgeschichte' V, *NMz* 39 (1918), Part 9, p. 134ff.; K. Geiringer, 'Der Instrumentenname "Quinterne" und die mittelalterlichen Bezeichnungen der Gitarre, Mandola und des Colascione', *AfMw* 6 (1924), p. 103; K. Nef, *Geschichte unserer Musikinstrumente*, p. 69; C. Sachs, *Handbuch*, 1st ed., p. 169, writes: 'there is no tangible difference between either the rebec and rubebe or between these two and the gigue.' [23] According to F. Hoerburger, it is not the shape of an instrument, but the way in which it is used and played which determines the designation and classification of musical instruments: F. Hoerburger, 'Correspondence between eastern and

Busant.[24] Concerning the construction of a fiddle it says: 'he ordered a fiddle (*videlen*) to be made.' Later, the text continues: 'when the *gige* was ready.'[25]

In the second category (with a definite neck) the picture is still more complex. During the Middle Ages, and especially in the thirteenth and fourteenth centuries, we frequently come upon instruments with elliptical bodies (Plate 45). Sometimes the resonator is slightly waisted,[26] rather like the modern guitar (Plates 3–6, 10, 11, 66–68). This type was referred to several times in the preceding descriptions of Byzantine instruments. Often the waist curves sharply inwards bisecting the body, which then looks almost like a figure-of-eight (Plates 51, 54–57, 59, 61–64). The figure-of-eight fiddle apparently derives from the primitive long-necked lute with double resonator – two half gourds or coconut shells, set one above the other. Thus the figure-of-eight body of the medieval Turkish *rabāb* shows two bellies and, unlike our guitar, has no flat bottom.[27] In addition, the sound-board of the medieval figure-of-eight fiddle invariably has either two circular or four semicircular sound-holes. These instruments therefore have a double resonator, which would strengthen the tone, but is not linked with a particular playing-technique. A special shape, widely used in medieval times, is the doubly indented fiddle (Plates 53 and 60), where a semi-circular arc rounds out the waist of the body, so that the sound-board is divided into three sections.[28] Bottle-shaped bowed instruments (Plates 1, 2, and 9) occur occasionally in Mozarabic and Byzantine miniatures. Finally, there are the spade-shaped instruments, their bodies sharply rectangular at the fingerboard end and rounded towards the end pin (Plates 22–24 and 26). These, with the exception of the hurdy-gurdy and the bowed rote, which will be treated separately,[29] are the main type of bowed instrument to appear on the European scene within the period of this study.

The number, location, and shape of the sound holes also varied according to the structure of the body. The first stage was the circular sound hole common to all plucked instruments, situated in the middle of the belly, under the strings. This type of hole was eminently suited to plucked instruments (where the sound quickly dies) since it made the strings more resonant.[30] But this was a disadvantage when the bow was used. To offset this, the central round hole was sometimes bisected by a wooden bridge,[31] leaving a flat open segment on either side. These semicircular openings predominate in eleventh and twelfth-century representations (Plates 32, 33, 35, 36, 39–42, 45, 46, 49, 69–71). Frequently they served

western Folk Epics', *JIFMC* IV (1952), p. 25. [24] Cf. p. 73, Note 16. [25] In Neidhard's Song 'Ein wehsel', 10, 2f. (Hagen, *Minnesinger* III, 211b), the poet speaks of 'playing good tunes on old fiddles' ('guote noten giget (man) uf alten videln'). [26] It has already been indicated in Chapter II, p. 39f., that 'waisted' sides on chordophones were not originally intended to increase the manouverability of the bow. [27] W. Friedrich, op. cit., p. 69. [28] This shape, frequently illustrated from the twelfth to the fourteenth centuries, is described as 'unnatural' by J. Rühlmann in *Die Geschichte der Bogeninstrumente*, p. 116. He considers fiddles of this type to be 'musically useless, foolishly conceived instruments'. [29] See pp. 105 ff. [30] H. Schultz, *Instrumentenkunde*, p. 82. [31] Curt Sachs, in his *Handbuch*, 1st ed., p. 171, quotes the Southern Slav

the additional purpose of ornamentation, and were carved in a great variety of decorative shapes (Plates 43, 44).

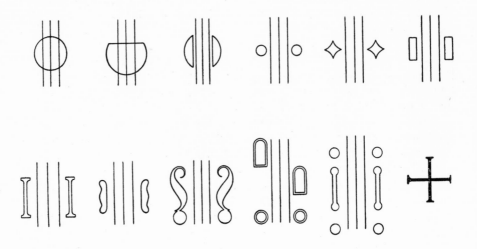

Methods of attaching strings

As we have already seen, the second method of classifying medieval bowed instruments is based (a) on the different ways of attaching the strings, and (b) on the position of the pegs. In the first case we distinguish between instruments with strings attached to an end pin and those with strings attached to a frontal stringholder; and in the second case, between those with lateral and those with frontal or rear (that is, sagittal) pegs.[32] Until the fourteenth century, nearly all Western representations of bowed chordophones show pegs inserted into the front or back of the peg-box, and an end-pin fastening (Plates 1, 22–27, 29 ff.). But in the Byzantine Empire and the Near East during the same period, most bowed instruments had lateral pegs, and the strings were attached to a frontal stringholder.[33] While sagittal pegs, inserted either from the front or from the rear in medieval times, were usually fixed in a round peg-disk, lateral pegs were inserted in a narrow peg-holder sloping slightly backwards, from which they jutted out on either side (Plates 4, 6, 10, 11, 28).

As with most long-necked lutes of primitive peoples, the strings on bowed instruments of the early Middle Ages stretched from the pegs to the end-pin, to which they were attached by means of a loop. This simple sling, though still

vijalo as an example. [32] Whereas Sachs (*Handbuch*, pp. IX and X) lays great stress on the method by which the strings are attached to the body as a means of distinguishing between various categories of instrument, K. Geiringer, in *Die Flankenwirbelinstrumente in der bildenden Kunst der Zeit zwischen 1300 und 1500* (Dissertation, Vienna, 1923), p. 1 ff, attaches much greater significance to the position of the pegs. [33] Cf. Chapter II.

occasionally identifiable on bowed instruments of the eleventh and twelfth centuries (Plates 29, 34, 48), was gradually superseded after the tenth century by a tail-piece, which assumed a variety of shapes and was often richly decorated. To raise the strings above the level of the belly, a piece of wood was jammed under

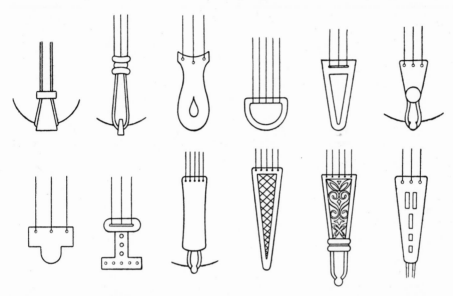

them. If this flat, bridge-like bar was glued to the belly to prevent the inconvenience of its falling out or being dislodged, it became possible to attach the strings to it instead of bringing them down to the end of the sound-board (Plates 4, 8, 10, 11, 21). The evidence shows that both methods were used. In each case the strings run close to the belly, since most early bowed instruments lack a bridge which would raise the strings away from the body of the instrument and transfer their vibrations to the surface of the resonator.[34] When a bridge is shown on instruments with an end-pin attachment[35] (Plates 29, 39, 43–46, 48), it is frequently some distance from the lower edge of the belly. It seems clear that in these cases the tailpiece had the additional function of preventing the section of string on the other side of the bridge from vibrating in sympathy with the bowed section. In some instances (Plates 61, 65, 68, 91) the illustrations show relatively high bridges, with feet.[36] Bridges were generally made of wood, bronze, amber, or bone.[37] At least in the beginning, their upper edge was usually straight, or

---

[34] The tailpiece would seem initially to have functioned simultaneously as a bridge, and served to lift the strings off the belly of the instrument. Where the strings were attached to a frontal stringholder, the lie of the strings corresponded roughly to that on bridgeless instruments with an end-pin fastening. [35] The bridge was almost entirely limited to instruments with strings were attached to an end pin. [36] A list of the most important types of bridge is given by J. Rühlmann, op. cit., p. 136 f. [37] Excavations have revealed a number of

only slightly curved,[38] and was often notched. The introduction of the rounded bridge, which made it possible where the resonator was similarly curved to apply the bow to each string individually, was a gradual process.

The strings

Turning now to the sound-producing component of medieval bowed instruments, the strings, the main points to consider are the materials used, the number of strings, and the processes of their manufacture. The question of the actual material used is of importance for two reasons. On the one hand it sheds a revealing light on the quality of the tone produced, since this is to some extent determined by the inherent properties of each material. Secondly, cultural interconnections and interrelationships are revealed by the use of similar materials for the strings of instruments from different regions.

Materials used

The use of silk strings, common in the early Middle Ages, undoubtedly originated in Asia.[39] Strings were made of silk in Eastern Asia in ancient times,[40] and are mentioned in Arabic literature from c. 800 onwards, as for instance by al-Kindī,[41] and in the treatise by the Ikhwān al-Ṣafā.[42] One of the first players to string his lute in this way was the Arab minstrel Ziryāb, who died in 809.[43] Later, in the thirteenth century, we find in the European literature, a fiddle 'mit sidinen seiten' ('with silken strings')[44] or stringed instruments 'quae per chordas

bridges in bronze, amber and bone, the sole remains of medieval stringed instruments. These bridges are reproduced in J. Werner, *Leier und Harfe*, and in the article 'Germanische Musik' (W. Niemeyer) in *MGG* (Plate 4).   [38] For the effect on the sound, as well as the technical usefulness of the various types of bridge, see F. Hamma, 'Besinnliches über den Steg', *Instrumentenbau-Zeitschrift* (Constance, 1952), 6th Year, p. 88.   [39] The breeding of silkworms originated in China, and it was from the Chinese that the Arabs learned the art of silkmaking in the early Middle Ages. In the mid-6th century, Justinian introduced silk and silkmaking into the Byzantine Empire. But it was not until the thirteenth century that the manufacture of silk material became of practical significance in Greece and Italy, and it only spread to the rest of Europe in the fifteenth century. The following works are devoted to the history of silk-making: H. Algond, *La Soie, Art et histoire* (Paris, 1928); O. von Falke, *Kunstgeschichte der Seidenweberei*, 2nd ed. (1921).   [40] See C. Sachs, *History*, pp. 164 and 185; also K. Robinson's article 'Chinesische Musik, I. Geschichtliche Entwicklung von der Frühzeit (Shang-Dynastie) bis zum Ende der Han-Zeit (1523 a. Chr. bis 206 p. Chr.)' in *MGG*.   [41] Information from Arab scribes about materials used in making strings has been assembled by H. G. Farmer in 'The Structure of the Arabian and Persian lute in the middle ages', *JRAS* (1939), pp. 41 ff., and W., Friedrich, op. cit., pp. 45 ff.   [42] F. Dieterici, *Die Propädeutik der Araber im 10. Jahrhundert* (Berlin, 1865), p. 117.   [43] H. G. Farmer, op. cit., p. 42.   [44] The phrase is taken from the *Busant*, a tale from the 14th or 15th century; cf. F. H. von der Hagen, *Gesammtabenteuer*, Vol. I (Stuttgart and

... sericinas exerceri videntur',[45] showing clearly the strong influence of the East on Western instruments.

In Europe, on the other hand, the prevalent use of strings made from twisted animal gut may be regarded as 'a relic of the ancient civilizations of the Mediterranean and the Near East'.[46] For instance, the strings of a surviving Egyptian lute dating from the sixteenth of fifteenth century B. C. are made of gut.[47] So too were the strings on the chordophones of the Sumerians and Babylonians.[48] Literary sources from classical antiquity refer more than once to the use of gut strings.[49] (Hindus refused to handle gut on religious grounds, since it was part of an animal.[50]) In the Islamic Empire, as in Europe, gut strings were known from early medieval times. As early as the eighth century, the Arab minstrel Ziryāb[51] strung his lute with gut as well as silk, though he preferred the latter, since it produced a clear tone and, being less susceptible to changes in temperature, kept its tuning better. In addition, it was more durable and resistant when the plectrum was used. In later Arab manuscripts, both materials are generally mentioned when the strings are discussed. Al-Kindī, comparing the two, comes to the conclusion that strings made of silk produce a better quality of tone and can withstand a greater strain than those of gut.[52] The Persian treatise *Kanz al-tuḥaf* and the instrumental descriptions of the Turk Aḥmed-oghlu Shükrullāh contain references to the use of strings made from silk as well as from gut.[53] By contrast, the predominance of the gut string was absolute in Europe during the Middle Ages, and it was especially favoured for bowed instruments because of its softer, more supple tone. During this period most strings were made from sheep-gut,[54] and Hugo von Trimberg[55] describes how the bow was 'drawn across sheep's intestines'. In a poem of Amarcius,[56] written about the middle of the eleventh century, we find another reference to a musical instrument, the strings of which were made from the damp gut of a wether; while the Colmar *Liederhandschrift* tells how 'sheep-gut on wood can make so sweet a sound'.[57] A fourteenth-

Tübingen, 1850), p. 348.   [45] The allusion to the use of silk strings occurs in the *Summa musicae*, a treatise written in Germany during the first half of the thirteenth century (at one time mistakenly ascribed to Johannes de Muris); *GS* III, 199 b.   [46] C. Sachs, *Handbuch*, 1st ed., p. 124.   [47] H. Hickmann, article 'Harfe' in *MGG*, col 1516.   [48] F. W. Galpin, *The Music of the Sumerians and their immediate Successors the Babylonians and Assyrians* (Cambridge, 1937).   [49] Evidence for the use of gut strings in ancient times is provided by the *Odyssey* (XXI, 407), the *Hymn of Hermes* (line 47) and the *Onomasticon* of Pollux (E. Bethe: 'Pollucis onomasticon', Libri IV, 62, *Lexicographi graeci*, Vol. IX [Leipzig, 1900], p. 219).   [50] C. Sachs, *Real-Lexikon der Musikinstrumente* (Berlin, 1913), article 'Saite'.   [51] H. G. Farmer, op. cit., p. 42.   [52] H. G. Farmer, op. cit., p. 45.   [53] W. Friedrich, op. cit., pp. 45 ff.   [54] Even in ancient times sheep-gut was used to make strings, as we know from the *Odyssey* (XXI, 407) and the *Hymn of Hermes* (Hom. hymn. in Merc. 47).   [55] This quotation is from the didactic poem *Der Renner* by Hugo von Trimberg (1260–1309). See J. and W. Grimm, *Deutsches Wörterbuch*, revised by I. Kühnhold, W. Mittring, and W. Pfeifer (Leipzig, 1957), under 'streichen' B 6 a.   [56] See P. A. Schubiger: *Musikalische Specilegien, Zur mittelalterlichen Instrumentalmusik*, Vol. V of the *Publikationen älterer praktischer und theoretischer Musikwerke*, IVth Year, Part II (Berlin 1876), p. 148 f.: 'Eminulis nimium digitis percurrere chordas quas de vervecum madidis aptaverat extis.'   [57] *Mei-*

century Middle English text describes a fiddle with wolf-gut strings,[58] while the Arab minstrel Ziryāb made his from the intestines of young lions.[59] In medieval times, gut strings were obviously more fragile than they are today, and it is not uncommon to read that 'dem videlaere sin seite zerbrochen was' ('the fiddler broke his string').[60] To prevent this, the player let down the strings of his fiddle whenever it was not in use,[61] thus protecting them at the expense of pitch constancy.

In thirteenth-century Europe, and in China, metal strings were already in use as well as those of silk and gut. They even take pride of place in the *Summa musicae*:[62] 'Chordalia sunt ea, quae per chordas metallinas, intestinales, vel sericinas exerceri videntur.' Yang Yü,[63] in his *Shan-chü hsin-hua*, gives particulars of a harp-like instrument with twenty strings made of copper wire, though this same Chinese source later implies that this was a relatively unusual type of stringing in Eastern Asia. During this period, bowed instruments were only rarely provided with metal strings, though they were gradually adopted for instruments that were plucked or beaten, in view of their superior strength and their louder, more penetrating tone quality. From this time we find occasional references to horse-hair strings, as for instance in the earliest Turkish account of musical instruments, written by Aḥmed-oghlu Shükrullāh in the early part of the fifteenth century.[64] Even today, bowed instruments with horsehair strings may be found in the Near East and the Balkans, in Northern Europe and Central Asia, but more especially in Turkey (*kemençe, kabak*),[65] Bosnia (*gusla*),[66] Croatia (*lirica*),[67] Scandinavia and Wales (bowed lyre),[68] in the Shetland Islands (*gue*),[69] Norway (*haar gie*),[70] Central Asia (*iklij*),[71] among the Uzbeks and Turkmeni (*kobuz, qā'us*),[72] the Kir-

sterlieder der Kolmarer Handschrift, ed. K. Bartsch (Stuttgart, 1862), No. CXX, lines 17 ff. [58] The relevant passage runs as follows: 'Strenges I maad of wolfes guttes ... I put in a fedele' (Trev. Barth 142 b/b); see H. Kurath, Sh. M. Kuhn: *Middle English Dictionary* (London 1953 ff.), s. v. 'fiddle'. [59] H. G. Farmer, op. cit., p. 42. [60] This quotation is from a Minnelied, which continues 'the same thing happens every week', F. H. von der Hagen, *Minnesinger*, Vol. II (Leipzig, 1838), No. 64a; a similar phrase occurs in the same work, Vol. II, No. 61 b: 'Heia, nu hei, des videlaeres seite der ist enzwei' ('hey, nonny no, the fiddler's string is broke in two'). [61] This information comes from Ulrich von Lichtenstein, cf. H. J. Moser, *Streichinstrumentenspiel im Mittelalter*, p. 12. [62] *GS* III, 199b. [63] H. Franke, 'Beiträge zur Kulturgeschichte Chinas unter der Mongolenherrschaft, Das Shan-kü sin-hua des Yang Yü', *Abhandlungen für die Kunde des Morgenlandes*, Vol. XXXII, 2 (Wiesbaden, 1956), p. 89 f. 'The Uigur Buddhist priest Lü-lü was at one time Superintendent of religious affairs ... During his lifetime he was wont to play upon the twenty-stringed (harp). Its strings were of copper. Each time when I asked instrument-makers about this, they could not use [strings of this type].' [64] W. Friedrich, op. cit., p. 45. [65] S. Y. Ataman, *Anadolu Halk Sazlari* (Istanbul, 1938); A. R. Yalgin, *Cenupta Türkmen calgilari* (Adana, 1940). [66] W. Wünsch, *Die Geigentechnik der südslawischen Guslaren*. [67] M. Gavazzi, 'Jadranska "lira-lirica"', *Narodna starina* IX (Agram, 1930); Fr. S. Kuhač, 'Prilog za povjest glazbe južnoslavjenske', *Rad Jugoslavenske Akademije znatosti i umjetnosti*, Vol. XXXVIII (Zagreb, 1877), pp. 62 ff. [68] C. Sachs, *Handbuch*, 2nd ed., p. 123. [69] O. Andersson, *Budkavlen XXXIII* (1954), p. 2. [70] O. Andersson, op. cit., p. 1. [71] *Great Soviet Encyclopedia*, article 'iklyj'. [72] M. G. Capus, 'La musique chez les Kirghizes et les Sartes de l'Asie centrale', *Revue d'Ethno-*

4

5

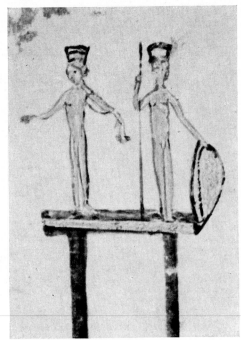

6

8

9

10

11

12

13

14

15

16

17

18

19

20

21

22

23

24

Iraxit abinfernif caprorum mille ciuernif

Consonancia   cuncta musica

27

28

Quatuor hos proceres psalmos dictare scientes Rex dauid elegit iur scs strennuus armis

ASAPH   DAVID   EMAN

Addauid cantuum cythariae   non cymbala desunt

ETHAN   IDITHVN

His armonius non organa non tuba desit   Rex ex azotis archam iubilando

29

30

31

32

33

34

35

36

37

38

39

40

41

42

43

44

45

46

47

48

49

50

52

anum: pfalterium iocundum c
ccinate in neomenia tuba: ininf

53

54

55

56

· DAVID ·

ATHAN· IDITHVN· HEMAN· ASAPH·

57

VIT
VIR
VNVS
DE

RAMAThaim sophim
demonte ephraim. &no
men e? helcana filius
ieroam. filii heliu. filii
thou. filii suph ephra
teus. Ramachaim ine

62

61

63

64

65

66

67

68

69

70

71

72

73

74

75

76

77

78

79

80

EATVS VIRQVINONABIIt

81

82

83

84

In confilio impiorum &

85

86

87

88

89

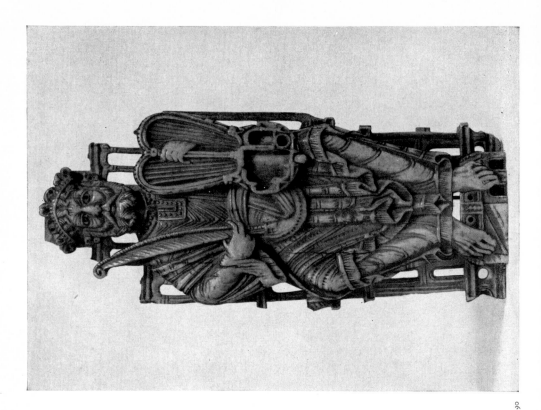

94

95

96

97

ghiz (*kyl-kyjak* = horsehair *kyjak*),[73] the Kazaks (*kobys*),[74] in the Altai (*ikili*),[75] among the Yakuts[76] and the Mongols (*morin-chur*).[77] In addition, musicians occasionally used 'chordae nervalis' favoured in antiquity – strings made from animal sinews[78] – for the stringing of bowed instruments until the late Middle Ages. This is chiefly borne out by the treatise on music by Paulus Paulirinus of Prague.[79] According to Yang Yü's *Shan-chü hsin-hua*, Ho Huai-chi, a Chinese musician of the T'ang period, strung his instrument with the sinews of a water-fowl.[80] Strings from vegetable materials – bast, hemp, flax and lianas – mentioned by ancient writers[81] and still in use on chordophones of primitive African tribes,[82] cannot be shown to have been used in the Middle Ages. Not until the seventeenth century do we hear of 'hempen strings from coconut, yucca, and aloe'.[83] However, among the different types of string known in medieval times, only the gut string came to be used throughout Europe, and it is of course still much used today.

Methods of manufacture

In the Middle Ages, the task of actually making the strings was usually carried out by the player himself. The process is described in fourteenth-century sources, above all in the *Secretum philosophorum*,[84] which includes several chapters on music, and describes the preparation of strings. This practical introduction recommends sheep-gut as suitable raw material. The gut should be soaked for at least half a day in water or lye,[85] until all the external layers or remains of flesh have separated from the fibrous intestinal connective-tissue membrane. The next step is to leave the cleaned guts to soak for two more days in strong lye, or in red wine, dry them in a linen cloth, and then twist together two, three, or four lengths of

---

graphie III (1885), p. 107; and V. Bel'aev, *Muzykal'nye instrumenti Uzbekistana* (Moscow, 1933), p. 53. [73] V. Vinogradov, *Kirgizskaja muzyka* (Frunze, 1958), p. 178. [74] *Great Soviet Encyclopedia*, article 'kobys'. [75] K. A. Vertkov, *Altaiskie muzykal'nye instrumenti* (manuscript), Lecture delivered at Leningrad, 1939. [76] *Muzykal'naja kul'tura avtonomnych respublik* (Moscow, 1957), p. 341. [77] E. Emsheimer, 'Preliminary Remarks on Mongolian Music and Instruments', *The Music of the Mongols, Part I, Eastern Mongolia* (Stockholm, 1943), pp. 82ff. [78] The use of sinews in the manufacture of strings is vouched for in particular by authors of the late classical era (Pollux, *Onomasticon* IV 62; Philostr., *Imag.* I 10; Luc. *Dial. Mar.* I 4; Porph., *in Ptolem. Harm.* 294; Schol. Aristoph. *Han.* 232). [79] J. Reiss, 'Pauli Paulirini de Praga Tractatus de musica', *ZfMw* 7, p. 263. Here we read of a bowed instrument 'habens cordam nervalem'. [80] H. Franke, 'Beiträge zur Kulturgeschichte Chinas unter der Mongolenherrschaft, Das Shan-kü sin-hua des Yang Yü', *Abhandlungen für die Kunde des Morgenlandes*, Vol. XXXII, 2 (Wiesbaden, 1956), p. 89f. [81] For proof of this see H. Abert's article 'Lyra' in *Realenzyklopädie der klassischen Altertumswissenschaften*, ed A. Pauly, rev. G. Wissowa (Stuttgart, 1894ff.). [82] C. Sachs, *Geist und Werden*, pp. 68ff. [83] G. Harsdörffer, *Deliciae mathematicae* (1677), Vol. II, p. 155. [84] The passage of the manufacture of strings is given by J. Handschin, *AMI* 16/17 (1944/45), pp. 1ff. [85] According to information given by the group working on the Medieval Latin Dictionary at the Berlin Academy of Sciences, the words *lexine* (lexiva) and *lestine* are mis-readings or corruptions of

the prepared intestines, while still damp, to make a string of the requisite strength. After this the finished gut string should be stretched out to dry. The author gives a final word of warning against storing the strings in too dry or too damp a place, since excessive dryness or damp causes them to snap easily. In the Old French epic *Le Bon Berger*[86] also we find a description of a lengthy process for making thin sheep-gut strings, and learn that the material was first washed, then dried, twisted, rubbed, and polished, and finally pulled and stretched. The *Kanz al-tuḥaf*,[87] a fourteenth-century Persian-Arabic treatise on music, describes both how gut strings were made, and how strings were made from silk threads. The Persian author stresses that care must be taken that the silk strings should be white, smooth, and as uniformly strong as possible. The raw silk cocoons must first be boiled, treated with wood ash, and finally washed and rinsed two or three times in clean water. The silk should then be placed to dry slowly in the shade. After it is dry, the threads are twisted together into a single strand, the number of threads being determined by the ultimate strength of the string required. The lowest string, according to this treatise, would be made of sixty-four threads, and the topmost string sixteen. The writer further recommended that the silken strings be rubbed with a viscous gum, tinted yellow with saffron, until they are thoroughly impregnated. In this way, the strings were rendered more elastic, and could sustain high tension. For gut strings the Persian author advocates sheep gut rather than goat. Depending on the strength of the material, the lowest string should be made from two or three lengths of gut, whereas the higher strings need fewer strands. To improve the appearance of gut strings, they were treated either with saffron or with white colouring.

When the usual medieval methods of making gut strings are compared with the processes used today,[88] the basic operations show a marked degree of similarity. Nowadays the gut is thoroughly cleaned and soaked in a solution of potash, or else – especially in Italy – in a mixture of water and winelees. It is then divided lengthwise, using a device invented by string manufacturers in Markneukirchen. The strands are then twisted together, from six to thirteen to each string, dried, stretched, and polished. The final step is the treatment of the strings with sulphur, which not only eliminates any unpleasant smell, but also blanches and strengthens them. (There is no mention of this last procedure in early sources.) Today, as in medieval times, the gut used comes primarily from sheep and lambs.[89]

lexivia (= lye), as in Johannes de Garlandia's *Dictionarius*. [86] Ed. by J. de Brie (Paris, 1879), p. 35: 'les menües cordes des boyaux bien lavez, sechez, tors, rez, essüez et filez sont pour la melodie des instruments de musique.' [87] These excerpts are published in English translation by H. G. Farmer, op. cit., p. 48 f. [88] The modern process of manufacturing strings is described by W. Albrecht in 'Vom Schafdarm zur Saite', *ZfI* 1940, p. 184 f.; H. Matzke in *Unser technisches Wissen*, pp. 289 ff.; P. O. Apian-Bennewitz in *Die Geige, der Geigenbau und die Bogenfertigung* (Weimar, 1892, 2nd ed., Leipzig 1920), pp. 318 ff. [89] Much of it from English animals, that which

The number of strings

An interesting question concerns the number of strings. From time to time it has been maintained that instruments with few strings are older, while many-stringed instruments are more modern; and this evolutionary theory forms the basis of Rühlmann's works, for example. Rühlmann was convinced that all bowed instruments 'appear at the outset with one playing string only, to which is soon added a drone-string'.[90] Grillet[91] likewise speaks of the early one-stringed fiddle and the later version with its plurality of strings. But this view is contradicted by the pictorial evidence from medieval sources. On almost every representation the bowed instruments are shown with from three to six strings. In particular, early Byzantine instruments dating from the tenth and eleventh centuries, and Western European fiddles and bowed rotes from the late eleventh and twelfth centuries (Plates 2, 4, 8, 11, 31, 38, 40, 41, 64, 90, 92–97), frequently have more than the three strings[92] prevailing during the eleventh century. Twelfth-century representations, too, show a preponderance of three-stringed instruments, and literary sources of the time refer to the *trichordum giga*.[93] The thirteenth century saw the spread of five-stringed bowed instruments, as confirmed by Elias Salomonis[94] in 1274: 'Sicut vidimus, quod in viella non sunt nisi quinque cordae.'

Side by side with these, however, instruments with fewer strings were frequently found in Central Europe. Several twelfth-century illustrations, for instance, show pear-shaped bowed instruments with one or two strings only (Plates 47, 48, 50) – such illustrations are almost all of German origin.[95] In addition, the narrow rebec is usually depicted as a two or three-stringed instrument. Jerome of Moravia describes the *rubebe* as an instrument with two strings tuned a fifth apart,[96] while in another somewhat later source[97] there is a reference to a *rebebe à corde terne*. It is to be stressed that, while as a rule the figure-of-eight fiddle remained three-stringed, the pear-shaped and elliptical instruments soon came to have five strings.

The increase in the number of strings was not at first designed to extend the compass of the instrument, since two of the strings were generally paired in unison, so that playing was not interrupted if one of the strings broke. In the case of the 'bordunus', which could be omitted if necessary, this precautionary measure was clearly felt to be superfluous.[98] Furthermore, tuning in double courses was pre-

comes from Yorkshire being of particularly high quality.   [90] J. Rühlmann, *Die Geschichte der Bogeninstrumente*, p. 89.   [91] L. Grillet, *Les Ancêtres*, pp. 23 ff.   [92] Cf. in particular the instrument shown on an eleventh century fresco in the Cathedral of St. Sophia, Kiev (Plate 8). Five-stringed Byzantine instruments corresponding to the Arab *rabab* are mentioned as early as the ninth century; cf. H. G. Farmer, *Ibn Khurdādhbih*, p. 512.   [93] For example, in a 12th century book of extracts, originating in Scheftlarn, now in the Bayrische Staatsbibliothek, Munich, Clm 17142 (*Old High German Glosses*, Vol. 4, p. 235, line 8).   [94] *GS* III, p. 20.   [95] The bowed instruments described as *lira* or *lyra* in 12th and 13th-century miniatures (cf. p. 35, Note 69) are likewise one-stringed instruments.   [96] S. M. Cserba, *Hieronymus de Moravia*, p. 289.   [97] F. Gennrich, 'Zur Musikinstrumentenkunde der Machaut-Zeit', *ZfMw* 9, p. 516.   [98] Only on the *lyra*

sumably an attempt to strengthen the melodic line relative to the drone. The doubling of strings is implied by the data on fiddle tuning given by Jerome of Moravia in his *Tractatus de musica*[99] (d Gg d′d′ and G G d c′ c′), and there is further evidence from medieval illustrations. Some twelfth-century pictures show bowed instruments with five strings, four of them arranged in pairs, while the fifth runs on its own along the edge of the fingerboard (Plates 43, 44 and 45). Johannes Tinctoris[100] testifies that three and five-stringed instruments were tuned in the same way, the only difference being that on the latter each pair of strings was tuned in unison. Similar stringing in double courses is occasionally found nowadays on folk instruments, for example, in Moravian peasant fiddles.[101] Here also the doubling is confined to the highest strings; these normally carry the melody, so that a broken string would be particularly disastrous.

We may therefore assume from the evidence available that the modern practice of playing on four strings was rare in the case of medieval bowed instruments, which were mainly strung with three or five strings.

The bow

Illustrations of the bow from the end of the tenth century show a wide variety of shapes and sizes. Extreme types appear almost simultaneously: the large, strongly curved, almost semicircular type, held in the middle of its arc (Plate 1), and the flat bow, of scarcely perceptible curvature, the hair of which lay along the shaft, almost touching it (Plates 3, 8, 62, 63, 92). There was the symmetrically round bow, and the bow curving at one end only (Plates 23, 26, 51, 54, 91), its otherwise straight shaft arching sharply at the tip.[102] On some bows the shaft protrudes at one end far beyond the point where the hair is attached (Plates 2, 4, 7, 10–12, 22, 24, 89). Initially this protruding section, which serves as a grip, is often as long as the bowing section itself. We find examples in illustrations of hair only 20 to 30 cm. in length, which would preclude any but the shortest bow strokes (Plates 28, 30, 64); while others, by contrast, have a total length around 120 cm., more than twice the length of the instrument itself, and generally wielded with the arm outstretched (Plates 4–7, 9–12). Pictorial evidence suggests that the tenth and eleventh centuries were a time when musicians were experimenting with a wide range of bows, those which proved unsatisfactory being discarded or modified. This indicates clearly that in the tenth century the bow was still in an early stage of development. Not until the late Middle Ages was a common type evolved, 50 to 80 cm. in length and moderately curved. The sub-

---

da braccio or da gamba of the 15th and 16th centuries do the separate drone-string appear in courses. [99] S. M. Cserba: op. cit., pp. 289 and 290. [100] In his description of the bowed 'viola', Tinctoris gives the following information: 'sive tres ei sint chorde simplices ut in pluribus: per geminam diapentam: sive quinque sic et per unisonos temperate: inequaliter', cf. K. Weinmann, *Johannes Tinctoris*, p. 41 f. [101] The Moravian *plaschprment* is generally tuned C G d d; cf. J. Zak, *Die Bauernfideln*, pp. 105 ff. [102] The tension of a bow-stick that curves sharply at

sequent history of the bow, traced largely through the studies of Dräger,[103] is marked by progressive straightening of the stick, by the axis of the shaft 'approximating to the direction of the hair',[104] and by the introduction of a 'nut'.

All theories of the development of the bow hitherto advanced break down when applied to the early history of bowing. No particular length of bow can be regarded as characteristic of any one stage of development, or be used as a basis for chronological arrangement of the material; nor can one say with any certainty whether or not a specific type of bow was used in conjunction with a particular instrument. Again, the hypothesis that the length and shape of the bow had a bearing on the way the instrument was held[105] cannot be applied to the early period. Long and short bows are shown indiscriminately with instruments propped against the player's shoulder or resting on his knee, that is, in front of the waist. These questions of technique will be discussed more fully in the following chapter.

The basic problem of bow-making lay in correlating the tension of the hair with the curve of the shaft. While the straightening of the bow-shaft meant, by and large, a decrease in tension, the resistance to deformation of the extended bow, curving sharply at one end, was greater than that of a bow of shallower and uniform curvature. Where there was no handle, and the player held in his hand not only the shaft, but the end of the hair as well, he could regulate the tension of the bow while playing by pressing his fingers against the hair. In the case of the flat bow, various types of nut were introduced from the thirteenth century onwards, in order to make the hair stand away from the shaft.[106] Sometimes a natural bifurcation in the wood was used for this purpose (Plate 75), in which case one twig was pared down to its stump, or a piece of wood (Plate 71) – or even a finger – was inserted between shaft and hair. This last device is already illustrated in an eleventh-century miniature (Plate 92).

As a rule, the shaft of the bow was made of wood, which not only had to be of great stiffness, but also had to have a certain degree of elasticity in order to withstand the necessary tension.[107] In spite of this, it was evidently not uncommon in medieval times for the player to break his bow.[108] In some illustrations from the thirteenth and fourteenth centuries it is possible to determine that the bow is made of bamboo, as in Eastern Asia today.[109] Nearly all such illustrations stem from regions where the Oriental influence was strong; and there is no evidence that this type of material was ever used in any other parts of Europe. The 'hair'

one end is greater than that of a stick describing a uniform shallow curve. [103] H.-H. Dräger, *Die Entwicklung des Streichbogens und seine Anwendung in Europa (bis zum Violenbogen des 16. Jahrhunderts)* (Dissertation, Berlin, 1937, printed in Kassel, 1937). [104] Dräger, op. cit., p. 22. [105] Dräger, op. cit., pp. 41 f., 56 and 64; also H. Matzke, *Unser technisches Wissen*, p. 259. [106] The various forms of bow nut are described in detail by Dräger, op. cit., p. 18. [107] W. Friedrich, *Die älteste türkische Beschreibung*, p. 67. [108] F. H. von der Hagen, *Minnesinger*, Vol. II (Leipzig, 1838), No. 63 a: 'nu is dem videlaere sin videlboge enzwei' ('now is the fiddler's bow in two'). [109] For example, in miniatures from the *Cantigas de Santa Maria*, Escorial Library, Madrid, MS.

of the tenth-century bow is described by al-Fārābī[110] as 'strings or similar material'. We know that horsehair was commonly used after the thirteenth century. Hugo von Trimberg[111] writes of stringed instruments being 'stroked with a horse's tail'; Paulus Paulirinus[112] describes them as 'quae traccione crinium de caudis equorum', and Johannes Tinctoris[113] refers to the bow (arculus) 'quom chorda ejus pilis equinis confecta'. The Turkish treatise of Aḥmed-oghlu Shükrullāh,[114] written c. 1400, gives more precise information relating to the fabrication of the bow: 'and the horsehair should be attached to the bow like bowstrings, the number of hairs being nine. And if they be more than nine, it is no matter; but let them not exceed forty.' The hair was therefore decidedly weaker than on our modern bows, which use from 100 to 120 horse hairs, and we may assume that the resulting tone was correspondingly thin.

There is good evidence that *Fidelharz* or rosin was rubbed into the hair in an attempt to increase the effectiveness of the bow in the Middle Ages.[115] It was similar to the rosin we use today, and according to a fourteenth-century Middle High German description was made from the resin of the incense tree (Boswellia Carterii) and from spruce resin (*Fichtenharz*). The Arabs also used cobbler's wax and mastic to annoint their bows, as we are told by the famous historian Ibn Khaldūn (1332–1406) in his voluminous *Introduction to History (Muqaddima)*.[116]

As with instruments, bows too might occasionally be made from costly materials and decorated, to draw attention to the wealth of the players or of his patron. 'J'ai un archon, noblement est ouvrés, pour vieler est fais' ('I have a bow, nobly wrought, and made for fiddling') says the Old French *Chanson d'Huon de Bordeaux*.[117] The *Romance of Alexander* tells of a bow set with precious stones,[118] while the *Nibelungenlied* has a reference to a red-painted fiddle-bow.[119] Many medieval illustrations show bows the point and grip of which are artistically curved or reflected, or fitted with a spherical protruberance, sometimes carved in the shape of an animal's head (Plates 2, 32, 35, 38).

T-i-I, and on the reliquary triptych in the Academia de la Historia, Madrid. [110] R. d'Erlanger, *La Musique Arabe*, Vol. I, p. 166. [111] See J. and W. Grimm, *Deutsches Wörterbuch, S. V.* 'streichen', B6a. [112] J. Reiss, *Pauli Paulirini*, p. 263. [113] K. Weinmann, *Johannes Tinctoris*, p.41 f. The Colmar Liederhandschrift likewise refers to stringed instruments being made to sound 'with horses' tails', cf. K. Bartsch, *Die Meisterlieder der Kolmarer Handschrift* (Stuttgart, 1862), No. CXX, verse 17 ff. [114] See Friedrich's translation, op. cit., p. 67. [115] One of the songs in the Colmar MS. lists all that is necessary for the bowing of strings. After noting the strings and the bow, the text mentions the rosin (colophonium): 'Daz harz im niht enliugt dar an, kan erz dar zuo bereiten, mit fiure, wîrouch unde bech vil eben zesamene leiten', ref. Bartsch edition, Stuttgart, 1862, No. CXX, verse 17 ff. [116] Cf. *Ibn Khaldun: The Mugaddimah, An Introduction to History translated from the Arabic by Franz Rosenthal*, Vol. II (New York, 1958), p. 397. [117] Ed. A. Graf (Halle, 1878), verse 2396. [118] 'The bow was of sapphire'; see L. Grillet, op. cit., p. 38. [119] 'His fiddle bow is painted red'; Bartsch edition, revised by H. de Boor, 12th edition (Leipzig,

TECHNIQUES OF PERFORMANCE

Although only fragments of medieval instruments have survived, it has been possible to gain a fairly clear picture of the structure of these early bowed instruments from the mass of secondary sources, and to draw certain conclusions as to the sound produced by these early fiddles, and hence to form some idea of the ideal sonority of that time. It is appreciably more difficult, on the basis of the available sources, to form any clear idea of the technique of performance which, in the last analysis, determines the form of musical expression for any instrument.

Positions

The question of technique embraces a complex of individual problems, including the position of the instrument, fingering and stopping, bowing, tuning, the use of the drone-strings – all issues that as yet have been little investigated. As the early illustrations show, the fiddler usually played standing, though in the early period of bowing he was often seated. Noteworthy is the fact that the musician often played while walking or even dancing. Fiddling seems to have been widespread as 'marching music' in the Middle Ages (Plates 30, 31, 33, 36, 37). By his extravagant dancing gait (Plates 2, 24, 27, 28), the fiddler – *musicus* and *joculator* in one – obviously sought to attract greater attention to himself and to his artistic prowess.

To some extent, position, fingering, and bowing are all contingent on the structure, size, and proportions of the instrument itself. A fiddle that exceeds a certain length can no longer be played with its body resting on the breast, or supported by the player's shoulder and chin, and must be either stood on the floor or propped on the knee. A very heavy instrument, similarly, should be propped up, if possible, to take the weight off the left arm (Plate 22). In the Middle Ages it is rare to find illustrations showing bowed instruments held in the position now universally adopted by violinists(Plates 8, 23, 24, 33, 47, 48, 58). In this, the instrument lies almost horizontal, its body being held by shoulder and chin, while the neck lies across the flat of the player's hand so that the fingers retain maximum freedom for stopping the strings and altering position.[120] There are two reasons for the limited use of this position during the Middle Ages: first, the weight of the heavy bowed instruments of the period quickly tired the player's left arm; and second, mobility of the hand stopping the strings was clearly not as necessary as it is today.

During the thirteenth and fourteenth centuries, fiddles were often played in a rather strange position. The instrument was held with its axis horizontal, the neck directed to the left. The body lay squarely across the player's body at shoulder level so that the strings had to be bowed vertically (Plates 67, 68). Such a position[121]

1949), stanza 2004, 4. [120] Cf. W. Trendelenburg, *Die natürlichen Grundlagen des Streichinstrumentenspiels* (Berlin, 1925). [121] Further illustrations showing bowed instruments held in this way

would be practicable only if the instrument were hung round the player's neck on a strap, and indeed slings can sometimes be discerned in illustrations. On one eleventh-century fiddle (Plate 8) played against the musician's chest, the sling hangs loose; while in another illustration showing the position described above (Plate 65) it rests round the player's neck. To this day it is possible to find isolated traces of this practice among village musicians, as for instance in Siebenbürgen, where instruments the size of our cellos are suspended from the players' necks by means of a strap.[122] Elsewhere, in Bohemia and Moravia, the *plåschprment*, another large bowed instrument, was played, according to early sources,[123] 'quite differently from the ordinary double bass; that is to say, it lay on a table if the player were seated, or hung like a guitar round his neck if he performed in a standing position.' The Polish fiddle (*suka*), now almost extinct, the *Klarfidel* and the *Grobfidel* of the Jihlava district (Czechoslovakia), and the large Sorbish *Fiedel* were all traditionally fitted with a strap.[124] When he had finished playing, the musician would sling his instrument on his back, again using the strap, thus recalling the medieval minstrel so often shown in miniatures carrying his instrument in just this way (Plate 66).

In the majority of medieval illustrations, the fiddle is propped or slanted against the player at a steep angle. His left arm, holding the instrument, hangs so low that the neck slopes downwards, sometimes almost vertically, while the resonator rests lightly against his shoulder or chest (for example, Plates 4–7, 10–12, 27–32, 35–40). By comparison with the first position[125] this undoubtedly reduced the strain on the left arm, but it also severely restricted the freedom of the fingering hand, which had the additional task of holding the instrument firmly. A further disadvantage is that an instrument resting against the player's chest in this way is liable to slip sideways whenever the left hand alters its position. 'This position', wrote Leopold Mozart,[126] 'doubtless looks natural and pleasing to the spectator; but for the player it is somewhat awkward and troublesome, for any sudden upward movement of the hand leaves the violin without support, so that it must inevitably slip, unless the player has learned, by long practice, to hold it in position between thumb and forefinger.' Such a position could only be regarded as rational and appropriate, if the player were to confine himself to playing single sustained notes. The performance he could achieve on an instrument held thus meets the demands of the standard form of accompaniment in the Middle Ages, which was in the main limited to supporting notes and sustained notes. Whenever bowed instruments appear in this position, therefore, what we are really looking at is a pictorial representation of fiddle-accompaniment. Quick runs and lively melodies would only be possible in this position if the instrument were somehow attached to the player's body. As parallel examples from the field

are given in A. Buchner, *Musikinstrumente im Wandel der Zeiten* (Prague, 1956), Plates 93, 98, and 99.   [122] O. Dincsér, *Zwei Musikinstrumente aus dem Komitate Csik* (Budapest, 1943), p. 86. [123] See L. Kunz, *Die Bauernfiedeln*, p. 141 f.   [124] See also the following page.   [125] That is to say, the afore mentioned aberrant horizontal position of the instrument.   [126] L. Mozart, *Treatise*,

of ethnomusicology clearly show, it was not unknown, even in the case of fiddles held at an oblique angle, for them to be attached to the musician by a strap,[127] a practice adopted by Sorbish *husla* players and by peasant musicians of Jihlava. Here the sling, fastened to the instrument, is looped around the crooked elbow to give some measure of support. However, there is no evidence that this type of armband was ever used in the Middle Ages. As a rule, medieval illustrations suggest that the neck of the steeply inclined fiddle was firmly held by the fingering hand, the main function of which, therefore, was to act as a support. This presupposes, however, that these are instruments with fingerboards, against which the strings were pressed. This type of instrument was mainly confined to Europe. Oriental instruments with no fingerboard would be automatically excluded from this position, since the wide gap between strings and neck would make it virtually impossible to stop the strings, on which gradations of pitch are achieved by only a light pressure of the fingers, while at the same time keeping the necessary firm hold on the steeply-slanting instrument. Such Oriental instruments are consequently always played in an upright position – propped either on the knee of the seated musician or on the floor. Thus the fact that in the East bowed instruments are almost invariably played upright, while most of their European counterparts are supported against the player's body, clearly stems from structural differences[128] already noted between Oriental and European instruments.

Until the thirteenth century only waisted instruments, more particularly the figure-of-eight fiddle, were played *a gamba* in Europe (Plates 51, 54–56, 61–63), whereas the pear-shaped and elliptical bowed instruments were always to begin with played on the shoulder. Many medieval illustrations showing waisted and unwaisted instruments side by side bring out this difference in technique (Plates 53, 55, 59, 60, 64, 81). The sitting or squatting position commonly assumed in the East for playing upright instruments was adopted by Western musicians only for the larger instruments – especially the figure-of-eight fiddles. The smaller sizes were nearly always played with the musician standing, resting the instrument against the upper part of his body. If, as sometimes happened, a musician performed on the waisted fiddle in a standing position, he still held the instrument vertically in front of the upper part of his body (Plate 57). One is tempted to doubt the factual reality of such illustrations, since the instrument is shown without any visible means of support, hanging loosely down, in circumstances where it would certainly have demanded the constant support of the player's right hand. These doubts are, however, dispelled by evidence from ethnomusicological parallels. The old Polish fiddle known as *suka* (bitch) was played in exactly the same way. We are told[129] that the musician supported the instrument by resting the end pin in a strap hung round the neck or over the shoulder, and down the

---

English ed. trans. E. Knocker, 2nd ed. (London, 1956), p. 54. [127] A. Buchner, *Musikinstrumente*, Plate 315, shows a Sorbic *husla* player whose instrument is attached in this fashion. The position of the *jihlava* fiddle is described in L. Kunz, *Die Bauernfiedeln*, p. 142. [128] Here the criterion is the use or non-use of a fingerboard. [129] According to information from Dr. Martin

front of the body. In medieval times the bowed instrument was held almost exclusively in the left hand and the bow in the right, just as it is today. This meant that the task of bowing fell to the more efficient hand.

Bowing

The style of bowing is an essential factor in the technique of playing medieval bowed instruments. As the illustrations show, the shaft of the bow was held in the closed fist and not, as today, with the fingertips. This firm grip was necessary if the player was to keep control of the clumsy bow while playing. A loose wrist, and hence elastic transition between changes in strokes,[130] were clearly unthinkable with the bow held in such a rigid fashion. Obviously the medieval bow, by virtue of its weight and the strength used by the player, pressed more heavily on the strings than in modern bowing, although even today folk musicians make a point of drawing as much sound as possible from the strings.[131] To do this, the bow is sometimes gripped with the whole hand. This increased pressure brings with it unpleasant scratching noises, particularly characteristic of Oriental bowing, and presumably also a feature of medieval fiddle tone.

Whereas the strongly curved bow, as shown in many medieval illustrations, was often held midway between the points at which the hair was attached (Plate 1), the flat bow was usually held at one end. In the first case, the bowing hand came in contact only with the wood; but in the second, the hand embraced both shaft and hair, and could increase the tension of the bow by applying greater pressure to the hair. Both methods occur side by side in medieval sources.[132] Only the end grip finally established itself in Europe, since a straight, more strictly linear bowing action, indispensable on instruments with more than one string, can hardly be achieved if the bow is held in the middle. To improve the 'stability of the bowing plane'[133] rounded bows with a long handle were widely used until the twelfth century, making it appreciably easier for the player to achieve an even bowing action.

Apart from end grip and middle grip, we must distinguish between the normal overhand grip and the reverse or underhand grip. The use of the reverse grip imposes its own limitations, since the forearm, bent forward in this position, can only be turned outwards until the bow is horizontal. An upward-pointing stroke of the bow, such as is necessary when the instrument lies against the player's shoulder, is therefore out of the question if the bow is held underhand. Only where the strings run almost vertically is there evidence that the reverse grip was used. Furthermore, this technique assumes a long bow, because the bowing

Sobieski, Warsaw. [130] The sequence of movements involved in bowing is discussed in F. A. Steinhausen, *Die Physiologie der Bogenführung auf Streichinstrumenten*, 5th edition, ed. F. von Reuter (Leipzig, 1928). [131] O. Dincsér, *Zwei Musikinstrumente*, p. 26, Plate 22, and p. 85. [132] The majority of illustrations show the bow held at one end, and it is mainly Oriental miniatures that illustrate the centre grip. [133] H.-H. Dräger, op. cit., p. 38.

hand, or forearm, strikes the side of the instrument well before the full length of the bow has been used.

Basically, then, the rule is that with instruments played on the shoulder or against the chest the bow is held overhand, while with upright instruments the reverse grip is used. If, exceptionally, instruments in the former position are shown with the bow held in the reverse grip, the neck of the fiddle points so steeply downwards that the strings run roughly as on upright instruments (Plates 4–7, 10–12). Again, musicians are sometimes shown playing knee fiddles using the overhand grip. The reason for this deviation lies in the unusual shape of the bow, which is here remarkably short and curved, making it unsuitable for the reverse grip (Plates 1, 2, 21, 22, 64).

The tone-quality of these medieval bowed instruments may be gauged from the point at which the bow is drawn across the strings. This can usually be determined accurately from the pictures. Whereas nowadays the bow is applied to the strings in the region of the bridge, about a tenth of the strings' length from the bridge,[134] in the Middle Ages it was drawn across about a third of the strings' length from the bridge – or across the middle of the strings (Plates 43–38, 45, 48–57, 60–65). This naturally resulted in a more muted tone, much thinner and weaker than that of modern bowing.

Stopping

'Viellatio autem ipsa finis est temperationis et modulationis chordarum.'[135] Albertus Magnus goes on to elaborate this statement as follows: 'Scientia compositionis chordarum docet componere et dividere chordarum ad sonum gravis vel acuti vel medii, et hoc per causas et rationis hujus compositionis.'[136] To form a clear idea of the medieval techniques of fingering and stopping on bowed instruments, we must turn to the relevant details given by Jerome of Moravia.[137] According to his description, only the 'first position'[138] was used at that time. The left hand always remained in the same position, therefore – a fact confirmed by various illustrations of medieval fiddles. On these instruments the neck is so short indeed as to preclude any change of position (Plates 3, 4, 22). The compass was restricted above, unlike modern violins, and frequently not fully used below, since the melody was played principally on the upper strings, with the lower strings frequently acting as a drone. The player used three fingers as a rule,[139] while the weaker fourth finger was used only on the top string.

Illustrations from European sources show that where the instrument was played in an upright position the strings were usually pressed against the finger-

[134] See F. A. Steinhausen, op. cit., p. 58 f.　[135] Albertus Magnus, *Ethics*, 6, 1, 6, p. 404 b.　[136] Albertus Magnus, *Ethics*, 1, 1, 2 p. 4 b.　[137] S. M. Cserba, op. cit., p. 289 f.　[138] Not until the second half of the 17th century do we find any reference to shifts of position in fiddling, and even then a change of position was only used as an expedient. Cf. K. Gerhartz, 'Die Violinschulen in ihrer musikalischen Entwicklung bis Leopold Mozart', *ZfMw* 7, p. 557.　[139] Adjacent semitones and tones

board with the fingertips; when the instrument lay against the shoulder or chest they were pressed with the inside of the finger. If we assume a certain degree of accuracy in the details of these medieval paintings, the position of the fingers[140] suggests that in the shoulder position two or three strings were often stopped simultaneously. If the strings affected were not tuned in unison, the result was a broadening of the sound like parallel organum or an organ 'mixture'. This conclusion, based on pictorial sources, is again strengthened by evidence from the folk tradition. Polish and Hungarian fiddlers in rural areas[141] commonly play their melodies in parallel fifths[142] to make them stand out more clearly. This practice also occurs among Turkish folk musicians. Examples of fiddle tunes from Asia Minor reveal the widespread use of organum in fourths resulting from the Turkish practice of tuning bowed instruments in fourths.[143] Analogous examples occur in Central Asia among Turkmen, Uzbeks, and Kirghiz. Both strings of the Kirghiz *kyjak* or the Sartish *qā'us*, tuned a fourth or fifth apart, are usually played simultaneously, either as melody and drone or as parallel organum.[144] The three-stringed *komuz* of the Kirghiz combines both practices. The melody is played on the highest string, which runs between the two others. The outer strings, tuned a fourth or fifth lower, sound simultaneously with the melody, the first sounding parallel to it at the fourth or fifth, and the other acting as a drone.[145] The *gydjak* of Turkmen and Uzbeks is played in a similar way.[146] Yakut bowed instruments double the melody at the octave, the three strings being tuned g' g g. Yakut round dances, the form of which is determined by the alternation of soloist and chorus, are interpreted on this instrument in an interesting way. First, the melody is played on the highest string; then all three strings play together: the melody is repeated by the first two at the octave, while the third string acts as a drone.[147] This practice, which broadens and intensifies the sound, obviously gave medieval bowed music its special characteristics. As in early vocal polyphony – the parallel organum of the *Musica Enchiriadis* – this 'mixture-stop' sound can be shown to have been produced by various other medieval instruments.[148] The technique of stopping two or three strings at a time implies that the bow excited several strings simultaneously. This was certainly the most widespread style of bowing in the Middle Ages – perhaps even the only one. Various structural features of the

were sometimes stopped with the same finger, which then had to change its position. [140] On many illustrations the fingers lie across several strings. [141] Tape-recordings of Polish folk musicians playing bowed instruments (Institute for the Study of Folk Art, in the Warsaw Academy of Sciences) confirm this practice. Cf. also O. Dincsér, *Zwei Musikinstrumente*, p. 44, Ex. 7. [142] O. Dincsér, op. cit., p. 86. [143] P. Collaer, 'Polyphonies de tradition populaire en Europe méditerranéenne', *Acta musicologica* XXXII (1960), p. 60. [144] V. Vinogradov, *Kirgizskaja narodnaja muzyka* (Frunze, 1958), p. 308, Ex. 14. [145] V. Vinogradov, op. cit., pp. 168 and 305, Examples 6a–c. [146] V. Uspenskij and V. Bel'aev, *Turkmenskaja muzyka* (Moscow, 1928), p. 68ff. [147] *Muzykal'naja kul'tura avtonomnych respublik* (Moscow, 1957), p. 341. [148] On the use of 'mixtures' on the medieval organ, hurdy-gurdy, psaltery, and other stringed instruments, and the spread of singing in parallel during the Middle Ages, see W. Bachmann, 'Die Verbreitung des Quintierens im europäischen Volksgesang des späten Mittelalters', *Festschrift für Max Schnei-*

bowed instruments of the time support this theory. The flat unwaisted resonator, the bridge scarcely arched or absent, and the occasional use of a crosspiece attached to the belly as anchorage for the strings – all these exclude any variation in the plane of the bow-stroke, in general. Thus the bow inevitably touched all the strings. Even when the body of the instrument showed a lateral inward curve, this was evidently not used, as it is today, to change the direction of the bow and allow it to touch individual strings only.[149] This is chiefly confirmed by the fact that in the majority of medieval illustrations showing waisted fiddles, the bow lies across the upper belly of the body, not across the waist itself (Plates 51, 56, 61, 64). The hurdy-gurdy[150] reveals this medieval string technique unambiguously, for it permits all the strings to be sounded simultaneously – it and the fiddle in their early forms were manifestations of the same sonorous principle.

A more advanced developmental stage was reached when, as Johannes Tinc-toris first describes, the bow could play each string individually on instruments with more than one string.[151] Before this could happen, a fully developed bowing technique which could vary the direction of the bow was necessary; and the strings themselves had to lie in a curving arc, while the body of the instrument had to be made with incurving sides. While the structure and playing technique of bowed instruments used in European art music were developed and perfected along these lines, folk music has preserved here and there the medieval style of bowing, where the bow, continuously or intermittently, excites several strings simultaneously.[152]

Tunings and drone-strings

The assumption that in medieval times the bow necessarily touched several strings simultaneously may appear strange, considered in relation to the modern practice of tuning modern bowed instruments in fifths or fourths. But if we consider the three different methods of fiddle-tuning used at that time, minutely described by Jerome of Moravia in his *Tractatus de Musica*,[153] this bowing technique appears entirely rational and comprehensible. In this context, the second method of fiddle-tuning mentioned by Jerome is particularly instructive. This was used for secular and other highly irregular melodies[154] with a wide compass. Here the strings were tuned in alternate fifths and fourths, thus: G d g d′ g′, sounding a bare root, fifth, and octaves. This type of tuning, based on the consonance of

der (Leipzig, 1955), pp. 25 ff. [149] C. Sachs, *Handbuch*, p. 173 f., and H.-H. Dräger, op. cit., p. 51, take the view that the 'waisting' of bowed instruments was designed from the outset to enable the players to bow individual strings. [150] The early hurdy-gurdy, which generally had a waisted body, supports the assumption that incurving sides were not originally intended to give the bow the freedom of movement necessary to bow individual strings. [151] In the treatise *De inventione et usu musicae* we read: 'ut arculus unam chordam tangens: juxta libitum sonitoris: alias relinquat inconcussas'. K. Weinmann, *Johannes Tinctoris*, p. 41 f. [152] Cf. examples in the following sections. [153] S. M. Cserba, op. cit., p. 289 f. [154] Op. cit., p. 290: 'propter laicos et

all the strings, only makes sense, however, if we assume that the player *intends* to bow several strings at once.[155] Again, this technique points indisputably to the use of drones, since playing in harmony was out of the question on primitive fiddles. We must suppose, then, that in medieval fiddling the melody was fingered (in the first position)[156] on the individual strings, and that all strings momentarily not participating in the melody sounded as a drone. Compared with that of the hurdy-gurdy, the compass of this medieval fiddle was much greater (G to d'); the melody could range over all five strings, always embedded in a complex drone of the fifth doubled at the octave.

Evidence from contemporary folk-instruments

Presumably a style of tuning similar to that described by Jerome of Moravia in the thirteenth century, together with its attendant drone-technique, was already in use on the earliest bowed instruments during the tenth century. This supposition is confirmed by ethnomusicological evidence from folk fiddles still played in various regions, which in shape, number of strings, and playing position correspond exactly to the bowed instruments in illustrations of the eleventh and twelfth centuries. This agreement between ethnological and historical material, particularly apparent in morphological aspects, tempts us to apply conclusions drawn from the technique and tuning of surviving fiddles to their early counterparts. Since medieval sources give no relevant information until the thirteenth century, any details of folk bowing techniques culled from folklore studies are of particular interest, especially as such practices often stem from very ancient traditions.

Fiddle-tuning of the type described by Jerome of Moravia in the thirteenth century is still to be found in Moravia today. In the Jihlava region in particular the locally made fiddles are tuned root – fifth – octave. This refers particularly to the bass *dynda*, also known as *plåschprment*, and tuned D G d d,[157] while the descant and tenor instruments (*dynda*, *niti*, *pajerki*) have been adapted to the usual tuning in fifths current today. The bass instruments in string ensembles of the Gorals, inhabitants of the Beskidy Mountains, are tuned like the Moravian *plåschprment*, and another feature common to both is their supporting drone-rôle when playing in consort with the descant and tenor fiddles. The bass has no melodic function, and either alternates between tonic and dominant, or sustains the tonic. This striking similarity between historical sources and modern folk musical practice indicates that traditions of tuning and performance, as well as of instrument making, often survive unaltered for hundreds of years in remote areas.

omnes alios cantus, maxime irregulares.' [155] In purely melodic playing, on the other hand, strings tuned to irregular intervals are disadvantageous. [156] Cf. Notes 137 and 138, p. 91 [157] For further details of tuning and playing cf. L. Kunz, 'Skripky', *Acta Musei Moraviae* XXXV (1950),

We know that tuning based on the harmonic consonance of all the strings was used in Northern Europe and in the Balkans as well as in the Near East and in Central and Eastern Asia. In addition to the Swedish *Schlüsselfidel*, there is the Hardanger fiddle from Norway, usually tuned c′ g′ c″ e″.[158] The lower strings usually sound a pedal-pointlike accompaniment.[159] While the open strings of the pochette-like small Polish fiddle are frequently tuned to the D major triad,[160] the Polish *suka* has a 'mixture' tuning – keynote, fifth, and octave.[161] In Turkey[162] and Northern Albania[163] fiddles are often tuned in the same way: keynote – fifth – octave – as is the three-stringed Bulgarian *gadulka* – this tuning again being based on harmonic consonance. The lowest string, exclusively used as a drone, is usually placed between the two others, the open strings being tuned either d″ a′ a″ or d″ g′ g″.[164] An account written in 1788 gives similar information about the bowed instruments used by Russian folk musicians.[165] 'The *gudock* is a violin with three strings, of which only the uppermost is stopped. A short bow bows all three strings, and the melody is played on the string tuned to the fifth [above the middle string]. The two strings sounding simultaneously are generally tuned to the fifth and the octave [below the top string], so that they often make horrid discords with the tune.'[166] It has already been shown that tuning in fourths and fifths, coupled with a drone accompaniment, was characteristic of Central Asian bowed instruments.[167] Particularly in earlier sources there is ample proof that this was so, while in Central Asia today tuning in fourths has been widely adopted in many areas. Mironov, in his book on the musical culture of the Uzbeks (1890) describes a seven-stringed bowed instrument, rather like a *gydjak*, the strings of which were tuned $A\flat'-E\flat'E\flat'-A\flat''A\flat''$.[168] We know, too, that the three strings on the Khirghiz *komuz* are tuned in various combinations of fourths and fifths, for example d′g′d′ or d′a′d′.[169] One of the two lower outer strings functions as a drone. In Kirghiz instru-

pp. 9 and 11; cf. also L. Kunz, *Die Bauernfiedeln*, p. 138.   [158] On the tuning of Old Norse stringed instruments cf. N. Bessaraboff, *Ancient European Musical Instruments*, p. 289; O. Andersson, *Altnordische Streichinstrumente*, pp. 252 ff.. and S. Walin, *Die schwedische Hummel* (Stockholm, 1952), p. 102.   [159] The technique of playing the Hardanger fiddle is described by A. Bjørndal, 'The Hardanger fiddle. The tradition, music forms and style', *JIFMC* VIII (1956), p. 14: 'The Hardanger fiddle plays a kind of polyphonic music in which the dominant has a specially important rôle, appearing almost like an organ point.'   [160] Information supplied by Dr. Martin Sobieski, Warsaw.   [161] *Grove's Dictionary*, 5th Edition (London, 1954), article 'Folk Music'.   [162] E. g. the tuning of the pear-shaped Turkish *kemänche*; A. Lavignac, *Encyclopédie de la Musique*, Vol. V, p. 3015.   [163] According to Dr. Erich Stockmann, Berlin, the fundamental-fifth-octave tuning of bowed instruments was also encountered during an expedition to Northern Albania.
[164] *Grove's Dictionary*, 5th Edition (London, 1954), article 'Folk Music'; cf. also I. Kačulev, 'Gdulkite v B'lgaria', *Izvestija na Instituta za Musika*, No. 5 (1958), pp. 131 ff.   [165] J. J. Bellermann, *Bemerkungen über Rußland*, Part I (Erfurt, 1877), p. 363.   [166] The *gudok* is a three-stringed bowed instrument with no sides, a rounded back and an oval or elliptical body. Details of its tuning and technique are given in Curt Sachs's *Real-Lexikon*, in the article 'gudok', and also in the article 'gudok' in the *Great Soviet Encyclopedia*. Cf. also L. Ginsburg, *Istorija violoncel'nogo iskusstva*, Vol. II (Moscow, 1957), p. 20 ff.   [167] P. 66.   [168] V. Bel'aev, *Muzykal'nye instrumenty uzbekistana* (Moscow, 1933), p. 56.   [169] V. Vinogradov, *Kirgizskaja narodnaja muzyka*, p. 168.

ments the highest string generally lies in the middle, even where the strings are tuned fundamental–fifth–octave, so that in these cases the strings lie in the order d'g'g.[170] In China and India, too, there are rare instances of bowed instruments being tuned G c g c' or c g c' g',[171] again in conjunction with a drone technique. However, bowing of this kind, where the melody is invariably accompanied by the sound of drone strings, is by no means confined to Europe and Asia. From Pennsylvania, for example, we also hear of fiddlers 'who doublestop continuously on open strings, and thus achieve a hypnotic drone resembling that of a bag-pipe'.[172]

In Siebenbürgen a practice of particular interest in connection with bowing is the division of labour when there is a drone accompaniment.[173] Here melody and drone are played on two different instruments. The fiddler who provides tunes for dancing and entertainment is accompanied by a second musician with a *gardon*, a bowed instrument resembling a cello. This drone instrument, the name of which derives etymologically from 'bourdon', has three or four strings, all tuned either to d, or to D d g or D A d.[174] Whereas a bow is used on the melody instrument, the strings of the 'gardon' are struck with a stick 40 to 50 cm. long. The accented beats of the dance or other tune are at times marked with a stroke while one of the strings is plucked on the weak beats. Since this 'beaten drone' is played on unstopped strings, with no variation in pitch, the instrument provides an accompaniment restricted to the pitch of the open strings. This example shows the close relationship between the beater – sometimes used as a friction stick – and the bow itself. The beater is obviously the more primitive form, reserved for producing sound on drone strings.

Plucked chordophones were tuned to keynote, fifth, and octave,[175] even more frequently than were bowed instruments, and in both cases this tuning was linked with the simultaneous striking or rubbing of several strings and hence with drone-accompaniment.

In many regions, however, tuning by fifths or fourths throughout is the pre-dominant tuning used for modern fiddle-like bowed instruments. Even here, however, the drone often plays a decisive rôle. Interesting evidence for this

---

[170] Op. cit., p. 171. [171] According to A Majumdar, *Die nordindische Musik der Gegenwart unter Berücksichtigung der alten Theoretiker* (Dissertation, Königsberg, 1941), p. 174, the Indian *sárangí* is frequently tuned G c g c'. Drone playing is particularly commonly met on Indian folk bowed instruments. [172] S. P. Bayard, 'Some Folk Fiddlers' habits and styles in Western Pennsylvania', *JIFMC* VIII (1956), p. 18. [173] O. Dincsér, 'Zwei Musikinstrumente aus dem Komitate Csik', *A néprajzi múzeum füzetei* 7 (Budapest, 1943). [174] Op. cit., p. 86. [175] Cf. for example the Perso-Georgian *tár*, the Carnatic *sitár* or the *tanbur* of Uzbekistan and Hindustan; C. Sachs: *Geist und Werden*, p. 251 ff. The playing of these instruments is described by P. Weiss, 'Usbekische Musik', *Die Musik* (August, 1931), pp. 831 ff.: 'The second and third strings act as a constant drone bass; the left hand stops only the first . . . the *tanbur* player plucks the first string on the instrument with the end of a steel point attached to his index finger, using his bare thumb for the faux-bourdon basses (comparatively rarely used)'. This instrument is frequently used to accompany, when the player strums with a plectrum across the open strings, creating an invariant drone bass,

tuning comes from North-eastern Asia Minor.[176] In the vicinity of the shores of the Black Sea elongated pear-shaped fiddles with three strings, played exclusively in the first position and tuned in fourths, are still to be found today. Where the melody is fingered on the top string, the middle string acts as a drone; but if the melody descends to the lower strings, the top string takes over the sustaining note. As well as the simple single-note drone, which can alter pitch by a fourth and lie now above, now below the melodic line, a double drone at the fourth is achieved by bowing all three strings at once.[177] This example demonstrates that tuning in fourths by no means excludes the use of drones. The methods of tuning and playing Turkish fiddles are strikingly similar to those of bowed instruments of Central Asia – Turkmenistan, Uzbekistan and Kirghistan – in particular to those of the two-stringed Kirghiz *kyjak* and the *kobuz* (*qā'us*) of the Sarts, as well as to those of the *iklyj*, widespread in Central Asia. These instruments are usually tuned in fourths. The melody is played on the top string, while the lower string is sounded as a drone. Sometimes the melody is transferred to the drone-string to extend the lower range; when this happens the upper string usually takes over the drone.[178]

Tuning in fourths is also known in the Balkan Peninsula. Like the Cretan fiddle, tuned as a rule d' g' b',[179] the pearshaped Greek *lira*[180] also uses the lowest string (d') or d' and g' as a drone. Greek refugees from the Black Sea Coast of Turkey, the ancient territory of Pontus[181] (see above), brought with them to Greece the elongated pear-shaped fiddle – known as the 'Caucasian' fiddle – the strings of which are tuned in fourths (d g c').[182] However, both the Caucasian[183] and the South-eastern European fiddles (which have retained the medieval pear-shape in Dalmatia, Bulgaria, and Greece) are much more commonly tuned in fifths than fourths. Thus the Bulgarian *gadulka* is generally tuned g d' a',[184] with the g and d' mostly acting as drones. It is true that where an instrument is tuned in fifths,

[176] This account is taken from L. Picken, 'Instrumental polyphonic Folk-Music in Asia Minor', *PRMA* 80 (1953/54), p. 76f. On pp. 78 and 79 the author gives several examples of fiddle pieces with simple drones and drones in fourth. [177] L. Picken, op. cit., p. 84f., takes the view that the medieval techniques of bowing and tuning have survived almost intact in this area of the Near East. 'The polyphonic fiddling of those who live on the Black Sea coast, in the belt of hazelnut cultivation between Giresun and Hope, may without exaggeration be described as quasi-medieval.' [178] V. Vinogradov, op. cit., p. 179. [179] L. Bürchner, 'Griechische Volksweisen', *SIMG* 3 (1901/1902), p. 409. Tuning in fifths – g d' a' – is also common (cf. *MGG*, article 'Griechenland, Volksmusik'). [180] W. Wiora, 'Europäischer Volksgesang', in *Das Musikwerk*, ed. K. G. Fellerer, p. 66 (Ex. 99e), reproduces a Greek dancing song with *lyra* accompaniment. The bowed instrument sounds the note d' as a constant drone. [181] This Turkish Black Sea province roughly corresponds to the coastal region between Giresun and Hopa, where (according to Picken's description) the unstopped strings generally sound as a constant drone on bowed instruments tuned in fourths (cf. Note 177). [182] S. Karas, article 'Griechenland, Volksmusik' in *MGG*. [183] The three strings on the elongated Caucasian fiddle are usually tuned in fifths (g d' a'); cf. the *Catalogue of the Exhibition of Ancient Music held by the City of Munich in the Bayrisches Nationalmuseum* (Nov./Dec. 1951), No. 119. [184] Ch. Obreschkoff, *Das bulgarische Volkslied* (Berne and Leipzig, 1937), p. 101; also B. A. Kremenliev, *Bulgarian Folk-Music* (Berkeley, 1952),

what should be the lowest string is frequently tuned an octave higher, giving a 4–1–5 tuning instead of 1–5–9.[185] In this way the lowest string, acting as a permanent drone, assumes the middle position, while the two outside strings carry the melody. The same arrangement of strings and tuning is found on the Dodecanese *lira* (c′ g d′),[186] the Croatian *lirica* (g′ d′ a′),[187] the *vijalo* of the Southern Slavs and Dalmatians (d″ a′ e″),[188] and certain Turkish fiddles (d′ a e′),[189] all instruments outwardly resembling the bowed instruments in medieval illustrations. In each case the middle string functions as a drone. The Kirghiz *komuz* is tuned in like fashion, although here it is usually the top string that lies in the middle, the two others being tuned a fourth and a fifth lower (d′ g′ c′).[190] The melody is played in consecutive fourths on the first and second strings, while the third acts as a simultaneous drone. A number of variants of this tuning in fourths and fifths are known from three-stringed fiddles of Central Asia, where the 1–4–5 arrangement is not uncommon. Thus in some districts the Kirghiz *komuz* is tuned d′ g′ a′.[191] The *gadulka* provides an interesting parallel (c′ f′ g′ or d′ g′ a′). The tune is played on the top string, while the two others are nearly always played as open strings, yielding a fixed drone of a fourth.[192] From these examples we may conclude that, notwithstanding variations in tuning, all these three and fourstringed fiddles have certain techniques in common, in particular the use of drone-strings. The fiddle-drone does not always lie below the melody and is not to be equated with a low, supporting or sustained note in the Western sense. In many cases there is as yet no clear distinction between drone-strings and melody-strings. As soon as the melody is transferred to a string previously acting as a drone, the vacated string is sounded as a drone. In contrast to the Western drone-string of the late Middle Ages, which lay close to the fingerboard and was sounded only at places harmonically appropriate to the melody, the drone strings here sound continuously like a pedal-point, regardless of the course of the melody. As we have seen, this technique, with its permanent drone accompaniment, is not confined to fiddles with strings tuned to be consonant when all are sounded together, but is also possible on those tuned in fourths and fifths. Indeed, where double drones are used, both fifths and fourths occur.[193]

In most of the examples previously mentioned some or all of the strings are bowed simultaneously; but in some regions players alternate between bowing several strings and one string, that is between drone-accompanied and solo performance. The Sarts of Central Asia use a slack bow[194] capable of exciting all the

p. 135. [185] Ch. Obreschkoff, op. cit., p. 101. [186] Cf. S. Karas, loc. cit. [187] *Grove's Dictionary*, 5th Edition (1954), article 'Folk Music, Jugoslavia'. [188] C. Sachs, *Real-Lexikon* article '*vijalo*'; also C. Sachs, *Geist und Werden*, p. 243. [189] Cf. S. Y. Ataman, *Anadolu halk sazları yerli musikiciler ve halk müzik karakterleri* (Istanbul, 1938), Plate 3. [190] V. Vinogradov, op. cit., p. 168. [191] Op. cit., p. 171. [192] M. A. Vasiljević in *JIFMC* IV (1952), p. 19 ff.: 'La chantarelle (sol), qui est en même temps la finale de la mélodie, sert à rendre l'exécution principale (mélodique), tandis que les deux autres (fa, do) donnent les tons d'accompagnement fixes et immuables.' [193] This type of organ-point accompaniment in fourths is thought by Vasiljević (op. cit.) to be older than drones in fifths in South-Eastern Europe. [194] M. G. Capus, 'La Musique

strings simultaneously, although on their instruments the strings lie in an arc, not in the same plane. However, the Sart musician frequently tightens the hair of the bow with the fingers of the right hand, to enable him to play on one string only. A similar type of bow is used by both the Yakuts[195] and the *kyjak*-players of Kirghistan.[196] The hair hangs loosely from the shaft, and is tightened by the hand while playing. Most East Asian bowed instruments demand a very special bowing action.[197] The hair of the bow passes between the two strings or two pairs of strings, so that instrument and bow are permanently attached to one another. By pressing the bow towards the body of the instrument, or pulling outwards, away from the instrument, the player can bow either string or pair of strings.

One last type of bowed drone-accompaniment, practised in many parts of Europe and firmly rooted in the folk tradition, remains to be mentioned. Here the open strings are only sounded *arpeggiato* at the beginning and end of each piece, at intermediate cadences, and at specially accentuated points.[198] Dissonant clashes between melody and drone are thus very largely avoided. This style of bowing is widespread in Europe, but is also known elsewhere, for example, among the Kirghiz. The lower of the two strings on the *kyjak* is primarily a drone-string, though it is only rarely sounded with the melody as snatches of a drone bass, while at cadences it provides a powerful and sustained pedal-point.[199]

The insight into techniques of fiddling given by ethnomusicological studies thus reveals certain general principles of drone-playing which in isolated areas appear to have survived intact over a period of several centuries.[200]

Medieval and later evidence

Having ventured briefly into the field of comparative musicology, let us turn once again to the Middle Ages. The evidence shows, or appears to show, that the three-stringed, pear-shaped fiddles of the eleventh and twelfth centuries were

chez les Khirghizes et les Sartes de l'Asie centrale', R. d'E. III (1884), pp. 97 ff., esp. p. 108. [195] Dr. A. Th. von Middendorff, *Reise in den äußersten Norden und Osten Sibiriens*, Vol. IV, Part 2 (St. Petersburg, 1875), p. 1588 (illustration). [196] V. Vinogradov, op. cit., p. 178. [197] A. Schaeffner, *Origine*, p. 222. [198] Here are a few of the many available examples of this practice: a *Polsdans* from Osterdal in Norway, played on a bowed instrument, with the fifth g d' sounding with the melody at the beginning of every line, is reproduced by O. M. Sandvik in 'Norwegian Folk Music and its Social Significance', *JIFMC* I, 1949, p. 13. Russian folk music provides many similar instances, cf. J. Jampol'skij, *Russkoje skripičnoje iskusstvo*, Vol. I (Moscow/Leningrad, 1951), pp. 42 ff.; Rumanian fiddlers often bow the open strings simultaneously with the melody, cf. B. Bartók, 'Volksmusik der Rumänen von Maramures', *SvglMw* 4 (1923), Example 155 a. [199] V. Vinogradov, op. cit., p. 179. [200] Even the one-stringed *gusla* and the Arab *rabāb* are constantly used as drone instruments when they accompany singing. As shown in various examples of Serbo-Croat folksong, transcribed by Béla Bartók, the accompanying bowed instrument confines itself to the two notes g and a, which act in alternation as drones to the melody. Cf. B. Bartók/A. B. Lord: *Serbo-Croatian Folk Songs*, New York 1951, p. 107 ff. (Ex. 7) and p. 184 ff. (Ex. 34 ff.). Examples of *rabāb*

played and tuned in the same way as their descendants, still to be found in the East and in the Balkans. Though there are no descriptions of techniques or the tunings which date from the early period of bowing, there are occasional references in medieval literature which lead to the conclusion that early bowed instruments had a drone-function. Johannes de Garlandia (*c.* 1225) hints that in its initial stages bowing was akin to the practice of organum, in the sense of the constant, simultaneously sounding *organicus punctus*. Among other things, he writes: 'Giga est instrumentum musicum de quo dicitur organicos imitata modos.'[201] Likewise the name of the instrument known as *organica lira*,[202] mentioned in a thirteenth-century manuscript, would seem to imply playing accompanied by a drone. In this example the kinship in name of this instrument with the *organistrum* or hurdy-gurdy is made clear; the technique of the latter can be related from the beginning to the simplest forms of polyphony. Albertus Magnus's observation[203] that fiddle playing is well suited to creating a pleasant harmony of strings ('viellatio bene suum habet ad harmoniam chordarum') would also seem to suggest that as late as the thirteenth century each stroke of the bow still touched some or all of the strings simultaneously, thus generating two or more sounds in the style of early parallel organum or drone polyphony. At the end of the tenth century, 'Oriental' fiddle technique, with its continuous sounding of drone-strings, seems to have spread, together with the bow, *via* Spain and the Byzantine Empire into Europe.[204] Here it quickly established itself. Within a short space of time the fiddle became the favourite instrument of medieval times, and the use of drones likewise attained such popularity that it quickly came to be one of the most essential elements in medieval musical practice.

From early in the twelfth century, however, European illustrations show certain changes in stringing and playing which suggest that the nature and rôle of drone-playing was gradually changing in the new environment. As the appreciation of harmony began to develop, together with a feeling for vertical, chordal structure, the character of drone-playing was gradually adapted to the changed musical situation. Whereas the continuous drone that accompanied fiddle-playing in the tenth and eleventh centuries was scarcely to be regarded as having a harmonic function in the Western polyphonic sense, by the end of the Middle Ages the drone-strings were used exclusively harmonically, that is to say, they were only sounded when they formed a perfect concord with the melody. This development, which remained for all intents and purposes confined to Europe, led to

accompaniment, where the bowed instruments supply sustained notes only, are given by H. G. Farmer in *Historical Facts of the Arabian Musical Influence* (London, 1930), p. 347 f., and C. Engel, *Researches*, p. 89.   [201] Quoted in J. Pulver, *A Dictionary of old English Music, Musical Instruments* (London, 1923), p. 117. Early vocal polyphony – medieval organum – was also regarded as an imitation of organ music. Thus John Cotton (*GS* II, p. 263) writes: 'Qui canendi modus (diaphonia) vulgariter organum dicitur; eoquod vox humana apte dissonans similitudinem exprimat instrumenti, quod organum vocatur.'   [202] The description of the *organica lira* occurs in the British Museum Arundel MS. 339, f. 110, dating from the thirteenth century.   [203] Albertus Magnus, *Ethics*, 2, 1, 10, p. 165 a.   [204] Cf. Chapter II, p. 61.

the separation of melody strings from drone-strings, and to delimitation of their functions. If a string ran near to (but not over) the fingerboard, so that the player could not alter its pitch by stopping, it was automatically excluded from melodic use. This isolation of single strings, only to be used as drones, never occurs on three-stringed fiddles, but only on bowed instruments with four, five, or more strings. Contrary tow hat has sometimes been supposed,[205] the fact that initially this isolated string appears only on unwaisted fiddles played on the shoulder, is not morphologically determined, but is obviously caused by the manner of holding the instrument. When a fiddle is played *a gamba*[206] the thumb lies behind the neck, and cannot normally pluck the drone-string which lies to one side of the fingerboard, though it can do so with ease when the instrument is in the shoulder position. According to Jerome of Moravia, such instruments were generally tuned d G g d' d'.[207] His treatise, written during the second half of the thirteenth century, stresses the fact that the d string, known as 'bordunus',[208] ran to one side of the fingerboard.

The divergent drone-string is clearly shown in illustrations from the first half of the twelfth century onwards. A miniature from the glossed Psalter manuscript in the municipal library at Lunel (Plate 69), which originated in England *c.* 1130, shows a narrow, pear-shaped fiddle with five strings. One string is separated from the others and runs alongside the fingerboard. This is the earliest illustration I have been able to trace where a bowed instrument is depicted with a laterally divergent drone-string. The same instrument is again represented in an Italian sculpture, dating from 1196, which occurs in the tympanum over the west door of the Baptistry in Parma (Plate 70). In construction (pear-shaped resonator, narrow tailpiece, and round soundhole) and in technique (held on the shoulder and played with a short, curved bow) it corresponds exactly to the fiddle in the English illustration previously described. Here again a drone-string running to one side of the fingerboard is visible. A similar drone-fiddle is illustrated in a tenth-century manuscript of the works of Boethius, now in the Biblioteca Ambrosiana, Milan (Plate 71), although the miniature showing the fiddler was added later, perhaps not until the thirteenth century.[209] In this case the drone-string lies even further from the fingerboard and is attached to a lateral peg or cross-pin jutting out from the peg-box.[210] From the thirteenth century onwards illustrations of such instruments occur in Germany and France (Plates 72–74), and there are fourteenth-century illustrations from Spain and Italy (Plates 75 and 76), so that this new kind of drone-accompanied fiddling had presumably spread throughout Europe. In the fourteenth century the pear-shaped drone-fiddle was replaced by instruments with elliptical bodies and a clearly defined neck, the structure of which

---

[205] Cf. C. Sachs, *Handbuch*, p. 173 f., and H.- H. Dräger, *Die Entwicklung des Streichbogens*, p. 51.
[206] In the early stages the instrument is nearly always held in front of the player's waist.   [207] S. M. Cserba, op. cit., p. 290 f.   [208] '...quae bordunus est aliarum ... eo quod extra corpus viellae id est a latere affixa sit, applicationes digitorum evadid.' (*CS* I, p. 153).   [209] The period from which the miniature dates is treated by G. Cesari in 'Tre tavole di strumenti in un "Boezio"

appreciably facilitated the separation of the drone-string, and made the instrument easier to handle (Plate 76).

Regarding the manner in which these instruments were played, full information is available both from comprehensive inconographical evidence and from Jerome of Moravia's treatise. The majority of the illustrations show clearly that the drone-string was no longer continuously excited with the bow, as on earlier three-stringed instruments. Instead it was usually plucked, either with the thumb or with a finger of the left hand. Frequently the player is shown in the very act of plucking the drone-string (Plate 72). According to Jerome of Moravia,[211] the art of fiddling at that time principally consisted in establishing a harmonic consonance between the centre of gravity of the melody and the drone. To avoid unnecessary dissonances, the player is advised to use the drone-string – either by plucking it with his thumb or touching it briefly with the bow – only when the note it produces will form a concord with the melody.[212] In these brief remarks the fundamental difference between this and Eastern drone-playing is clearly expressed. Whereas in the East the drone took no account of course of the melody, the concept of harmony is here all-important. The drone, which originally lay in the middle, is removed from the fingerboard so that its use is fully under the control of the player. Although the information concerning the use of the drone-string quoted above comes, not from Jerome himself, but from fourteenth-century glosses, the illustrations of drone-fiddles are sufficient confirmation that this method of playing was widely used shortly after 1100.

This technique was still known in the sixteenth and seventeenth centuries, especially for *lira da braccio* or *lira da gamba*,[213] which were organic developments of the medieval drone-fiddle. The process of evolution from the old fiddle to the bowed *lira* and the *viola da braccio* occured almost exclusively in Italy, and can be followed in great detail with the help of the available iconographical materials. This new type of instrument makes its first appearance at the close of the fifteenth century.[214] Characteristic differences between the *lira* and the medieval drone-fiddleare its heart-shaped peg-board, waisted body and altered stringing. The medieval drone-string, laterally diverging from the fingerboard, is reinforced by an octave string on the *lira*, and the number of strings lying along the fingerboard has also increased by comparison with the fiddle. Certain deviations from the

del X secolo', *Festschrift für G. Adler* (Vienna, 1930).   [210] According to the inscription, this pen-and-ink drawing is meant to represent the minstrel 'Nicolo dala viola fiorentino'. [211] S. M. Cserba, op. cit., p. 291.   [212] The relevant passage runs as follows: 'Quod bordunus non debet tangi pollice vell arcu, nisi cum ceterae chordae arcu tactu faciunt sonos cum quibus bordunus facit aliquam praedictarum consonantiarum, scilicet diapente, diapason, diatessaron etc.'   [213] For further details regarding the musical rôle of these instruments cf. M. Greulich, *Beiträge zur Geschichte des Streichinstrumentenspiels im 16. Jahrhundert* (Dissertation, Berlin, 1933), B. Disertori, 'Practica e tecnica della lira da braccio', *RMI* XLV (1941), pp. 150 ff.; C. Sachs, *Handbuch*, pp. 177 ff., and G. Kinsky, *Musikhistorisches Museum*, Vol. II, pp. 383 ff.   [214] One of the earliest illustrations of a *lira* occurs in a painting of Our Lady by B. Montagna from Vicenza

old fundamental–fifth – octave tuning[215] as given by Jerome – and rarely used in the seventeenth century[216] – indicate that change must also have occurred in the playing technique of these instruments. The tuning was no longer suitable for stopping one string while the others sounded as a drone – a point confirmed at different places in sixteenth and seventeenth-century texts. All stress that on the *lira* only chordal-polyphonic playing was possible – there was no question of the player's bowing any of the fingerboard strings individually.[217] As with the twelfth and thirteenth-century fiddle, the drone-string lying to one side of the fingerboard of the sixteenth-century *lira* is played with the thumb. Again, the drone is only used to give a tonal foundation to the polyphonic structure at suitable points. At this time, European drone-fiddling had in some respects reached a final stage. When finally whole courses of strings were introduced alongside the fingerboard,[218] they had lost completely their original drone-character, and served the function of a plucked accompaniment. In the meantime the technique still used today, whereby the bow touches only the string on which the melody is being played, had long since been adopted in Europe. Johannes Tinctoris's description of the viola of his day[219] shows that the bow touched only one string at a time because of the arched arrangement of the strings, leaving the others untouched. Though this technique precluded a continuously sounding drone, the term 'bourdon' for the lowest or next-to-lowest string on any bowed instrument was retained for centuries. Thus in 1556 Philibert Jambe de Fer[220] lists the strings on the gamba as bordon, quarte, tierce, seconde, and chanterelle. Both Leopold Mozart[221] and Marin Mersenne[222] refer to the G string on bowed instruments as 'bordun' or 'bourdon'.

(1499); cf. G. Kinsky, *Geschichte der Musik in Bildern*, p. 111. [215] Three examples of *lira* tuning should suffice to illustrate the relationship to medieval fiddle tuning:

Drone	Fingerboard
dd'	g g' d' a' e'' (G. M. Lanfranco)
dd'	g g' d' a' d'' (M. Praetorius)
Gg	c c' g d' a e' b f'♯ c'♯ (Sc. Cerreto)

cf. G. Kinsky, op. cit., Vol. II, pp. 383 ff. [216] A piece of 17th-century French viola notation is thus based on the tuning D G d g (b♭) d'; cf. J. Wolf, *Handbuch der Notationskunde*, Part 2 (Leipzig, 1919), pp. 227 and 229. In particular the viola d'amore kept to this harmonic, chordal tuning, the main function which is to facilitate the playing of arpeggios and chords. [217] S. Ganassi, *Regola Rubertina*, Book II, Chapter 17, observes that the *lira* was eminently suited to polyphonic playing in three or four parts and for this reason found it difficult to perform two-part music; L. Zacconi, *Prattica di Musica* (1592), Chapter 46, also mentions its special aptitude for polyphonic playing; M. Praetorius, *Syntagma musicum*, Vol. II, p. 26, writes that it was possible to achieve 'tricinia and more besides' on this instrument; M. Mersenne, *Harmonie universelle*, Vol. II, Book IV (1636), pp. 204ff., and Sc. Cerreto, *Practica musicale et instrumentale* (1601), Book IV, Chapter 10, stress that the strings on the *lira* could not be bowed individually because of its flat bridge. [218] Especially on the lira da bordone and the lira da braccio. [219] K. Weinmann, *Johannes Tinctoris*, p. 41 f. [220] Ph. Jambe de Fer, *Epitome musical* (1556); see M. Greulich, *Beiträge zur Geschichte des Streichinstrumentenspiels*, p. 26. [221] L. Mozart, *Gründliche Violinschule*, Facsimile edition, ed. H. J. Moser (Leipzig, 1956), p. 4. [222] *Harmonie universelle*, Vol. II, Book IV, Prop. VIII,

In addition to the two methods of medieval fiddle-tuning already mentioned, Jerome of Moravia[223] gives details of a third, according to which the open strings were tuned G G d c′ c′. The editor of Jerome's treatise attempts to explain this unusual pattern, with its gap of a seventh between d and c′, as a slip of the pen, and would replace the d by an e.[224] This interpretation is not very convincing, as there are no other known examples of strings tuned in sixths. The following explanation of Jerome's statement may lie nearer the truth. It is possible that this tuning pattern was originally designed for instruments on which only one string – usually the highest – carried the melody. Fiddles tuned thus had a very limited compass, therefore, and their musical use corresponded to that of the hurdy-gurdy. The c string was perfectly adequate for the vast repertory of archaic four and five-note melodies, and its doubling strengthened the melodic line, while the remaining strings obviously functioned as a drone fifth – G d. This hypothesis is supported by the fact that the scholiast describes the G string on instruments tuned G G d c′ c′ as the 'bordunus'.[225] For melodies of greater range, such a tuning was unsuitable, since the then customary technique of playing in the first position ruled out any possibility of achieving a connected scale across all the strings. Inevitably, there was a gap between the three lower (G G d) and two upper strings (c′ c′), which could, however, be bridged by a leap to the lower octave. As already mentioned,[226] the G d g d′ g′ tuning was preferable for melodies of wide compass, whereas the G G d c′ c′ tuning was better suited to medieval folkmusic, with its constant repetition of motifs of limited range. In medieval times and, with certain limitations, until recent times, the tuning of bowed instruments was based on g and d, which obviously played a crucial rôle in medieval music-making, since drone-pipes and strings were nearly always tuned to these two notes at that time.[227] Given this uniform tonal basis, a consort of several drone-instruments, such as is often depicted, was perfectly possible.

As far as we can judge, the development of fiddling in Europe is characterized by the increasing independence of individual strings, and progressive differentiation in playing technique. On the one hand the technique and construction were tailored to the demands of Occidental music, that is to say, to the performance of polyphonic or chordal compositions. One example of this type of instrument was the seventeenth-century *lira*, which was not designed to play a single melodic line at all. On the other hand, an effort was made to obtain greater musical flexibility. To cope with the technical demands of a melodic line elaborated to the point of virtuosity, both instrument and technique had to undergo change; in particular, polyphonic playing had to be abandoned.[228]

pp. 191/192. [223] Cserba, op. cit., p. 291. [224] Op. cit., p. LXXV; G. Reaney, 'Voices and Instruments in the Music of Guillaume de Machaut', *RBM* X (1956), p. 14, takes Cserba's conjecture into account. [225] Cserba, op. cit., p. 290f. [226] Cf. p. 93. [227] For further details relating to the tuning of drone-strings and pipes see p. 131 of this book. [228] This relationship between rhythm, melody and harmony is discussed by H.-H. Dräger in *Prinzip einer Systematik*, p. 9: 'Basically, it is the varying use of the elements of rhythm, melody and harmony which determines the attitude, that is, the styles of different peoples and different eras. No race can have

THE HURDY-GURDY

The common source of these differing streams of development was the drone-fiddling of the Middle Ages, most clearly demonstrated by the hurdy-gurdy. For this instrument, there could be no question of any change in technique, such as is to be observed in the use of the bow. Accordingly, it was only suitable for art music so long as European polyphony was based on the principle of the pedal-point.

Origin

In spite of many studies,[229] the origins of hurdy-gurdy playing, which had reached a peak in its development by about 1200, at the time of the Notre Dame Organum, remain completely obscure. The widely-held view that the hurdy-gurdy came into being in the ninth or tenth century is based on the evidence of one pictorial and one literary source, both of which have in fact been wrongly dated. The illustration of a hurdy-gurdy published by Gerbert[230] and taken from a Codex (since destroyed by fire) in the library at St Blasien, is not from the ninth century but from the thirteenth. Furthermore, the short essay on the construction of the hurdy-gurdy, *Quomodo organistrum construatur*,[231] which occurs at the end of the treatise by Odo (died 942) in an omnibus manuscript now in the Vienna Staatsbibliothek, is in itself no indication that the hurdy-gurdy was known in the tenth century. Since this manuscript dates from the thirteenth century,[232] 'in view of the fact that such compilations were common in the Middle Ages, we may safely assume that the writer of the Codex added a later essay on the organistrum, which was not the work of Odo.'[233] Not until the twelfth century do we find a number of illustrations which prove that the hurdy-gurdy was in use. These early illustrations are mainly from Western Europe, which suggests that the hurdy-gurdy may have been a creation of the West.[234] Oriental sources give no sign that it was known in the East at this time. Only the tenth-century essay by the Ikhwan al-Ṣafā brotherhood[235] appears to contain a reference to the hurdy-gurdy; but the passage is by no means clear. In the classification of musical instruments undertaken as part of the treatise, the names *dūlāb* and *nā'ūr* are listed next to the wind

---

all three elements simultaneously in its music to the highest attainable level.' [229] In his article 'Drehleier' in *MGG*, Dräger lists the most important literary contributions. [230] *De cantu*, Vol. II, Plate XXXII, 16. [231] *GS* I, 303a. [232] E. Buhle, *Die musikalischen Instrumente*, p. 7, Note 2. [233] Professor Heinrich Hüschen informs me that the treatise *Quomodo organistrum construatur* was not written by Odo, but by an anonymous author of a later period. The date given for the essay (10th century) in the 'Drehleier' article in *MGG* should therefore be corrected. [234] According to J. Rühlmann, *Die Geschichte der Bogeninstrumente*, p. 69, the hurdy-gurdy is a 'specifically German' instrument, 'foreshadowing the fiddle family'. J. Rousseau ascribes its invention to Guido d'Arezzo; cf. H. M. Schletterer, *Die Ahnen moderner Musikinstrumente* (Leipzig, 1882), p. 357, Note. [235] F. Dieterici, *Die Propädeutik der Araber im 10. Jahrhundert* (Berlin, 1865),

instruments and the *rabāb*, among those instruments able to sustain notes and join them smoothly together. Both have the meaning of 'water-lifting wheel'. As names of instruments both would be suitable for wheel-lyres, and this would certainly fit in with the text, and with their inclusion in the class of instruments that sound continuously. However, this hypothesis would hardly be worth mentioning were it not that a reference in the early fifteenth-century treatise by Ibn Ghaibī,[236] describing the *dūlāb* as a species of hurdy-gurdy,[237] apparently supports it. It is therefore possible that the hurdy-gurdy was known in Mesopotamia as early as the tenth century[238] and was not after all Western in origin but, like the bow, had its roots in the East.

The fact that the earliest iconographical evidence for the hurdy-gurdy occurs in carvings in Spanish cathedral doorways also suggests that it may have been introduced from the Islamic world. One of the oldest of these sculptures, dating from *c.* 1150, is on the archivolt of the West door of the Church of Santo Domingo in Soria (Plate 78), while the stone door sculptures in Toro, Estella, and Santiago de Compostela (Plate 80) are from the second half of the twelfth century. Evidence from the latter part of the twelfth century points to the presence of the hurdy-gurdy in France and England. The stone carvings on a capital (Plate 77) in the transept of the Abbey of St Georges de Boscherville, near Rouen, do not as has often been assumed date from the Abbey's foundation in the eleventh century, but from the middle of the twelfth century. From the same period comes a painting of a hurdy-gurdy in an Alsatian illumination from the *Hortus deliciarum* of the Abbess Herrad von Landsperg;[239] a miniature in the English Psalter manuscript 299, now in the Hunterian Museum in the University of Glasgow (Plate 60), the lower right-hand corner medallion of which shows a hurdy-gurdy; and a sculpture from the St Anne door of the Cathedral of Notre Dame in Paris (Plate 79) – here however the handle of the hurdy-gurdy is missing.

The various names by which the instrument was known[240] do not appear in medieval literature before 1150. During the twelfth and thirteenth centuries the hurdy-gurdy is usually described as either an *organistrum* or a *symphonia*. The term *organistrum* is used from time to time as a caption to illustrations of hurdy-gurdies.[241]

gives a German translation on p. 110. [236] Djami'al-Alḥān, Oxford, Bodleian Library, Marsh 282. [237] Cf. H. G. Farmer, in *Oriens* 15 (1962), pp. 242ff., esp. p. 246. [238] This 10th-century Arab source was written by members of the Order of the Brothers of Purity, whose headquarters were in Basra (Mesopotamia). [239] Illustrated in L. Grillet, *Les ancêtres du violon et du violoncelle*, Vol. I (Paris, 1901), p. 26, and H. Besseler, *Musik des Mittelalters und der Renaissance*, Plate 50. [240] F. Dick, *Bezeichnungen für Saiten- und Schlaginstrumente in der altfranzösischen Literatur* (Dissertation, Giessen, 1932), p. 84; D. Treder, *Die Musikinstrumente in den höfischen Epen der Blütezeit* (Dissertation, Greifswald, 1933), p. 33 f. [241] M. Gerbert, *De cantu*, Vol. II, Plate XXXII, 16, reproduces a copy of an illustration showing a hurdy-gurdy, once part of the 13th century Codex in the library at St. Blasien (destroyed by fire), and bearing the legend 'organistrum'. The same word may also be seen on the aforesaid miniature from Herrad von Landsperg's *Hortus deli-*

The *Summa musica*[242] refers to the hurdy-gurdy as 'symphonia seu organistrum'. The three essays on the hurdy-gurdy: *Quomodo organistrum construatur*,[243] *Mensura organistri*,[244] and *Organistrum/Organica lira meciendo laboras . . .*,[245] in thirteenth-century manuscripts, are in all probability no older than the iconographical evidence.

Construction

Although these essays are mainly concerned with measurements – the arrangement and spacing of the tangents on the hurdy-gurdy – fourteenth and fifteenth-century descriptions[246] also throw some light on the main structural features. We learn among other things that the hurdy-gurdy possessed a disc-like wheel (*rotula, rota parvula*)[247] the outer rim of which was coated with pitch (*pix*)[248] or the resin of the incense tree (*thus*).[249] Set in motion by means of a crank ('vertibulo girante'),[250] the wheel caused all the strings to sound simultaneously. Thick and strong gut strings were used ('cordas nervales grossas et fortes'),[251] which were stopped by tangent-like keys (*plectra, claves*).[252]

Further structural details are revealed by medieval illustrations. Very strikingly, up to the middle of the thirteenth century the hurdy-gurdies shown are almost invariably figure-of-eight shaped, with a waisted resonator (Plates 60, 77, 78, 80, 81). While it is generally supposed nowadays that the incurving sides of bowed instruments were designed from the beginning to give the bow greater freedom of movement and to facilitate the bowing of individual strings, the example of the hurdy-gurdy unambiguously refutes this, since that particular consideration is irrelevant here. Another striking feature of these early hurdy-gurdy illustrations (Plates 77 and 78) are the two large, circular sound-holes, over which the strings pass. Basing his argument on general evolutionary principles Norlind[253] regards the figure-of-eight hurdy-gurdy as a later parallel development of the genus,

ciarum. [242] *GS* III, 199. [243] *GS* I, 303a. [244] *GS* II, 286b. [245] British Museum Arundel MS. 339, fol. 110. [246] The following medieval descriptions of the hurdy-gurdy have been selected from the available material: a) Johannes Gerson: 'Symphoniam putant aliqui Viellam, vel Rebeccam, quae minor est . . . Haec sonum reddit, dum una manu resolvitur rota parvula thure linita, et per alteram applicatur si cum certis clavibus chordula nervorum prout in cithara, ubi pro diversitate tractuum rotae varietas harmoniae dulcis amoenaque resultat' (*Opera omnia Johannis Gersonis*, ed. L. Ellies du Pin, Vol. III, Part I, p. 627f., Antwerp, 1706). b) Paulus Paulirinus of Prague: 'Ysis est instrumentum in modum rote introrsus habens cordas nervales grossas et fortes et rotam interius cum pice registratam et exterius clavos cerastes quos eciam canens registrat cum digittis' (J. Reiss, 'Pauli Paulirini de Praga Tractatus de musica', *ZfMw* 7, p. 264). c) A glossary from the year 1468: 'lira, leyr, est instrumentum musicum, quod habet in alveo vasis cordas et per rottulam de suptus vertibulo girante tactus in pulso clavorum proporcionabiliter distantium consonantium variantes' (J. and W. Grimm, *Deutsches Wörterbuch* (Leipzig, 1885), s. v. 'leier'). [247] Cf. Note 246, source a and c. [248] Note 246, source b. [249] Note 246, source a. [250] Note 246, source c. [251] Note 246, source b. [252] Note 246, sources a, b and c; cf. also *GS* I, 303a. [253] *Systematik der Saiteninstrumente*, Part 2, *Geschichte des Klaviers*, (Stock-

the prototype being the rectangular, box-shaped instrument. Norlind's thesis is contradicted by the chronology of the iconographical evidence. The box-shaped instruments do not appear until the middle of the thirteenth century, and then primarily in England (Plates 82–84). Before this, hurdy-gurdies are exclusively waisted instruments, with, after 1160, an occasional example of the slender, pear-shaped version (Plates 79, 85), the form of which corresponds exactly to that of the fiddles of the time. Obviously, therefore, the hurdy-gurdy represents a modification of the bowed instruments of the period, intended to simplify the process of bowing and mechanize the stopping of the strings. Nearly every instrument shows a number of strings, presumably tuned like the strings of the fiddle. After 1200 many variations on the original three-stringed pattern occur. Already in the fourteenth century there are instruments with five and six strings (Plate 88), and Mersenne even considers the possibility of six bourdon strings.[254]

Techniques of performance and musical character

Unfortunately we have only a vague idea of the technique of playing medieval hurdy-gurdies; indeed, we cannot even be certain that the *organistrum* of the twelfth and thirteenth centuries was in fact a drone-instrument in the later sense. However, the various names by which it was known – *organistrum, organica lira, symphonia (chifonie)*, and *armonie* – suggest that the music it played must have been closely related to early polyphony, to organum. But what this 'polyphony' of the medieval hurdy-gurdy was like in detail we can never know, since the type of music played by this instrument and the style of medieval performance were never recorded. Unfortunately, even the early descriptions of the *organistrum* which have been quoted leave us in this respect completely in the dark; so that we are thrown back on the interpretation of iconographical evidence.

The crank-operated wheel inevitably excited all strings simultaneously, thus steadily generating certain harmonies. Essentially there were two different possibilities of creating a harmonic structure. Either only one string was stopped by means of the tangents, to yield a melody, while the others were strummed as an invariant drone-accompaniment; or each tangent touched all the strings simultaneously, so that while the wheel was in motion the instrument sounded a strict parallel organum – like an organ 'mixture'.

Since the hurdy-gurdy's key-mechanism is concealed by a protective cover in most medieval illustrations, it is very difficult to form a more accurate picture of how it was played in its early stages. As far as we can judge, both the above procedures were used in the Middle Ages. On one thirteenth-century illustration of an *organistrum*, reproduced by Martin Gerbert,[255] the tangents are clearly visible. The broad rotating tangents, sometimes referred to as 'revolving bridges', pressed against all three strings by a slight rotary action, obviously rule out a

holm, 1939), col. 5 ff. [254] *Harmonie universelle* (Paris, 1637), Vol. II, Book 4, p. 212. [255] *De*

constant drone and suggest rather a strengthening and broadening of sonority by means of organum at the fifth.[256] Until the middle of the thirteenth century illustrations show only instruments for two players, where the technique, as well as the structure of the instrument, seem to correspond to the instruments with rotating tangents just discussed. One player operates the crank, while the other is fully occupied by the manipulation of the *plectra*. The instrument lies across the knees of the players as they sit side by side. In the twelfth-century hurdy-gurdy the unwieldy mechanism was very similar to that of the contemporary organ, where the keyboard worked on the principle of individual handles which were pulled out or pushed in to admit air to the appropriate pipe.[257] Such instruments could not be used for the lively melodies of the medieval minstrel, and were presumably used mainly for slow-moving airs or, in ensemble with other instruments, to provide long, drone-like supporting notes or chords. Both of the instruments suited to producing sustained notes – the twelfth-century hurdy-gurdy and organ – seems to indicate the use of drones in the sense of purely drone-instruments able to produce nothing but long, supporting and sustaining notes, not simultaneously moving melodic line. In their use of accompanying 'mixtures', both instruments, until early in the thirteenth century, have some connection with parallel organum which, according to *Musica enchiriadis*, was played in slow, measured style and therefore suited both instruments admirably.

The thirteenth century saw a marked change in the structure of the hurdy-gurdy. The large instruments for two players disappeared, to be replaced by smaller forms fitted with a more practical type of key-like, sliding tangent, so that only one player was necessary, turning the crank with one hand and depressing the *claves* with the other (Plates 82–84, 86, 88). About this time the organ also adopted a more manageable key mechanism, and showed a similar development towards the less cumbersome, one-man instrument, the portative.[258] These new instrumental types and their improved mechanism were symptomatic of a changed musical ideal, which expressed itself in the combination of two diametrical opposites: a fast-moving variable melodic line and a rigid, invariant drone. The use of striking tangents (instead of rotating tangents) on the hurdy-gurdy after *c.* 1200 meant that any movement of the player's fingers affected one string only, the melody string, while the others kept up a constant, inflexible

cantu, Vol. II, Plate XXXII, 16. [256] Examples of 'mixture'-type, strict parallel organum in medieval instrumental music are given in W. Bachmann, 'Die Verbreitung des Quintierens im europäischen Volksgesang des späten Mittelalters', *Festschrift für Max Schneider* (Leipzig, 1955), p. 26; for further medieval evidence of organ mixtures see H. Avenary-Löwenstein, 'The Mixture Principle in the Mediaeval Organ', *Md* IV, 1 (1950), p. 51. [257] The keyboard of the medieval organ is fully described in E. Buhle, *Die musikalischen Instrumente*, pp. 84ff.; on p. 97 of this work he writes: 'The manipulation of the organ presented certain difficulties because of its unwieldy construction; a legato performance in our sense would have been inconceivable. The pulling out and pushing in of the keys took time, so that a break between one note and the next was inevitable. [258] The earliest representations of portatives date from the 13th century. The illustration published by H. Hickmann, *Das Portativ* (Kassel, 1936), p. 15, as the earliest evidence

pedal-point. Quick runs, which were also possible, were executed on the hurdy-gurdy as on the portative:[259] the forearm was held parallel to the strings, enabling the fore and middle fingers to depress the keys in quick succession (Plates 83 and 84) and avoiding the awkwardness of passing one finger over another. In playing, the instrument either rested on the player's knees (Plates 82, 84–87) or hung from a strap (Plates 83 and 88).

The compass of the hurdy-gurdy initially was relatively restricted for, as the illustrations show, twelfth and thirteenth-century instruments usually had only six to eight keys. An exception to this is the hurdy-gurdy shown in a sculpture on the Portico de la gloria in Santiago de Compostela (Plate 80) which, though it dates from the second half of the twelfth century, already has eleven or twelve tangents. Not until the thirteenth century was the compass extended, in some cases to two octaves. Marin Mersenne tells us that in the seventeenth century some hurdy-gurdies had as many forty-nine keys.[260] From the medieval treatises that discuss such questions as the arrangement of the tangents,[261] and from illustrations, it is clear that hurdy-gurdy melodies were based on the diatonic scale in the twelfth and thirteenth centuries. Slides and slurs (*portamenti*), possible on the fiddle, could not be produced on the hurdy-gurdy, and in its early stages any form of chromaticism, or narrow-interval melody, was ruled out. But for the variable leading-note, some medieval hurdy-gurdies were provided with two tangents. The instrument illustrated by Martin Gerbert, for instance,[262] includes in the diatonic scale of C – as clearly shown by the tangents marked with the names of the notes – both B♭ and B. The letters used to name the degree of the scale were often inscribed on the keys of the instrument as a guide to the player, as may be seen in a fourteenth-century Spanish fresco (Plate 88), for example.[263] It is known that this was also done on the contemporary organ.[264]

On some hurdy-gurdies (Plate 85) the tangent mechanism had been abandoned, and the strings were stopped against the fingerboard with the fingers, as on the fiddle. One fifteenth-century illustration[265] shows a hurdy-gurdy without keys, where the thumb alone performs this function. All three strings are stopped simultaneously to alter their pitch, so that the musical potential of such a technique would be equivalent to that of Martin Gerbert's instrument,[266] with its broad rotating tangents.

is not from the 12th century, as the author suggests, but from the 14th. [259] On the technique of playing the portative cf. Hickmann, op. cit., p. 155 ff. [260] See J. Rühlmann, op. cit., p. 77. [261] See above, p. 107, Notes 243, 244 and 245. [262] *De cantu*, Vol. II, Plate XXXII, 16. [263] The following scale can be read from the keys: GFEDCBAG. The letters underlined are partly obscured by the player's fingers. [264] On the organ shown on Plate 50, the letters of the alphabet are discernible on the organ case, inscribed above the keys. Cf. also Bernelius: 'quod propter facilitatem et ut melius agnoscerentur factum est, ut eis potius litteris, quibus organa nostra notata sunt, hos numeros praesignavimus.' (*GS* I, 318). [265] Illustrated in G. Schüne-mann, 'Die Musikinstrumente der 24 Alten', *AfMf* I, p. 56, Plate 13. [266] Cf. p. 108, Note 255.

Tuning

We know little about the structure of medieval hurdy-gurdy melody. We know even less about the tuning of the instrument. In view of the close relationship between the hurdy-gurdy and the early fiddle, we can assume that the strings of both were originally tuned in roughly the same manner. This supposition is strengthened by the evidence of an illustration showing a medieval hurdy-gurdy[267] with three strings, and above them on the body the letters m d G, which can be interpreted as an indication of their tuning. M could be an abbreviation of 'melodia', while d and G could represent the tuning of the drone-strings. As the letters on the tangents unambiguously show, the melody string of this instrument is tuned to c,[268] so that the full tuning would be G d c which, allowing for string doubling, exactly corresponds to the third type of fiddle-tuning given by Jerome of Moravia (G G d c' c').[269] If this interpretation is correct, we must suppose that the tangents are inaccurately represented and touch only the top string, while the other two sound without change. However, organological treatises from later centuries, together with the evidence from hurdy-gurdies in use in some areas to the present, show that the tuning of melody and drone-strings did not follow a uniform pattern, but was frequently varied.

To sum up, as far as this is possible. The hurdy-gurdy, which emerged in Europe later than the bowed fiddle, was derived from early bowed instruments and served to simplify the process of bowing, to avoid bow-changes, to mechanize the stopping of strings, and to establish a definite, precisely calculated scale. Whereas today the hurdy-gurdy ranks with the bagpipe as pre-eminently a drone-instrument the musical function of which is entirely different from that of other friction instruments, in the Middle Ages the boundaries between the various genera of bowed instrument were less sharply defined. Their common starting point, as we have seen, was the drone style of playing.

THE BOWED ROTE

Like the hurdy-gurdy, the bowed rote[270] also has a special place among the friction instruments of medieval times, on account of its structure. During the nineteenth century this instrument was believed to be the ancestor of our modern bowed instruments, from which the fiddle developed by discarding the yoke and adding a fingerboard. Later studies led, however, to the conclusion that the

---

[267] M. Gerbert, *De cantu*, Vol. II, Plate XXXII, 16.   [268] The first tangent sounds the note d, so that the open string is tuned to c.   [269] S. M. Cserba, op. cit., p. 291.   [270] To distinguish them from the ancient lyres, lyre-type medieval instruments are here described as *rotes*, a name often applied to them. The most important medieval literary sources that mention this instrument are noted by Curt Sachs in his *Handbuch*, 1st ed., p. 161. The name is related etymologically to *hrôtta*, the tortoise or turtle, and thus corresponds to the Greek term chelys, applied to a musical instrument. The most common versions of this name in medieval literature are given in G. Kinsky,

bowed rote was not the beginning of a development but the last stage in the history of the European lyre.[271]

When the bow came to Europe during the tenth century, the possibility of using it was tested on a number of different instruments, among them the rote, which as a plucked instrument had won a prominent place among the instruments of the early Middle Ages. Many illustrations from the eleventh century onwards show the rote being bowed.[272] The earliest iconographical evidence comes from Auch, in South-west France (Plate 91), Hildesheim (Plate 89), Werden an der Ruhr (Plate 94), St Bertin (Plate 90), and Southern England (Plate 92) – that is to say mainly from Western and Central Europe. In the later Middle Ages (thirteenth–fifteenth centuries) illustrations, literary references, and descriptions of the bowed lyre abound, especially in Northern Europe. Some of the most valuable material comes from St Fianian's Church, Waterville, Co. Kerry, in south-west Ireland, dating from c. 1200 (Plate 93), from Trondheim Cathedral (Plate 97), and from Wales.[273] Another most important find was the thirteenth-century bowed lyre which came to light in the excavations of old Danzig.[274] There is no evidence that this instrument – which was not very susceptible of further development, but satisfied the demands of medieval music-making – survived on the Continent after 1400. It survived as a folk instrument in remote areas of Scandinavia and the British Isles until recent times.[275]

Structural characteristics

Structurally, the bowed rote resembles the plucked types of this genus known from the early Middle Ages, sometimes found in excavations, and shown on many illustrations.[276] Notwithstanding unmistakable relationship with the ancient lyre, the medieval rote exhibits various characteristics that clearly distin-

---

Heyer-Katalog, Vol. II, p. 363 f.   [271] P. 8 f.   [272] The following illustrations of the bowed rote date from the 11th century: Paris, Bibliothèque Nationale, MS. lat. 1118, fol. 104r (Plate 91); Klosterneuburg, Library of the Augustiner-Chorherrenstift, Cod. 987, fol. 11v (Plate 89); Berlin, Staatsbibliothek, MS. Theol. lat. Fol. 358, fol. 1v, now in the University Library, Tübingen (Plate 94); Cambridge, University Library Ff. 1.23, fol. 4v (Plate 92).   [273] For illustrations from the 12th and 13th centuries cf. J. Rühlmann, *Atlas zur Geschichte der Bogeninstrumente* (Brunswick, 1882), Plate VI, and O. Andersson, *The Bowed-Harp*, pp. 167, 239, 242, 254.   [274] E. Emsheimer, 'Die Streichleier von Danczk', *STMf*, 1961, pp. 109 ff.   [275] Several excellent studies deal specifically with the Nordic bowed lyres, with special reference to material in various museums, and to evidence available from folklore studies. Among more recent works are: O. Andersson, *The Bowed-Harp* (London, 1930), S. Walin, *Die schwedische Hummel* (Stockholm, 1952); C. Dolmetsch, 'The crwth', *The Consort*, No. 13 (1956), p. 23 f.; cf. also J. F. W. Wewertem, 'Zwei veraltete Musikinstrumente', *MfM* XIII (1881), pp. 151 ff.; H. Panum, 'Harfe und Lyra im alten Nordeuropa', *SIMG* VII (1905/06), pp. 1 ff, and O. Andersson, 'The Shetland Gue', *Budkavlen* XXXIII (1954), pp. 1 ff.   [276] Lyres from excavations are described by J. Werner, *Leier und Harfe*, pp. 9 ff. The abundant inconographic materials relating to the plucked medieval rote have not yet been fully evaluated. Cf. also E. Emsheimer, 'Die Streichleiter von Danczk', *STMf* (1961), pp. 109 ff.

guish it from the lyre of antiquity. While the lyre was constructed from several separate parts – the resonator, the yoke, and the pillars – the rote was made in one piece, its curving yoke and body forming an organic whole.[277] Examples from excavations reveal that the desired shape was wrought from a block of oak 3–4 cm. thick. The resonator and pillars of the yoke were hollowed out and covered with a thin sheet of maple, secured with small bronze nails.[278] The extant instruments are from 40 to 80 cm. long. Judging by the relative sizes of the players and their instruments in medieval illustrations, the majority of rotes fit the measurements of the instruments found by archaeologists. The only exception to this pattern is the bowed rote, some 130 cm. long, which appears in a miniature from the *Psalterium Sancti Leopoldi* at Klosterneuburg, Codex 987, fol. IIv (Plate 89), playing in consort with a similar instrument 50 to 60 cm. long. Another distinction between the medieval rote and the ancient lyre is the entirely different method used to attach the strings: on the rote pegs were almost invariably inserted into front or back of the upper part of the yoke.[279] A tuning key was frequently used to turn the pegs. Some illustrations show this key fastened to the yoke with a thread, hanging down to one side of the instrument,[280] while others represent the musician in the act of tuning his instrument with the key.[281]

Techniques of performance

In attempting to discover the technique of playing the lyre or rote, we are faced with very special problems.[282] The bowing action is perhaps easier to reconstruct, since the instrument's shape is such that it is only possible for the bow to touch all the strings, lying invariably in one plane, simultaneously. Only

[277] Only a few medieval reproductions of ancient lyres deviate from this principle: Utrecht University Library, Psalterium (formerly in the Cotton Collection, Claudius C. VII), fol. 83r; London British Museum, Add. 24199, fol. 18; Harl. 603, fol. 18v; Cleop. C. VIII; Paris, Bibliothèque Nationale, Ms. lat. 11550, fol. 7, v. Transitional shapes, where the yoke is firmly joined to the arms, are represented by rotes found in the Oberflacht excavations and in a miniature from the Ms. lat. 7211 in the Bibliothèque Nationale, Paris, fol. 140. [278] Further details in J. Werner, op. cit., pp. 9ff., and E. Emsheimer, op. cit., *STMf*, (1961), pp. 109ff. Illustrations and descriptions also given by F. Behn in *Vor- und Frühgeschichte*, Part 6 of *Musikgeschichte in Bildern*, ed. H. Besseler and M. Schneider (Leipzig, in preparation). [279] The thirteenth-century bowed lyre found in the course of excavations in the old town of Danczk had rear pegs, as the peg-holes show; E. Emsheimer, op. cit., p. 111. [280] Clearly visible in the following miniatures: Cividale, Library, Cod. Gertrudianus (Photograph in A. Goldschmidt, *Die deutsche Buchmalerei*, Vol. II (Munich, 1928), Plate 20); St. Gall, Stiftsbibliothek, Cod. 21 (Photograph in K. Schlesinger, *The Instruments*, Vol. II, Plate IV); St. Blasius, Stiftsbibliothek (copy in M. Gerbert, *De cantu*, Vol. II, Plate XXVI). [281] For example, in miniatures from the following manuscripts: Ivrea, Bibl. Capitolare, Cod. 85, fol. 25v; Munich, Staatsbibliothek, Clm 343 (Photograph by Foto Marburg, No. 102143). [282] Nowadays it is generally agreed that a variety of techniques were used in lyre-playing. This was particularly true of the plucked lyre. Possible techniques are discussed in detail by O. J. Gombosi in *Tonarten und Stimmungen der antiken Musik* (Copenhagen,

rarely is there a bridge shown to raise the strings off the resonator, and those that are shown are straight, not arched.[283] The use of the bow to play the lyre only makes sense if we assume that the bow set up a constant drone-accompaniment on separate drone-strings as background to a melody. This supposition is supported by an abundance of ethnological parallels – the Celtic crwth from Wales, the Swedish Talharpa, the Finnish Jouhikantele, and similar Nordic bowed lyres.

Whereas the early medieval plucked rote had at least five or seven strings and was played, like harp and psaltery, on open strings, the medieval bowed rote had fewer, at least to begin with – during the eleventh and twelfth centuries generally no more than three or four (Plates 89, 91, 92). This by no means implies a reduction in the number of notes obtainable on the instrument. In its bowed form, the lyre managed with fewer strings because one of these was stopped, and could therefore produce several notes. The other two served almost exclusively as drones. The Northern European bowed lyres have clung to this technique right up to the present.[284] It seems not to matter whether the strings pass over a fingerboard or are strung freely over the frame of the lyre. In the latter case, the strings were stopped (as ethnological material shows) either by touching them tangentially with the fingernails[285] – like hurdy-gurdy tangents – or by gentle pressure with the inside of the finger, without pressing the strings against a fingerboard, even where this was present.[286] The latter method of fingering is shown on several medieval miniatures. The player either inserts his left hand into the opening formed by the curving arms of the yoke (Plate 91), or brings his hand round from behind the instrument and stops the strings from the side, touching the one nearest his hand with the fingertips or the inside of the fingers (Plates 89, 92, 94, 96).

Besides these bowed rotes with three and four strings, there is evidence from the twelfth century onwards of instruments with five or six strings, also played with the bow (Plates 90, 93, 95). Where this increase in the number of strings was not due to simple doubling or octave-doubling of the drone-strings, it is possible that the old method of playing the lyre on open strings was used, as it still was for plucked instruments of the same genus during the eleventh and twelfth centuries:[287] the instrument was held at the point where the strings were attached

1939), pp. 39ff. and 116ff., and C. Sachs, *History*, pp. 264ff. [283] Bridges from medieval lyres found during excavations are illustrated by J. Werner, op. cit.; cf. also W. Niemeyer's article 'Germanische Musik' in *MGG*, The bridge is clearly recognizable in the following 11th and 12th century illustrations: Paris, Bibliothèque Nationale, MS. lat. 1118, fol. 104r; London, British Museum, MS. Harl. 2804, fol. 3v. [284] O. Andersson, *The Bowed-Harp*, p. 252f. [285] Loc.cit.; cf. also A. Koczirz, 'Über die Fingernageltechnik bei Saiteninstrumenten', *Festschrift für G. Adler* (Vienna, 1930), pp. 164ff. [286] A similar technique is commonly used in playing bowed folk instruments of South-Eastern Europe and the East. Cf. pp. 87ff. of this book. [287] The rote is shown in this position in the following miniatures *inter alia*: Munich, Staatsbibliothek, Clm 7355, fol. 5v; Rome, Vatican Library, Pat. lat. 39, fol. 44v; Cambridge, University Library, Ff. I. 23, fol. 4v; St. Gall, Stiftsbibliothek, Cod. 21; Heiligenkreuz, Library, Hs. 10. F. 9;

to the frame-like curve of the yoke, so that either the strings that were not to sound could be stopped with the fingers of this hand, or their pitch could be changed by a tone or semitone, by finger-pressure. This technique is illustrated in an English miniature dating from the eleventh century (Plate 92). With regard to technique, a special position is occupied by an illustration from an archivolt in the west transept of the Grossmünster in Zürich (Plate 96). Here the scutiform lyre is held upright in front of the cross-legged player's body. His right hand manipulates the bow, which passes across all the strings simultaneously, while the splayed left hand is clearly employed in damping those strings that are not meant to sound at that moment. This technique is commonly used on Ethiopian lyres.[288] Occasionally, we meet medieval bowed lyres with more than ten strings. One example of this type of instrument is clearly shown on an ivory carving of the eleventh or twelfth century from the St Bertin region (Plate 90), only later used as a cover for the Carolingian Lothar Psalter. The instrument, with its back turned to the observer,[289] reveals at least twelve strings of which, however, only the few that pass over the narrow fingerboard[290] were stopped or fingered, to all appearances. Since the bow must inevitably have touched all the strings simultaneously at each stroke, the only explanation of this unusual portrayal is that either the aim was to produce as loud as possible a drone bass for the melody, or that the illustration does not represent the instrument as it really was.[291] Nevertheless, such multi-stringed instruments were exceptional in medieval times, and as a rule we find that once the rote became a bowed instrument, its stringing and technique were very similar to those of the early fiddle.

The position in which both these instruments were played was also roughly the same. The plucked lyre was held in front of the player's body, while its bowed counterpart was usually played with the resonator resting against the chest, or shoulder and chin (Plates 89, 92–94). Where the bowed lyre is shown supported on the player's knee (Plates 89–91), the picture usually represents a resting position. The musician has stopped playing, and has therefore put down his instrument.[292]

There was obviously a further point of similarity between the bowed rote and the fiddle in the tuning of their strings, but precise details are not available until a later date. We are, therefore, thrown back yet again on comparative ethno-

Wolfenbüttel, Library, MS. Helmst. 1057, fol. 5r; Bamberg, Staatsbibliothek, A. II, 47, fol. 10r; Munich, University Library, MS. 24, fol. 2r. etc.   [288] There is evidence that this technique was also used on the plucked rote of early medieval times. A miniature from an eighth century Anglo-Saxon Psalter MS. (British Museum MS. Cotton, Vespas. A. I, fol. 30b) depicts King David in the company of his musicians, holding a rote. With the splayed fingers of his left hand he dampens the strings from behind, while his right hand wields the plectrum.   [289] The back of the resonator is obviously open.   [290] Since the fingerboard is very narrow, it seems clear that two strings only run over it.   [291] On p. 155 of his *Musikleben*, F. Behn expresses his doubts about this rather dubious representation. 'The author of this ivory relief clearly wished to represent a bow, which was still a novelty to him, but has associated it with the wrong instrument.'   [292] This also applies to Plate 91. The bow lies across the strings below the bridge, show-

8*

logical evidence, as provided by present-day bowed lyres of Northern Europe. The earliest data we have relating to the tuning of the Nordic bowed lyres agree remarkably with the 'mixture' tuning of medieval fiddles recorded by Jerome of Moravia[293] in the thirteenth century. The strings of the Finnish Jouhikantele, for instance, were originally tuned g d′ g′[294] for the most part, a pattern eminently suited to drone-playing, whereas the strings on the plucked medieval lyre were clearly arranged in diatonic or pentatonic order, as befitted open-string playing. At the same time, documentary evidence confirms that triadic tuning (fundamental-third-fifth-octave) was used on bowed lyres.[295] Not until recently was the tuning of the kantele changed to tuning by fifths (g d′ a′),[296] frequently varied, however – especially in Karelia – by tuning the lowest string an octave higher (g′ d′ a′).[297] This same pattern of tuning (g′ d′ a′) is often encountered on bowed instruments of South-Eastern Europe and the East.[298] With respect to technique also Scandinavian bowed lyres agree with South-eastern European fiddles: the two outside strings were fingered, while between them the lowest string sounded as a drone.[299] On the Welsh crwth, a fundamental change in tuning resulted from transferring the drone-strings to the side of the fingerboard[300] (as on European fiddles since the late Middle Ages), so as to ensure their independence of the bow, and to make possible their harmonic use. Here, too, the drone-strings were almost invariably tuned to d or g,[301] as on the fiddle.

In short, we see that, through the use of the bow, the rote approximated to the medieval fiddle, both in structure and technique. In the process it became a drone-instrument, at the same time meeting the need for cantabile performance· In the sphere of art music the bowed rote was able to maintain its position only so long as this was based on a melodic restricted compass with drone-accompaniment. As a folk instrument it has survived to the present.

ing that the instrument is not being played at the moment. [293] S. M. Cserba, op. cit., p. 289 f. [294] O. Andersson, *The Bowed-Harp*, p. 64. [295] S. Walin, *Die schwedische Hummel*, pp. 65 ff.; further details relating to the tuning of both plucked and bowed Nordic lyres are given. [296] O. Andersson, op. cit., p. 189. [297] Op. cit., p. 68. [298] Cf. above, p. 98, Note 187. [299] O. Andersson, op. cit., p. 69 f. [300] Op. cit., p. 225. Even the drone-strings (which did not run off to the side) were only used 'now and then' in the 19th century, and did not sound continuously with the melody (from Malmberg's account of the technique); cf. S. Walin, *Die schwedische Hummel*, p. 68. [301] Details regarding the tuning of the drone-strings on Nordic stringed instruments are given by S. Walin in *Die schwedische Hummel*, pp. 64 ff., and O. Andersson, op. cit., p. 226.

IV

BOWED INSTRUMENTS IN MEDIEVAL SOCIETY

Their social standing

The question of the social function fulfilled by bowed instruments in medieval times is important since instruments of the period stand in close relationship to different strata of the social hierarchy.[1] The right to play certain instruments – for example, oliphant and buzine – was a privilege of the feudal aristocracy; certain instruments only were sanctioned or tolerated by the Church. Others again were chiefly confined to the peasantry. As time went on, however, the social standing and prestige of the various instruments was liable to change. The hurdy-gurdy is a case in point. Among ecclesiastical music theorists of the twelfth century it was held in high esteem. But it remained so only as long as European art music was based on the pedal-point principle.[2] By the fourteenth and fifteenth centuries it was frequently to be found in the hands of beggars and wandering minstrels.[3] In the sixteenth century it had become the favourite instrument of country folk, the 'lyre for peasants and traipsing women'.[4] In the eighteenth century it became the fashionable instrument of aristocratic dilettanti and was used to express pastoral moods and feelings; but the nineteenth century returned it to the sphere of folk music where it has remained ever since.

By contrast, the general development of bowed instruments lies in the oppo-

---

[1] Various aspects of this problem are outlined in E. A. Bowles, 'La hiérarchie des instruments de musique dans l'europe féodale', *Revue de musicologie* XLII (1958), pp. 155 ff.; cf. also W. Salmen, 'Zur sozialen Schichtung des Berufsmusikertums im mittelalterlichen Eurasien und in Afrika', *Les Congrès et Colloques de l'Université de Liège*, Vol. 19 (1960), *Ethnomusicologie* II, pp. 23 ff. [2] Cf. pp. 105 ff. [3] From the following quotations it emerges that the hurdy-gurdy was associated with beggars in the 15th century, and more specifically with blind beggars: J. Gerson (died 1429), *Opera omnia*, Vol. 3, Part I (Antwerp, 1706), col. 627 f.: 'Symphoniam putant aliqui viellam, vel Rebeccam, quae minor est. At vero rectius existimatur esse musicum tale instrumentum quale sibi vindicaverunt specialiter ipsi caeci'; J. Cocleus, *Tetrachordum Mus. Tract.* I, Chapter 10: 'Rota vero instrumentum est, quo coeci mendicantes utuntur'; Paulus Paulirinus de Praga, *ZfMw* 7, pp. 264 ff.; 'Ysis (hurdy-gurdy) . . . est repertum quo instrumento communiter mulieres solent victum querere'; Berthélémy l'Anglais, Bibliothèque Nationale, Paris, MS. Fr. 22532, 340 v: 'On appelle en France une symphonie un instrument dont les aveugles jouent en chantant les chansons de geste'; Bertrand du Guesclin (A. W. Ambros, *Geschichte der Musik*, Vol. II (Breslau, 1891), p. 41): 'ens ou pays de France et ou pays Normant / ne vont tels instruments fors aveugles portant / ainsi vont les aveugles et li povres truant . . . et demandant leur pain.' [4] M. Praetorius:

site direction. As has been shown in some detail,[5] bowed instruments were originally used exclusively for the performance of folk music, and were disdained by the cultured musicians and theorists of Islam. They were described as imperfect,[6] and are mentioned only in parenthesis for the sake of completeness. Only the lute and lute-playing were aristocratic. The Chinese described bowed chordophones as *hu* (= barbarian), and as such they rarely participated in the court music or religious ceremonies of Asian peoples. One of the few early descriptions of one such occasion occurs in an account[7] of music at the court of the Ghaznavids who caused drums to be beaten and *rabāb* and *chang* (harp) to be played during a reception for friendly princes and ambassadors. From the thirteenth century onwards we find further isolated references to the use of bowed instruments at the courts of other Oriental potentates;[8] but *rabāb* and *kamanja* remained essentially folk instruments.

The advent of the bow in Europe brought a significant change in the social status of fiddling, for the use of bowed instruments in Europe was at first mainly restricted to the circles of feudal aristocracy and courtly minstrels. Medieval sources tell us that instruction in fiddling was an integral part of a nobleman's education, and members of the nobility are frequently mentioned as fiddlers. Thus the *vieleor* of the German Emperor Conrad was the son of a count.[9] 'Vièlent li noble jogleor' ('the noble minstrels play') runs one Old French poem,[10] while Ulrich von Zatzikhoven[11] relates in the *Lanzelet* how at that time it was the custom (*landsite*) for youths and maidens of noble blood to learn *gîgen*, that is, to play the fiddle. At all events, the courtly minstrel was expected to be thoroughly proficient in fiddling. Many accounts list the accomplishment of the medieval minstrel, and a certain competence as a fiddler is invariably demanded of him. 'I was a courtly minstrel' says Tristan, in Gottfried von Strassburg's epic of that name,[12] 'and well-versed in the ways of courtly life: speaking out or holding my peace, playing lyre and fiddle, harp and rote, and rail and mock.' The minstrel Estrumens[13] expresses it in much the same way: 'Here is my harp, on which I

Syntagma musicum II, *De organographia* (Wolfenbüttel, 1619), p. 49.   [5] Above, pp. 55 ff.   [6] The defects of the *rabāb* are stressed by al-Fārābī in his *Kitāb al-mūsīqī* (R. d'Erlanger, *La Musique Arabe*, Vol. I (Paris, 1930), p. 285 f. The Berlin MS. We 1233 fol. 47 v, also reveals that educated Arabs regarded the *rabāb* with some disdain (cf. H. G. Farmer, *Historical Facts*, p. 265, Note 1.).   [7] Cf. B. Spuler, *Iran in frühislamischer Zeit* (Wiesbaden, 1952), p. 270.   [8] According to al-Maqrīzī, I, 1, p. 136, the kemânche was popular at the courts of the Aiyūbid ruler al-Kāmil (died 1238) and the Mameluke Baibars (died 1277); cf. H. G. Farmer's article 'rabab' in *Enzyklopädie des Islam*. The rabab's sporadic appearences in the sphere of court music are less surprising if we take into account the fact that in the ancient East, musicians were nearly always slaves, who brought their own familiar instruments with them from their native countries. Cf. J. Fück, '"Arabische" Musikkultur und Islam', *Orientalische Literaturzeitung*, 48th Year (1953), col. 24.   [9] *Le Roman de la Rose ou de Guillaume de Dole* (12th–13th century), ed. G. Servois (Paris, 1893), vv. 636–42.   [10] *Les Enfances Godefroy*, ed. Hippeau, v. 230.   [11] Ulrich von Zatzikhoven, *Lanzelet*, ed. K. A. Hahn (Frankfurt am Main, 1845), v. 262; cf. also *Tristan*, by Gottfried von Strassburg, vv. 3675 and 7987.   [12] W. Golther's edition (Berlin, 1888), v. 7564 ff.   [13] J. Sittard, 'Jongleurs

know well to harp, and my viele, on which I fiddle; and I can also drum and dance.' Other necessary skills included hunting, fishing, and playing chess. In the Old French *Roman de Brut*, by Robert Wace,[14] the capabilities of the minstrel Blegabres are set out: 'Master of all instruments and skilled in song, and familiar with many lays and tunes. Able to play viele and rote, lyre and psaltery, harp and bagpipe, gigue and symphonie, if he were well enough versed in harmony'. Another interesting picture of the minstrel of his age is painted by Guiraut de Calançon (1210) in his Sirventes *Fadet Joglar*:[15] He must be 'good at story-telling and rhyming, and acquit himself creditably in trials of skill. Know how to strike drums and cymbals, and to play the hurdy-gurdy. Know how to throw and catch little apples on knives, to imitate birdsong, do card-tricks and be able to jump through four hoops. Know how to play citola and mandoline, know how to handle monochord and the guitar, string a rote with seventeen strings, be proficient on the harp, accompany well on the gigue, so as to enhance the spoken word. Jongleur, you should be able to handle nine instruments (vielle, bagpipe, pipe, harp, hurdy-gurdy, gigue, decachord, psaltery, and rote); and when you have mastered these, you will be equipped to deal with every eventuality. And do not neglect the lyre or the cymbals.' Medieval minstrels were thus not only musicians, but jesters, jugglers, and acrobats as well. Finally, there is another interesting report in the Old French tale *Les deux Bordéors ribaus*,[16] according to which the medieval minstrel was expected to be thoroughly familiar with contemporary poets and their works. Furthermore, he was required to tell stories in both Latin and French, and to know every conceivable game. He should be able to relate the adventures of Charlemagne's knights, or of King Arthur, sing, declaim or recite all manner of poetry, give advice to the lovelorn, and play all the standard musical instruments. 'I shall tell you what I can do: I am a fiddler, I play the bagpipe and flute, harp, chifonie and giga, psaltery and rote, and I can sing a song well.'

In the face of the amazing range of accomplishments expected of the professional musician of medieval times, a high degree of virtuosity on all the various instruments was scarcely to be expected. Outstanding individual performers on the vielle are famous as such, and we know that the troubadours Perdigos and Pons de Capdueil[17] were excellent fiddlers who were also gifted as poets and singers.

---

et Menestrels', *VfMw* I (1885), p. 197. [14] This story dates from the 12th century. See Le Roux de Lincy's edition (Paris, 1836), vv. 3769ff. [15] See W. Keller, 'Das Sirventes "Fadet Joglar" des Guiraut von Calanzo', Romanische Forschungen XXII (1906), p. 144f. [16] L. Grillet, *Les ancêtres*, p. 74. [17] Op. cit., p. 77. Other medieval sources also testify to the great skill of fiddlers: Heinrich von dem Türlin, *Diu Crône*, ed. F. Scholl (Stuttgart, 1852), v. 652; Rudolf von Ems, *Der gute Gerhard*, ed. M. Haupt (Leipzig, 1840), v. 3615; Wolfram von Eschenbach, *Parzival*, ed. K. Bartsch (Leipzig, 1923), v. 639, 9f. Indifferent players are also occasionally mentioned, and Giraut de Cabreira, a 13th century troubadour, upbraids his assistant Cabra (v. 167): 'You play the vielle badly, your fingering is bad, and your bowing is bad'. He goes on 'You can neither

The high social status of the medieval fiddle is further demonstrated by the esteem in which it was held by European music theorists. One of these, Johannes de Grocheo,[18] writes: 'Further, among all the stringed instruments I have seen, the viella deserves to take precedence' – an opinion shared by Jerome of Moravia.[19] Another tribute comes from a poem by the German/Bohemian poet Ulrich von Eschenbach:[20] 'Now see, for all this play I will the fiddle praise'. This implies that the fiddle was the favourite instrument in court circles. The rebec also appeared from time to time at the royal court.[21] Costly fiddles, lavishly embellished or studded with precious stones, were illustrated and described in books;[22] they were witnesses to their owners' wealth. By contrast, unless a minstrel happened to be under the patronage of a member of the ruling class, his instruments were much simpler, and undecorated. The price of one of these minstrel's fiddles is given in an English source of the late fourteenth century, *Sir Beve of Hamtoun* (3905 ff.). On her return from Armenia, Josian, Sir Beve's wife, purchases a fiddle from a minstrel 'for fourti panes' (= pence).

If we assemble all the available eleventh-thirteenth-century literary evidence relating to the use of bowed instruments in knightly society,[23] the fiddle stands in first place, taking precedence over harp and trumpet. Whole 'orchestras' of fiddlers were maintained at the court of Alfonso the Wise of Castile, and at that of Manfred of Hohenstaufen, in Sicily.[24] Fiddlers accompanied their lords on journeys, playing a *reisenot* as they rode, to please him and keep him in good heart.[25] Fiddlers also formed part of the Queen's retinue:[26] 'At court the Queen is preceded by many a fiddler, and they walk apart, two by two'. In Gottfried von Strassburg's epic,[27] Tristan is obliged to spend his days in the hunting field with the king, and his evenings entertaining him with songs, accompanying himself on harp and fiddle. The fiddler was greatly in demand during or after

sing nor dance, nor do tricks, like the wandering jongleurs from Gascony.' [18] See J. Wolf, 'Die Musiklehre des Johannes de Grocheo', *SJMG* I (1899), pp. 96f. [19] S. M. Cserba, *Der Musiktraktat des Hieronymus von Mähren*, p. 290f. [20] See H. J. Moser, *Das Streichinstrumentenspiel im Mittelalter*, p. 12. [21] 'At the royal courts, however, everyone is keen to play the trumpet, gittern and rebec.' *Œuvres complètes d'Eust. Deschamps*, ed. G. Raynaud (1878–1903), Vol. VIII, p. 232f., vv. 19ff. [22] See pp. 73 and 86; a 'vièle délicieuse' is mentioned in the Roman de A. Mahomet. See Grillet, op. cit., p. 40. [23] Cf. esp. F. Dick, *Bezeichnungen für Saiten- und Schlaginstrumente in der altfranzösischen Literatur* (Dissertation, Giessen, 1931); D. Treder, *Die Musikinstrumente in den höfischen Epen der Blütezeit* (Dissertation, Greifwald, 1933); G. Schad, *Musik und Musikausdrücke in der mittelenglischen Literatur* (Dissertation, Giessen, 1911); F. Brücker, *Die Blasinstrumente in der altfranzösischen Literatur* (Dissertation, Giessen, 1926), pp. 62ff. [24] An account of music at the court of King Manfred is given in Ottokar's *Reimchronik*, ed. Seemüller in *Monumenta germanica hist.* V, 1, pp. 5ff. [25] Ulrich von Lichtenstein, *Frauendienst*, 165, 4; cf. H. J. Moser, *Die Musikergenossenschaften im deutschen Mittelalter* (Dissertation, Rostock, 1910), p. 18. [26] The quotation is from the story 'Laurin' in *Das helden buch mit synen figuren* (Strasbourg, 1509), v. 1748. [27] Ed. F. Ranke (Berlin, 1930), vv. 3721 ff. The 'Wigalois', ed. F. Pfeiffer (1847), p. 217, 11, tells how six fiddlers had to provide music to dispel the ill humour of their lord, Count Adân.

festive banquets,[28] at weddings, receptions, and other celebrations,[29] and not infrequently for dancing at court[30] also. Dance music was often performed by a single fiddler, with no support from other instruments.[31] Bowed instruments were also very popular for accompanying singing, both the solo art-song of the minnesinger and also group singing at social gatherings, as described by the thirteenth-century writer Durmart le Galois:[32] 'And some of them fiddled, while harps and gigas joined in, and ladies and young maidens sang.'

With the growth of towns there was a marked desire among the burghers to demonstrate their affluence by engaging players to provide musical services. Johannes de Garlandia[33] is able to report that in the houses of the rich, 'vidulatores cum vidulis, alios cum sistro, cum giga, cum symphonia,' were to be encountered. Adam von Salimbene, a native of Parma and a Minorite friar of the thirteenth century, gives a vivid account of a concert at the house of a leading citizen.[34] He tells of 'Viéles, citharas and other instruments in the hand of men and women, playing sweetly to songs beautiful in words and melody, so that the heart was made beyond measure joyful. All listened in silence.' Other similar descriptions of music in the home are to be found in fourteenth-century texts.

But the thirteenth century also witnessed the admission of the fiddle into the Church. The barriers erected by the clergy against the minstrel and his instruments were breached more and more often after the twelfth century. Thus the writings of John of Salisbury[35] and Honorius Augustodunensis[36] sanction the use of musical instruments in church worship.[37] St. Francis of Assisi no longer prohibits the activities of Italian minstrels, but accepts their practices and their instruments. We know from some of his pupils that they occasionally used the fiddle in church and in the context of their pastoral duties. The polemical question

---

[28] 'The banquet over, the fiddlers were ordered to strike up', *Lohengrin*, ed. H. Rückert (Quedlinburg, 1858), v. 320, 6. Other instances occur in Heinrich von Veldeke, *Die Eneide*, ed. L. Ettmüller (Leipzig, 1852), vv. 12953 ff., and Heinrich von dem Türlin, *Diu Crône*, ed. F. Scholl, (Stuttgart, 1852), v. 29287. References in Old French texts include *Galerent*, v. 4814, *Manekine*, vv. 2297 ff., *Cleomades*, vv. 2879 ff. (cf. F. Brücker, *Die Blasinstrumente in der altfranzösischen Literatur* (Dissertation, Giessen, 1926), pp. 74 ff.). Similar Middle English evidence is given by G. Schad, *Musik und Musikausdrücke*, pp. 72–73. [29] Many references are quoted in the dissertations (p. 120, Note 23) of F. Brücker, F. Dick and D. Treder. [30] 'Let us then tread a courtly measure to the sound of the fiddlers' (Neithart), see F. H. von der Hagen, *Minnesinger*, Vol. III (Leipzig, 1838); 'Come on, all those who wish to dance to the fiddlers' (Walther); 'Karsic ... bade the fiddlers strike up a merry tune so that they might dance', *Tristan*, continuation, ed. F. H. von der Hagen (Breslau, 1823), vv. 620 ff. [31] In Wernher der Gartenaere's *Meier Helmbrecht* ed. F. Panzer (Halle, 1924), v. 944, the *gige* accompanies the dancing on its own. [32] See E. Stengel's edition (Tübingen, 1873), vv. 15076 ff. [33] *Magistri Johannis de Garlandis Dictionarius*, LXXX; see L. Grillet, op. cit., p. 62. [34] Quoted in Latin in Fr. X. Haberl, *Bausteine für die Musikgeschichte* (Leipzig, 1885–8), Vol. III, p. 27. [35] Cf. M. Gerbert, *De cantu*, Vol. II, p. 98. [36] Op. cit., p. 100. [37] Other contemporary accounts demonstrate the forceful resistance offered by the clergy to the use of musical instruments in public worship. The Spanish Franciscan friar Johann Aegidius Zamorensis (*c.* 1260) observes that in general only the organ was tolerated inside the church, whereas all other instruments 'propter abusum historionum' were usually

'unde quaeso, in ecclesia tot organa, tot cymbala, tot monstruosa?' formulated by Guibert de Tournay[38] in his sermon of 1283 *Ad monachos nigros sermo primus*, demonstrates the speed at which instrumental music had gained ground in divine service.

Master Lambertus (the Pseudo-Aristotle) records in his *Tractatus de musica*[39] that the fiddle – in addition to the organ and certain plucked instruments – was introduced into church music in his lifetime; and Gautier de Coinci[40] stresses that the fiddle was used to glorify God, and that the clergy set store by the sound of harp and fiddle (*vièle*), of psaltery, organ, and *giga* (*gigue*). Finally Eustache Deschamps[41] testifies that the fiddle was also popular in medieval monasteries. In polyphonic church music it was occasionally used to support the voices and provide long, sustained notes.[42] It is interesting to note the comment by the Abbé Aimery de Peyrac, from Moissac (*c.* 1300), that the Choral or cantus firmus lost none of its beauty if played from time to time on a bowed instrument.[43]

Nowhere in any of the pre-fourteenth century sources do we find reference to the use of the fiddle among the 'lower' social strata – the world of serfs and villeins, artisans, and day-labourers.[44] Not until the last years of the Middle Ages is there evidence from vernacular literature that bowed instruments were sometimes played by village folk. These would of course be the more primitive types of bowed instrument – the rebec, the pearshaped gigue, and the hurdy-gurdy which, together with shepherd's pipe and bagpipe, were played not only by farmers and shepherds but by beggars and vagabonds also. Thus the *Bellefoière*[45] speaks of the sound of the bagpipe and the hoarse rebec of the cowherds ('du son de la musette, du rebec enroué des vachers'); and the *Banquet du boys*[46] similarly refers to the rebec as a shepherd's instrument.

Medieval fiddlers were graded according to their education, as were *musicus* and *cantor*.[47] The practical musician was by far the most common type. Though in time he had acquired a certain degree of technical expertise on his instrument, he lacked a formal musical education, and above all a basic training in the liberal

---

banned (Gerbert, *Scriptores*, Vol. II). [38] See P. Aubry, 'Les abus de la musique d'église du XIIᵉ au XIIIᵉ siècle', *Tribune de Saint-Gervais* IX (1903), pp. 57 ff. [39] *CS* I 253 a: 'Artificiale est ut organa, vielle, cythara, cythole, psalterium et similia … valdeque fores ecclesie ausa est subintrare.' [40] Gautier de Coinci (1177–1236), *Miracles de la Vierge*; cf. L. Grillet op. cit., p. 77; F. Dick, *Saiten- und Schlaginstrumente*, p. 81, and W. Krüger, *Mf* X (1957), p. 282. [41] *Œuvres complètes*, IV, 127, v. 13: 'The fiddle is played in monasteries.' [42] A theory supported by Y. Rockseth among others, in her *Polyphonies du XIIIᵉ siècle*, IV, p. 44; many references to the use of instruments in the church are noted by W. Krüger in 'Aufführungspraktische Fragen mittelalterlicher Mehrstimmigkeit', *Mf* IX (1956), pp. 424 ff. Cf. also W. Krüger, Singstil und Instrumentalstil in der Mehrstimmigkeit der St. Martialepoche', *Congress Report* (Bamberg, 1953), pp. 240 ff. [43] Quoted in English by E. Bowles in 'Haut and bas', *Musica disciplina* VIII (1954), p. 128 f. [44] Until the fourteenth century the music of rustics and shepherds shows a striking bias towards wind and percussion instruments; cf. F. Brücker, *Die Blasinstrumente in der altfranzösischen Literatur* (Dissertation, Giessen, 1926), p. 73 f. [45] F. Dick, *Saiten- und Schlaginstrumente*, p. 95. [46] F. Dick, *Saiten- und Blasinstrumente*, p. 94. [47] W. Gurlitt, 'Die Bedeutungsgeschichte von

arts. Such men were for the most part self-taught, or had spent a few years taking lessons from a minstrel.[48] Albertus Magnus[49] neatly outlines the educational attainments of this type of musician: 'Many are masters of the fiddler's art, though they know nothing of harmony; accordingly, they act more from practical experience (*ex usu*) than from any scholarly or theoretical background (*ex arte*).'

The educated musician is in a very different category from that of the purely practical performer. We know of a number of men – important medieval composers and theorists, and other notable scholars and members of the aristocracy, all of them presumably learned in the *artes liberales* (or at least in the topics of musical theory) – who could perform on a number of instruments, including the fiddle. Nevertheless they rarely appeared in the role of practising musician. Among the privileged classes, playing the fiddle (and the hurdy-gurdy) was regarded as one of the *exercitia liberalia*,[50] to be practised, not for its usefulness, but for its own sake.

The artist who appeared in public, the 'bonus artifex in viella', had seldom enjoyed the benefits of a comprehensive practical and scholarly training. As a rule he would spend several years as apprentice to an experienced minstrel, and thereafter courses of instruction and minstrel schools carried his studies a stage further, though they dealt for the most part only with his practical needs. We read of one such *vedelerscole* in Ypres, run by 'meistre Symon, maistre des menestrens de la vièle'.[51] In 1328 and 1365 fiddlers gathered together in Malines, and in 1354 in Deventer, for 'advanced courses of instruction',[52] and many medieval sources tell of sizable conventions held by minstrels at which champion pipers and fiddlers were chosen, though such assemblies were primarily designed to strengthen ties between minstrels, and to deal with questions of organization.

Their repertoire: conditions of performance

Before turning to the special problems of performance and the musical use of medieval bowed instruments, we must ask: what could be played on these instruments? In his treatise *De musica*,[53] Johannes de Grocheo answers clearly that a good fiddler could play anything 'every cantus or cantilena, and in general every type of music ... It combines in itself the attributes of all other instruments, and distinguishes most sensitively between all forms of music.' The fiddle's all-round versatility was in large part due to its wide compass, to its technical sophistication and musical flexibility, and to the cantabile character of bowed instruments. The smallest intervals, slurs, quick passages, figuration, and long

musicus und cantor bei Isidor von Sevilla', *Neue Studien zur Musikwissenschaft* 7 (1950). [48] The minstrel's rôle as a pedagogue is discussed in W. Grossmann's *Frühmittelenglische Zeugnisse über Ministrels* (Dissertation, Berlin, 1906), pp. 88 and 99. [49] Albertus Magnus, *Ethics* (ed. Borgnet, Vol. VII), 2, 1, 10, p. 165a. [50] Albertus Magnus, *Metaph.* 1, 2, 7, p. 32a. [51] Cf. *Bergmans, Simon, maître de vièle* (1911), p. 763. [52] W. Salmen, *Der fahrende Musiker im europäischen Mittelalter* (Cassel, 1960), p. 183. [53] Ed. by J. Wolf in *SIMG* I (1899), pp. 96–97.

sustained notes could all be executed without difficulty, and open strings could be sounded as drones to the melody. And whereas the majority of medieval instruments were restricted to fixed single notes or fixed scales, the fiddle could produce every conceivable intermediate pitch on the scale, and bring out in performance every dynamic nuance too. Bowed instruments were thus peculiarly suited to the musical conceptions of the Middle Ages, as expressed in vocal music of the time.[54] The special characteristics of that music included richly differentiated ornaments and slides, a continually flowing melodic line, and a restrained, veiled quality of sound.

The gap between instrumental and vocal spheres, not conspicuous in medieval music, is almost wholly bridged by the bowed instruments. The forms of instrumental music played by the fiddler corresponded to the main categories of vocal music in the minstrel's repertoire, from the various types of *lai*, strophic songs and songs with burdens, to the round-dance songs derived from dance rhythms. The syllabic sequence, too, with its uniformly regular beat, provided suitable material.[55] Since no manuscripts of instrumental music survive from the period up to the thirteenth century – the medieval musicians played without music – we are dependent on information concerning the minstrel's repertoire. We read frequently of the '*lais de vièles*', compositions based on strophic songs (*Leich, lais*) and transformed by a process of diminution into 'decorated paraphrases' of the original. According to a poem by Colin Muset,[56] it was mostly songs that were played on the *vielle* (en lors vièles vont les lais vièlant); while in the *Roman de la Violette*[57] we find the phrase 'the minstrels play lais on their vieles, together with tunes and songs and accompaniments'.[58] Another reference, this time in the *Chronique de l'abbaye du Mont St Michel*,[59] confirms that minstrels performed songs and instrumental pieces ('Lais et sonnez vunt vièlant') and a longer list, from a poem by Jeannin Allart,[60] mentions that 'songs, rondeaux and estampies, dances, tunes and baleries, love-songs, and ballads' are played on the *viella*. Guillebert of Metz[61] also quotes the hurdy-gurdy as an instrument on which songs were played, and Juan Ruiz[62] in his *Libro de amor* writes of the 'dulces debayladas' performed on the *vihuela de arco*. Songs for dancing (*balades, baleries*) are likewise included in the repertoire of fiddlers in Central and North-Western Europe.

[54] For further details see P. Marquart, *Der Gesang und seine Erscheinungsformen im Mittelalter* (Dissertation, Berlin, 1936), cf. also G. Pietsch, 'Der Wandel des Klangideals', *AMl* (1932), and A. Schering, 'Historische und nationale Klangstile', *JP* (1927), pp. 31 ff.   [55] For the instrumental rendering of sequence and trope cf. H. Besseler, 'Spielfiguren in der Instrumentalmusik', *Deutsches Jahrbuch der Musikwissenschaft*, I (1957), p. 25.   [56] See L. Grillet, op. cit., p. 63. 'Lais de vièles' are mentioned several times in the Old French *Roman de Brut*; cf. F. Dick, *Bezeichnungen für Saiten- und Schlaginstrumente*, p. 22. – Minstrels also played 'rotruenges et sons' on their fiddle; cf. Du Cange, suppl., article 'rocta'.   [57] According to this evidence, therefore, the conductus was also performed by bowed instruments on occasion.   [58] *Le Roman de la Violette ou de Gerart de Nevers* (13th century), by Gerart de Montreuil, ed. Douglas L. Buffum (Paris, 1928), vv. 3089/90.   [59] See F. Gennrich, *Grundriß einer Formenlehre des mittelalterlichen Liedes* (Halle, 1932), p. 160, N. 1.   [60] See L. Grillet, op. cit., p. 39.   [61] F. Dick, *Bezeichnungen für Saiten- und Schlaginstrumente*, p. 84.   [62] Cf.

A particularly extensive list of songs played on bowed instruments is contained in an Italian manuscript of the late fourteenth century.[63] This is a most valuable and informative source, since it gives the first lines, or at least the titles, of the songs performed instrumentally. Most of them seem to have been well-known popular tunes ('vièles qui font les mélodies bèles'),[64] and served the minstrel as a basic melodic repertoire which he could elaborate according to his capabilities as a performer.

Apart from these types of song, where words and music were closely linked, and the melody often conditioned by the text, the fiddler's repertoire also included pieces of purely instrumental origin. These were concert pieces or dance tunes, variously described as *nota*, *estampida* (stantipes), *ductia*, and *dance*.[65] The *nota*, according to Johannes de Grocheo,[66] was a dance form, akin to the lively, strongly rhythmical *ductia*. By contrast, the *estampida* was a virtuoso piece, the extreme difficulty of which, according to Johannes de Grocheo, kept young people's thoughts from straying to baser things.[67] The special criterion of these string pieces, according to the anonymous author of the treatise *De mensuris et discantus* (c. 1275)[68] was duple time, whereas the religious vocal music of the period was predominantly in triple time. These virtuoso pieces are characterized by their clear subdivision into separate sections (*puncti*). Their melodic shape is determined by the extempore nature of all such instrumental music, based on the repetition and variation of characteristic string figuration.[69] A fully-fledged fiddler was expected to be able to furnish his listeners with a constant stream of new melodies, improvised on the spot, and it was taken amiss if he served up old music. We read, for instance, in Wolfram von Eschenbach's *Parzival*:[70] 'Then Sir Gawain asked if there were no good fiddlers present. There were indeed many worthy fellows, and their artistry was so great that they were not constrained to play old dances.' From these sources we realize that the music of the medieval minstrel was spontaneous, impromptu, and ephemeral.[71]

In medieval times the fiddle was important not only for solo performance, but also as an accompanying instrument. Monodic artsongs were usually accompanied by a bowed instrument, played either by the singer himself, or by a min-

article 'Hita' in *MGG*. [63] See A. Schering, *Studien zur Musikgeschichte der Frührenaissance* (Leipzig, 1914), p. 107. [64] In the *Roman de Renard* we find: 'The harps play, and the fiddles (vièles), which make sweet melodies'; see L. Grillet, op. cit., p. 41. [65] See the following works: H. J. Moser, 'Stantipes und Ductia', *ZfMw* XVI (1934); J. Handschin, 'Über Estampie und Sequenz', *ZfMw* 12 (1929); J. Wolf, 'Die Tänze des Mittelalters', *AfMw* 1, (1918/19). [66] Translated by J. Wolf in *SIMG* I (1899), p. 98; cf. R. de Fournival, *La Panthère* (L. Grillet, op. cit., p. 63): 'en vièles, oi faire notes nouvelles.' Jehan Maillart, *Roman du Comte d'Anjou*, 14, speaks of 'Dansses, notes et baleries'. [67] J. Wolf in *SIMG* I (1899), p. 93 f.: 'Stantipes . . . facit animos iuvenum et puellarum propter sui difficultatem circa hanc stare et eos a cogitatione prava devertit . . .' [68] *CS* I, p. 338 (Anon. IV): 'Consimili modo quattuor currentes pro uno brevi ordinatur, sed hoc raro solebat contingere; ultimi vero non in voce humana, sed in instrumentis cordarum possunt ordinari.' [69] H. Besseler, 'Spielfiguren in der Instrumentalmusik (II. Spielfiguren im Mittelalter)', *Deutsches Jahrbuch der Musikwissenschaft für 1956* (Leipzig, 1957), pp. 23 ff. [70] V. 6394. [71] W. Salmen, *Der fahrende Musiker im europäischen Mittelalter* (Cassel, 1960), p. 226.

strel. How are we to imagine this collaboration between voice and fiddle? What form did the bowed accompaniment take? Until now these questions, which have long exercised scholars, have never been clearly and convincingly answered. A valuable clue as to the minstrel's usual rôle is given in a gloss to the Martianus-Capella manuscript in the Biblioteca Ambrosiana, Milan (M 37 sup. fol. 65 v), dating from the first half of the thirteenth century.[72] This leaves us in no doubt that the minstrel used to set down his instrument as soon as the voice joined in, so that voice and instrument alternated. The fiddle's main rôle in this case was to give the singer his note by providing short preludes and interludes, to keep him in tune, and to allow him to rest between verses. A similar pattern was followed in the East where, according to al-Fārābī's treatise, the instrumental music of the tenth century served primarily to 'accompany and embellish singing, and consisted basically in preludes and interludes, to afford the singer some respite. It (instrumental music) completes the music, in that it expresses that which cannot be communicated by the human voice.'[73] Sometimes the songs were rounded off by adding short, instrumental, coda-like postludes – Johannes de Grocheo calls them *modi*.[74] In one Old French source (thirteenth century) the singer is performing a *chançon*, and sometimes plays the refrain on his fiddle.[75] These preludes, interludes and postludes were originally improvised; but from the fourteenth century on occasional examples in staff-notation survive. The instrumental component, based for the most part on broken triads, is clearly distinguishable from the melodic line of the song. In some cases the fiddle introduction is a 'division' on the beginning of the song.[76] These instrumental preludes and ritornelli almost invariably show a very strong tonal relationship to a common keynote and implicit harmony. As a rule, the interludes and postludes resume the keynote of the prelude, which usually coincides with the pitch of the drone-strings (d or g). All but two of the preludes in the so-called *Berlin Liederhandschrift* (fourteenth century), for example, have d as keynote, and often consist merely of variations on the drone notes d and g. All these factors point to drone-fiddling. It is also possible that the implicit harmony of the ritornello, based on broken triads, was underlined by drones. Among the songs of Oswald von Wolkenstein[77] there is hardly one the instrumental sections of which could not be played on a drone-instrument. The picture changes markedly for fifteenth-century sources, for example, the *Lochamer Liederbuch*. Here, in almost a third of the preludes and interludes, the drone principle no longer applies.

[72] Cf. J. Handschin, 'Über Estampie und Sequenz I', *ZfMw* 12 (1929), p. 6.   [73] R. d'Erlanger, op. cit., Vol. I, p. 17.   [74] Cf. J. Wolf in *SIMG* I (1899), p. 122: a fiddle coda is tacked on to the *cantus coronatus*.   [75] *Li Romans di Claris et Laris*, ed. J. Alton (Tübingen, 1884), v. 9940.: '. . . who sang them a song, and also played its refrains on a fiddle'. In the Anglo-Norman song of the valiant Ritter Horn (R. Brede and E. Stengel, *Ausgaben und Abhandlungen aus dem Gebiet der romanischen Philologie* VIII (Marburg, 1883), v. 2830, a combination of harp and voice is described in detail.   [76] An interesting example of provided by H. J. Moser in *Das Streichinstrumentenspiel im Mittelalter*, p. 11.   [77] *Denkmäler der Tonkunst in Österreich* IX, 1.

Side by side with this practice of alternating voice and fiddle, there is literary evidence of simultaneous participation. This made greater demands on both singer and instrumentalist, and presupposed a high degree of adaptability, as well as complete familiarity with the principles of melodic structure and the problems of part-writing and two-part harmony. A singer who lacked the requisite musical background was never able, according to Elias Salomonis's treatise,[78] to adapt his voice to the fiddle accompaniment. In Trouvère Thomas's *Tristan*[79] it is considered remarkable that the Queen was able to make her song agree with the instrumental accompaniment. A singer of noble birth would generally have in his service a minstrel fully familiar with his repertoire and performing style. The *Roman de la Rose*[81] tells of a Norman nobleman who begins his song when his minstrel strikes up on the fiddle – 'commença cestui a chanter, si la fist Jouglet vièler'; his song is new, and the minstrel duly accompanies him on the fiddle – 'car et a chantée avoec Jouglet en la vièle cese chançonete nouvele.' However, a good minstrel was expected both to sing and at the same time to accompany himself on the fiddle, as we learn from an incident in the Old French *Roman de la Violette*.[82] The noble Gerart, disguised as a minstrel, is asked, in front of a whole company of people, to sing and play the fiddle simultaneously. This he is unable to do, though skilled in song and accomplished as a fiddler. Huon de Mery[83] reports as follows: the minstrels rose and, taking up their fiddles and harps, sang us 'chançons, lais, sons, vers et reprises et de geste'. Rambaud de Vaqueiras[84] tells of a player who accompanied himself on the rebec while reporting a splendid tournament that had taken place in Provence. In a twelfth-century *chanson de geste*,[85] minstrels sing heroic songs to a fiddle-accompaniment; and in the *Roman de la Poire*[86] they perform new songs 'en leur vièles'. Johannes Tinctoris[87] also observes that the fiddle was used 'ad historiarum recitationem', and to this day bowed folk instruments frequently provide both song and epic accompaniments in the Balkans, the Near East, and Central Asia.

The relation of instrumental to vocal parts, and the implications of ensemble playing

We have now to discover whether in these medieval examples of accompanied song the fiddle had a free and independent rôle, or always played in unison with

---

[78] *CS* III, p. 61 b: 'ignorans cantor ignorat habilitare vocem suam ad cantandum cantum qui cum instrumento ligneo, cum viella, cantaretur.' [79] See A. W. Ambros, *Geschichte der Musik*, Vol. II (3rd ed.) (Leipzig, 1891), p. 260, Note 6: 'La reine chante dulcement, la voix accorde al estrument.' [81] Ed G. Servois (Paris, 1893), vv. 2225 and 1843; a similar passage occurs in: *Cortège d'amour des Roman de la Poire*, ed. Stehlich, v. 1140: 'The minstrels with their fiddles sing these new songs.' [82] Ed. Michel, p. 72. [83] See L. Grillet, op. cit., p. 40. [84] See F. Dick, *Bezeichnungen für Saiten- und Schlaginstrumente*, p. 94. [85] *Les deux Rédactions en vers du Moniage Guillaume, chanson de geste du 12ᵉ siècle*, ed. W. Cloëtta (Paris, 1906–11), v. 2071/12; Egidius Parisiensis, in his *Carolinus*, observes that the deeds of Charlemagne were sung to a fiddle accompaniment (cf. L. Grillet, op. cit., p. 40); cf. also J. Sittard, 'Jongleurs et Menestrels', *VfMw* I, p. 183. [86] Ed. Stehlich, v. 1140. [87] K. Weinmann, *Johannes Tinctoris,*

the voice.[88] To this question, so often raised, the scarcity of sources containing indications of methods of performance precludes a definitive answer. It has been pointed out[89] that persistent unison with the voice would have inhibited freedom of performance and the execution of florid passages; and for this reason is less to be considered. It seems clear that, during this period, accompaniments might take quite different forms, dictated on the one hand by the nature of the melody, and on the other by the capacity of the instrumentalist. Where a steadily progressive tune was sung, the fiddler could demonstrate his talent for 'divisions', improvising ornamental passages around the principal notes of the melody. But often the bowed instrument must have confined itself during the song to single sustaining notes, especially where the singer accompanied himself. This supporting drone-like accompaniment was often played at a low pitch, not in the same tessitura as the vocal line. Giraldus Cambrensis[90] observes that the vocal line was supported by 'the dull sound of a low string', and that an accompanying instrumental part 'droned constantly in the bass'. Thomas's *Tristan*[91] also reveals that the instrumental line lay lower than the song. Sources from North-western Europe refer at various times to special technique of accompaniment, whereby voice and fiddle moved in parallel fifths, in a strict organum. Chaucer, in the *Canterbury Tales*, shows us a jovial English parish clerk, who was wont to 'pleyen songes on a smal rubible; Ther-to he sang som tyme a lowde quynyble'.[92] This practice was still common in England during the sixteenth century; as John Skelton says:[93] 'They play on their fiddles and sing in fifts.'

However, the fiddler's role was not confined to playing solos and accompanying singers. Most literary and pictorial sources describe or show bowed instruments playing in consort with other instruments, and it is striking that purely instrumental ensembles, without the collaboration of singers, appear much more frequently than groups with solo singers, and that as a rule the instruments taking part are completely heterogenous with respect to sonority. Often ten or more types differing in character, compass, and timbre are united. A particularly clear example of this occurs in a description of the music played during the celebrations at Westminster in 1306,[94] where the following instrumentalists are listed: five

p. 40.   [88] R. Haas, *Aufführungspraxis der Musik* (Potsdam, 1931), p. 78, expresses the view that the song of troubadours and Minnesinger were accompanied by a bowed instrument playing in unison with the voice.   [89] Among others by K. Nef, 'Gesang und Instrumentenspiel bei den Troubadours', *Festschrift für Guido Adler* (Vienna, 1930), pp. 58ff.   [90] Giraldus Cambrensis, Opera VI, Descriptio, p. 189 (*Rerum Britannicarum medii aevi Scriptores*, XXI); cf. Marius Schneider, *Geschichte der Mehrstimmigkeit*, Vol. II (Berlin, 1935), p. 20f.   [91] He is referring to the vocal line in relation to the instrumental accompaniment: in this context the phrase reads: 'dulce la voiz, bas li tons'. Cf. A. W. Ambros, *Geschichte der Musik*, 3rd ed. (Leipzig, 1891), p. 260, Note 6.   [92] *The Works of Geoffrey Chaucer*, ed. A. W. Pollard (London, 1899), p. 46.   [93] *The Poetical Works of John Skelton*, Vol. II (London, 1843), p. 434a; cf. W. Bachmann, *Die Verbreitung des Quintierens*, p. 27; further examples may be found in W. Salmen, 'Bemerkungen zum mehrstimmigen Musizieren der Spielleute im Mittelalter', *Revue Belge de Musicologie* II (1957), p. 17ff.   [94] This source is quoted by E. H. Meyer in *Die Kammermusik Alt-Englands* (Leipzig, 1958), p. 61.

and twenty-two trumpeters, nine violists, eight chrottists, six men with tabors, three fiddlers, two organists, two men with psalteries, two bagpipers, a lutenist, a guitarist, a citola player, a drummer, and a glockenspieler. The effect of the common medieval practice of juxtaposing instruments dissimilar in sound, which led Arnold Schering to formulate his theory of split sound,[95] was so rich and colourful that definite standard types of scoring cannot be demonstrated. It would nevertheless be a mistake to conclude that 'instrumentation' was purely a matter of chance. A careful study of the sources suggests that specific instruments were selected or favoured, depending on the occasion and the nature of the music. There are, for example, several descriptions of funeral music,[96] for which chordophones were used almost exclusively, whereas festive or military events were marked by a preponderance of wind instruments.[97]

The diversity of techniques demanded by the individual instruments resulted in a 'heterophonic' ensemble, characterized by simultaneous variation and varied sonority (a 'multi-coloured unison'). 'Each instrument performs the same melody in the position and manner peculiar to itself – with variations and omissions.'[98] Evaluation of all the available medieval evidence (literary and iconographical) for mixed instrumental groups, shows a preponderance of bowed instruments, juxtaposed with other types of instrument in every conceivable assortment of sonorities.[99] A combination that recurs with remarkable frequency in the eleventh and twelfth centuries is that of bowed instrument and horn – two highly contrasted timbres.[100] In an eleventh-century illustration (Plate 27) which bears the legend *Consonancia – cuncta musica* the artist indicates the differences between these two instruments as regards the character of their musical expression, by adding neumes to his illustration. The rhythmically and melodically lively pattern of the notation by the side of the fiddler is contrasted with the stereotyped repeated notes of the horn-player. In this way, the audible contrast between the supple fiddle-melody and the shapeless, drone-like background provided by the horn is demonstrated.

References to homogeneous instrumental ensembles are much less common; but among types of instrumentation where contrasting timbre is dispensed with must be listed the consorts of bowed instruments mentioned from time to time by medieval scribes. According to Ottokar's verse chronicle,[101] King Manfred had in his service a string band of seventeen master fiddlers and numerous apprentices. In his autobiography,[102] Ulrich von Lichtenstein tells how he was accompanied on a journey by a company of fiddlers. Another Middle High German

[95] 'Historische und nationale Klangstile', *JP* 34 (1927), p. 34. [96] E. Deschamps, I, 245/46, and *Mystère de St. Quentin*, vv. 3529ff.; cf. F. Brücker, *Die Blasinstrumente in der altfranzösischen Literatur* (Dissertation, Giessen, 1926), p. 71f. [97] F. Brücker, op. cit., p. 62ff. [98] H. Besseler, *Die Musik des Mittelalters und der Renaissance* (Potsdam, 1931), p. 78. [99] The same conclusions are reached by Marius Schneider in *Die Ars nova des XIV. Jahrhunderts in Frankreich und Italien* (Wolfenbüttel-Berlin, 1931), p. 29; H. Hickmann, *Das Portativ* (Cassel, 1936), p. 203; D. Treder, *Die Musikinstrumente in den höfischen Epen*, p. 37. [100] For examples, on Plates 22–27, 30, and 31. [101] *Monumenta germanica hist*, *Reimchroniken* V, i, p. 5 ff. [102] See H. J. Moser, *Die Musikergenos-*

text[103] describes how 'sixty German fiddlers were heard playing' and in *Laurin*[104] we read that in the Queen's train there were 'many courtly fiddlers, playing in pairs'.

What did the music of one of these medieval 'string orchestras' sound like? It seems improbable that they played in strict unison. Surely improvisation played an important rôle here too. We have a somewhat clearer picture of the practice of small string groups of from two to six players, since these attracted more attention from both artists and writers in the Middle Ages. The following are only a few examples dealing with this particular form of 'scoring'. Jean de Condé's poem *Messe des oiseaux*[105] mentions that four 'viella' players performed an 'estampie nouviele'; such a fiddle quartet is illustrated in the Spanish Mozarabic manuscript Hh 58 in the Biblioteca Nacional, Madrid.[106] The *Wigalois*[107] contains a reference to a group of six fiddlers who seek to banish Count Adân's melancholy with their 'expert fingering' ('künsteclîchen griffen'). Around 1200, two Provençal jongleurs arrived with their fiddles at the Court of Boniface II of Monferrat, and performed an estampida as a duet.[108] Subsequently the Troubadour Raimbault de Vaqueiras wrote words to this melody, and the result was the well-known maying song, 'Kalenda maya.' In 1375 two German *menestrerii* appeared before the Duke of Savoy, playing 'violam et gigam';[109] while the Old French poem *Bueve de Hantone*[110] tells of two fiddlers whose playing delighted the Queen and Buevon. Sometimes these fiddlers played alternately, sometimes together. Since they had no written parts at that time, each player had to pay close attention so as to fit in with what the other was doing. Wirnt von Gravenberc[111] observes that minstrels took great pains 'lest one should overlook a single note of the other'. The *Bueve de Hantone*[112] implies that the same applied to an ensemble of harp and fiddle. The music described here opens with alternating solo passages for both instruments, with or without the voice; in conclusion, fiddle and harp combine in a marvellous duet.

So far as illustrations of these instruments permit conclusions about pitch and compass, they suggest that, in medieval instrumental ensemble, musicians played for the most part within the same compass, roughly corresponding to the middle register of the voice. From time to time this conclusion has been quoted in more recent literature in support of the theory of differentiated monody, of unity of range, and of the 'heterophonic' structure of medieval instrumental music.[113] This, however, ignores the evidence of high- and low-pitched instru-

senschaften im deutschen Mittelalter (Rostock, 1910), p. 18. [103] *Der Stricker; Daniel von dem blühenden Tal*, ed. G. Rosenhagen (Breslau, 1891), v. 8153. [104] A poem from *Das helden buch mit synen figuren* (Strasbourg, 1509), v. 1748. [105] A. Scheler, *Les dits et contes de Baudoin de Condé* (Brussels, 1866/67), III, 20. [106] Plate I. [107] *Wirnt von Gravenberc: Wigalois*, ed J. M. N. Kapteyn (Bonn, 1926), v. 7425 f. and 8479 f. [108] H. J. Moser, *Das Streichinstrumenspiel im Mittelalter*, p. 7; cf. also F. Ludwig in *Handbuch der Musikgeschichte*, ed. G. Adler (Frankfurt am Main, 1924), p. 159, and J. Handschin in *ZfMw* 12 (1929), p. 1. [109] S. Cordero di Pamparato: 'Emanuele Filiberto de Savoia protettore dei musici', *RMI* 34 (1927), p. 234. [110] Ed. A. Stimming (Dresden, 1914–20), vv. 12, 183 ff. [111] Cf. Note 107. [112] A. Stimming, op. cit., vv. 12069 ff.; cf. F. Dick, *Bezeichnungen für Saiten- und Schlaginstrumente*, p. 21 f. [113] H. Besseler, 'Spielfiguren in

ments playing together which therefore contradicts the notion of unison playing. However, examples of this type are relatively rare. In a miniature from the Codex 987 in the Library at Klosterneuburg,[114] three bowed rotes are represented of different sizes: descant and bass instruments and one of intermediate range. From the respective string-lengths, the difference in pitch between the smallest and largest of these three instruments would be at least two octaves. A further reference, this time in an Italian text from the Codex pal. parmense 286,[115] deals with a composition for *rebecchette*, *rubebe*, and *rubicone*, three types of *rubebe*, each with a different compass. These two pieces of evidence can only mean that the ensemble-playing described must have been a kind of organum – either playing in octaves in the style of parallel organum, or melody supported by sustained notes, or other, similar forms of improvised polyphony.

Within larger instrumental groups in medieval times, we have to distinguish between those instruments that carry the melody, and others which merely provide a drone. To these are added a variety of instruments – chiefly idiophones and membranophones – which were not specifically pitched, but generated noise-like sounds. A distinction is drawn between melodic and accompanying instruments in the English poem on the vision of Tundalus (*c.* 1400). Organ and harp, combined with a percussion instrument, produce 'trebull and mene, and burdowne', regarded by the author as an exquisite sound. Many other instruments, not mentioned by name, played 'a full sweet melody'. 'Trebull, mene, and burdowne' are here clearly opposed, as voices supporting and filling out the harmony, to the melody. Significantly, the accompaniment is executed by instruments suited to chordal and drone-playing. This late fourteenth-century source confirms that we should not think of ensemble-playing by a variety of instruments, as shown in medieval representations, as exclusively unison playing.

Every form of collective music-making presupposes a uniform scale system, and every form of instrumental ensemble presupposes a uniform pattern of tuning. We know from many contemporary sources the value placed by medieval musicians on well-tuned instruments.[116] Illustrations also show the act of tuning. One of the most revealing of these is a miniature in the Latin Psalter manuscript 11550, in the Bibliothèque Nationale, Paris, representing King David, with a lyre, in the company of four musicians with a horn with fingerholes, harp, fiddle, and syrinx. While horn and syrinx give the note, the strings on the harp and lyre are tightened with a tuning-key, and the fiddler checks the tuning of his instrument by plucking the strings with his fingers.[117]

Many medieval illustrations show a group of drone-instruments playing in consort; this implies uniform tuning of drone-strings or pipes. The assumption

der Instrumentalmusik', *Deutsches Jahrbuch der Musikwissenschaft* I (1957), pp. 12ff., esp. p. 24. [114] Plate 89. [115] Cf. A. Schering, *Studien zur Musikgeschichte der Frührenaissance* (Leipzig, 1914), p. 102. [116] Tuning of instruments is one of the things mentioned in Heinrich von dem Türlin's *Diu Crône*, ed. F. Scholl (Stuttgart, 1852), v. 22085, and in *Les Narbonnais, chanson de geste*, ed. H. Suchier (Paris, 1898), Vol. I, v. 7852. [117] This illustration is interpreted in detail by E. Buhle,

is confirmed by medieval sources, where they contain more detailed information concerning the pitch of the drones. G, d, or both are always used in the three tunings described by Jerome of Moravia, and the hurdy-gurdy's drone-strings are also known to have been tuned in this way. According to the treatise of Anonymus IV, the drone-pipes on the organ were also tuned to G. In this highly informative document, produced after 1272, the author refers among other things to an organum in which the tenor remains fixed on G and ends on the same note, 'like the organ drone' ('ut in burdone organorum'). We know, too, that in the fourteenth century the bagpipe sounded a drone of a fifth, g–d. As evidence of this, a three-part *virelai* from the first half of the fourteenth century may be cited. Where the text uses the word 'cornemuse', the music imitates the sound of a bagpipe. While the top voice with its monotonously repeated phrases within the compass of a fourth imitates bagpipe-melody, the two lower voices sound a fifth drone, g–d'.

Their tone-quality, and their effect on the listener

For the early periods of musical history, the ideals of sonority and conceptions of music of different peoples can only be inferred from the stage of development reached by their musical instruments.[118] To some extent this also applies to the Middle Ages. If we are to try and form some idea how the music of that time sounded, we must take account of organological research. Neither the surviving texts in notation, nor the writings of the theorists, shed any real light on the sound of medieval music or on how it was played. In this context the question of the quality of sound produced by the medieval fiddle – the numerically dominant and characteristic sonority in instrument music of that time – assumes particular significance. We have already[119] reached certain conclusions regarding the tone quality and compass of early bowed instruments, on the basis of morphology, construction, and playing technique, as revealed by iconographical evidence. At this point, therefore, we can confine ourselves to an assessment of contemporary literary sources.

Among the cultured music theorists of the East, bowed instruments were sometimes regarded with disapproval – initially at least – on account of their thin, unattractive tone.[120] Al-Fārābī[121] insists that the volume of sound produced on the *rabab* was less than that obtainable on other instruments because of its

---

Die musikalischen Instrumente, p. 25, Note 1, and by H. Besseler, 'Spielfiguren in der Instrumentalmusik', *Deutsches Jahrbuch der Musikwissenschaft* I (1957), p. 24.   [118] Instruments did not always measure up to the musician's ideal or to the requirements of the music. 'Often developments in instrument-making did not keep pace with the contents of the music. Conversely the structural development of new instruments can also be in advance of the progress of musical style', E. H. Meyer, *Musik im Zeitgeschehen* (Berlin, 1952), p. 75.   [119] Chapter III.   [120] Cf. p. 55 f.   [121] R. d'Erlanger, *La Musique Arabe*, Vol. I (Paris, 1930), p. 285.

structure. In essence, however, the rough, nasal, forced tone of the *rabāb* corresponded to the Oriental ideal of the singing voice. In Europe, on the other hand, the sound of Asiatic bowed instruments was considered unpleasing. In the *Newe Chronika Türkischer Nation*, Hans Lewenklaw von Amelbeurn[122] describes a festive procession to mark the reception of a delegation in 1584: 'First came . . . three Zingani or gypsies, mistaken by some for Egyptians and by others for Arabs, dressed in the Turkish fashion. The middle one of the three was striking a lute, while each of the two others played on a little fiddle [Geige], which gave such a sharp, disagreeable sound . . .' The same verdict of European writers on the tone quality of Oriental bowed instruments is already voiced in a thirteenth-century source. The Spanish Arch-Priest Hita[123] speaks of the 'screeching' *rebab* (rabé gritador), contrasting it with the 'vihuela de arco' which produces 'dulces debayladas, voces dulces, sobrosas, claras et bien puntadas'. The Old French tale *Bellefoière*[124] likewise refers to the 'hoarse' rebec played by the cowherds. It is clear from these examples that already in medieval times obvious differences in sonority existed between Asiatic and European bowed instruments.

By the eleventh and twelfth centuries, bowed chordophones in Europe had already developed further, and their tone quality had been greatly improved.[125] The sources are unanimous in praising the beauty of medieval fiddle-tone. In the *Nibelungenlied* we read:[126] 'Volker the bold . . . makes sweet music on his fiddle.' Other Middle High German texts[127] refer to a 'welsche fidel', played by touching its 'susse sît', and to the 'sueze symphonie'. In his *Ethics*,[128] Albertus Magnus describes the agreeableness (suavitas) of the sound of the fiddle which the fiddler's performance leaves with the listener. Caesarius von Heisterbach, in a passage from his *Dialogus Miraculorum*, tells how a *joculator* rouses a sleeper with the sweet sound (dulcedine) of his fiddle;[129] and there are similar references in Old French literature. Gautier de Coinci[130] refers to the beauty of the fiddle's tone, and in the *Roman de la Rose* it is described as bright, clear, and distinct. Konrad von Megenberg[131] advanced the theory that the sound of the instrument was affected by changes in the weather: when the air is damp the organ and fiddle sound less sweetly than when the weather is fine'. By comparison with our modern bowed instruments, the volume of tone obtainable on the medieval fiddle was decidedly smaller, and the sound was muted.[132] It was customary in the Middle Ages to classify instruments according to whether they were loud (*haut*) or soft (*bas*); and the bowed instruments were invariably listed as *bas*.[133]

[122] See W. Friedrich, *Die älteste türkische Beschreibung*, p. 13.   [123] Cf. *MGG*, article 'Hita'.   [124] See F. Dick, *Bezeichnungen für Saiten- und Schlaginstrumente*, p. 95.   [125] Cf. pp. 61–64 of this book. [126] Ed. K. Bartsch, v. 1705.   [127] H. Georg, 2437, and Heinrich von dem Türlin, *Diu Crône*, ed. F. Scholl (Stuttgart, 1852), v. 22094.   [128] Albertus Magnus, *Ethic*, ed. Borgnet, Vol. VII, 6, 1, 6, p. 404b. [129] *Caesarii Heisterbacensis Monachi Dialogus Miraculorum*, ed. J. Stange (Cologne, Bonn, Brussels, 1856), p. 358.   [130] Ed. G. Servois (Paris, 1893), v. 2339.   [131] K. von Megenberg, *Buch der Natur* (14th century); ed. by F. Pfeiffer (Stuttgart, 1861), p. 16, line 1 ff.   [132] Cf. above, p. 91   [133] E. A. Bowles, 'Haut and bas', *Musica disciplina* VIII (1954), pp. 115 ff.

It is obvious from the illustrations that medieval bowed instruments varied considerably in size, and hence in compass. Some are approximately the same length as the modern double bass,[134] while others are smaller than our violins. In general, however, the compass of bowed instruments roughly corresponded to that of the human singing voice. The fiddle, the compass of which approximated to that of our viola, was equivalent to the male voice in pitch and range and was generally used to accompany male singers. Its lowest string was tuned to G and its top string to g'. The rebec, on the other hand, had a compass more like that of the female voice, and according to Jerome of Moravia[135] was tuned c' g'; while in a poem by Aymerie de Peyrac[136] we find the phrase: 'Some bowed the rebec as if imitating a woman's voice'. The Spanish Archpriest Hita[137] also refers to the rebec (rabé) 'con sua alta nota'. It seems clear that the fiddler preferred the upper register of the instrument, using the lower strings mainly as a drone-accompaniment. 'Many fiddlers were grateful that I pitched the melody so high', says Ulrich von Lichtenstein in his autobiography[138] – and elsewhere in the same work we find:[139] 'Two fiddlers rode behind, and kept my spirits up by playing a traveller's song at high pitch, which pleased me greatly'.

There are repeated allusions in medieval literature to the cheering and exhilarating effect of fiddle-music on the listener, and the fiddle itself is described as a merry instrument (*Vidula jocosa*),[140] which found especial favour with the fair sex: 'The ladies refused to be entertained either with the drum or the busine: they would hear nothing but fiddles, harps, rotes and other sweet sounding instruments.'[141] Albertus Magnus[142] interprets the effect of fiddle-music in the light of Greek conceptions of ethos, claiming that 'certain pleasures, such as singing, fiddling (viellatoria), dancing and play-acting, are essential to the proper government of the state'. The sound of the fiddle was said to possess magic power, and a certain healing quality. According to the Count of Anjou[143] fiddle-music made the sick forget their misery and pain ('pour esbatre ces genz malades'). In his essay *De morborum cognitione et curatione*, Constantinus Africanus,[144] who lived in the eleventh century, recommended the healing powers of such instruments as glockenspiel, fiddle, and rote; and a poem by Ulrich von Eschenbach[145] also suggests that the sound of the fiddle is 'good for the health'. It was held

---

[134] See Plate 1. [135] Cserba, op. cit., p. 289. [136] Grillet, op. cit., p. 132; J. Rühlmann, *Die Geschichte der Bogeninstrumente*, p. 47, and M. Gerbert. *De cantu et musica sacra*, Vol. II, pp. 153 ff. [137] Cf. *MGG*, article 'Hita'. [138] *Ulrich von Lichtenstein*, ed. Lachmann (Berlin, 1841), 165, 4. [139] Op. cit., 422, 18. [140] This description is in the *Medulla Grammatica Coloribus Rhetoricis* by Galfridus de Vim Salor (*c.* 1200): 'Cymbala praeclara, concors symphonia dulcis, fistulae, somnifera cythara, vitulaeque jocosae.' Cf. K. Schlesinger: *The Precursors of the Violin Family*, p. 427 f. [141] *Tinturel*, v. 1807; see H. J. Moser, *Geschichte der deutschen Musik* (Berlin, 1930), p. 146. [142] Albertus Magnus, *Ethic* (ed. Borgnet, Vol. VII), 1, 3, 1, p. 30 b. [143] *Altfranzösische Romanzen und Pastourellen*, ed. K. Bartsch (Leipzig, 1870), XIX, p. 31; Johannes de Grocheo also takes the view that folk music provides an excellent means for distracting the attention of the poor and the wretched from their dismal situation. [144] Book I, p. 14. [145] See H. J. Moser, *Das Streichinstrumentenspiel*

that its sound not only comforted, but served to express grief and pain.[146] Furthermore, the fiddle was used to lull people to sleep.[147] The fiddle also appeared frequently in illustrations of the Dance of Death.[148] In this magical rôle ascribed to the fiddle are traces of pagan associations which would account for the earlier repudiation of musical instruments by the Church.

im Mittelalter, p. 12.   [146] The relevant passage from *La Belle Dame sans Merci* runs as follows: 'Si m'en tient plus doulloureux chacune vielle son deul plaint' (*Rom.* XXXIV, p. 569, vv. 583/4). [147] In Coquillart's *Blason des Dames* we find: 'Qui s'endort au son du rebec'; see F. Dick, *Bezeichnungen für Saiten- und Schlaginstrumente*, p. 94.   [148] S. Cosacchi, 'Musikinstrumente im mittelalterlichen Totentanz', *Mf* VIII (1955), pp. 11 ff.

V

CONCLUDING SUMMARY

The development of bowing should not be regarded as a fundamentally instrumental phenomenon; in essence it was a tonal one. We have to do, not with the invention of new species or varieties of instruments, but with the opening up of new regions of musical expression. The use of the bow must at the outset have been brought about by a number of musical factors. The most important of these were the quest for new sonorities which would match contemporary ideals of timbre and performance; the desire for an unbroken melodic line, which would bring instrumental music closer to vocal music; and above all the trend towards playing in 'organum' style, with parts moving in parallel and an accompanying drone. Thus the origins of bowing should also be considered in the context of the birth and early stages of polyphony.

The crucial issue is the way in which the sound is produced, and, related to this, the performer's technique. Bowing keeps the string in a permanent state of oscillation, producing a continuous sound: moreover, several or even all the strings on chordophones adapted to this style of playing can be made to sound simultaneously. Thus it was perhaps a new application of techniques already widespread in folk music; conversely some plectrum techniques, and the use of the friction stick to rub the strings, must also be considered as early forms of bowing. From such practices as these the bow may have evolved quite independently in different places.

The origins of bowing

The first clear literary and artistic references to the bow as a means of drawing sound from stringed instruments occur at the beginning of the tenth century. At that time the area within which bowing was practised corresponded roughly to the territories of the Islamic and Byzantine Empires. Outside these territories there is no evidence that any stringed instruments were played with the bow before A.D. 1000, either in Europe or in Eastern Asia: the theories that the bow originated in Northern Europe or India have not been confirmed by recent research. Although bowed stringed instruments appear with remarkable frequency in tenth-century Byzantine illuminations, there are many indications that bowing developed somewhere in Central Asia – in Khwārizm, in Sogdian Transoxiana, and in Khurāsān. The earliest entirely incontrovertible pictorial evidence for the use of the bow or friction stick comes in fact from Central Asia in the ninth century.

The motivation for the appearance and early development of bowing sprang from the appreciation by the peoples of the Near East and Central Asia, in medieval times, of continuity of sound. Contemporary Arab scholars imply that the pleasure of listening to vocal music was by no means unalloyed, since the melodic line was constantly interrupted by pauses for breath. The remedy was clearly to design musical instruments which could join the notes together and provide a continuous melodic line. This demand was met by musical automata, to which many Arabic sources refer, by the bagpipe, by the organ, and by the various types of bowed instrument. The musical potential of bowed instruments closely matched the essential character of oriental musical performance, based as it was on vocal monody, a high degree of skill in improvisation, a melodic style built up of small intervals, a flowing, richly ornamented line, a continuous accompanying drone, and an assimilation of instrumental music to the vocal idiom. Whereas in medieval times other instruments were restricted to single notes or series of notes – the wind instruments by their natural harmonic series or the distance between their holes, the harps by the tuning of their strings, and the lutes by the spacing of their frets – bowing allowed the player to produce slides and slurs, as well as every conceivable intermediate note within the natural compass of the instrument. He was thus able to follow the vocal line in all its melodic intricacies.

In the Middle Ages, nevertheless, cultured Arab musicians and theoreticians regarded bowed instruments with some disparagement because of their thin and rather unattractive tone, and pride of place in the instrumental hierarchy was still reserved for the plucked instruments, with their clear and more precise sound. Bowed instruments continued to be associated predominantly with folk music in this territory, and to begin with only rarely appeared in the context of court music.

By the eleventh century, the bow had indubitably penetrated into Europe by way of Arab Spain and Byzantium. Once there, it was applied to native instruments of the fiddle and lyre family, which, the evidence suggests, had previously been played by plucking their strings. The earliest known evidence pointing to the use of the bow in the West is found in Northern Spanish and Catalan miniatures dating from the first half of the eleventh century. By 1100, bowing had spread over the whole of Western Europe. Pictorial evidence reveals that it had penetrated to Northern Spain, Southern France, Italy, Hainault, the Rhineland, and Southern England. (Not until the thirteenth century is there any sign that the bow was used in Eastern Asia and India.) With the proliferation of bowed instruments in Europe, instrumental music entered a new phase in its history. Playing became increasingly cantabile in character, so that, towards the end of the Middle Ages, musical instruments could frequently be substituted for the human voice. With the organ, bowed instruments played a significant role in the making of European polyphony. Medieval writers on music tell us that bourdon and the parallel movement of parts, the two main principles of early polyphonic vocal music, were borrowed from instrumental playing.

Types of bowed instruments

In the Middle Ages, a name was never applied exclusively to any one type of instrument, but was used to describe different instruments if these had a common function, use, or technique. (The reverse was also true, and one and the same instrument might be designated by a number of terms.) Thus in the eleventh and twelfth centuries the names applied to bowed instruments might also be used for plucked instruments. Again, the word 'fidula' occurs repeatedly in early medieval texts, but until the turn of the millennium does not refer to a bowed instrument.

The first bowed instruments show a bewildering multiplicity of styles, both in the basic principles of construction and in the details of their manufacture. To begin with there are no visible differences between the structure of bowed and plucked instruments: these emerge at a later date, probably in Europe. The earliest bowed instruments, in particular those of Byzantium, frequently display the typical characteristics of the lute; strings attached to a frontal string-holder and arranged in fan-formation, and lateral pegs. They also sometimes have a circular sound-hole in the middle of the sounding-board, which increased the resonance of the strings and was proper to plucked instruments.

Striking divergences appear between the bowed instruments of regions influenced by Arab or Byzantine culture, and those of Central and Northern Europe. In the West, the fiddle and its early bowed relations nearly always had end-pins and sagittal pegs. In the eleventh and twelfth centuries, regional European types emerge: slender, pear-shaped fiddles in Western Europe, spade-shaped bowed instruments in the South, and, in Central Europe, instruments with an almost round body. The figure-of-eight fiddle appears from the twelfth century onward, particularly in Western Europe. The 'waisting' of this instrument was not intended to give the bow greater freedom of action: incurving sides are a characteristic of any instrument with a double resonator. There is little point in classifying medieval chordophones according to whether or not they were ribbed, since there were as yet no glued ribs in the modern sense. In early instruments the resonating chamber was hollowed out of a single block of wood, either convex or box-shaped, and then covered over with a flat sounding-board. Spruce was considered particularly suitable for the sounding-board of the resonator, which was given a coat of lacquer. The evidence suggests that instrument-making had already reached an advanced level, and was mainly in the hands of the players themselves.

Strings

In medieval Europe bowed instruments were almost invariably strung with gut strings, and the materials used in the East – silk, horsehair, metal, and bast – were rarely employed. In the earliest representations of oriental bowed instruments the number of strings varies from one to six; but in the eleventh and twelfth centuries the western fiddle nearly always had three, and few medieval examples have four strings. In the thirteenth century it became standard European practice to use five strings, except on the pear-shaped fiddles, usually one-stringed, which appear chiefly in Central Europe during the twelfth and thirteenth centuries.

Bows

Initially, the bow took a great variety of shapes, some of them extreme. This experimental period, when both instruments and bow were subject to constant change in an effort to discover what size they ought to be and how best they might be made, is a sure sign that bowing was still in its infancy. The different shapes of bow illustrated in medieval sources cannot accordingly be assigned to specific types of instrument, nor may they be used to arrange illustration in any chronological order. Nor is the hypothesis that the length and shape of the bow was determined by the position in which the instrument was played valid in the early stages of bowing. Not until late in the Middle Ages did the multiplicity of shapes and sizes eventually resolve into one or two standard types of bow – its subsequent evolution is marked by a gradual flattening, with the stick running parallel to the hair, and by the introduction of various forms of nut.

As a rule, the medieval bow was strung with horsehair, though this was appreciably weaker than the hair on modern bows, and consequently did not have as firm a grip on the strings. The hair was rubbed with a kind of colophony (rosin) made from the resin of the incense tree and from spruce resin. The bow was held in the closed fist, in a grip which enabled the player to make a strong stroke and press harder on the strings, but which prevented a flexible wrist-action and any variation between one stroke and the next. A distinction must be drawn between the middle and end grip in bowing. The first was used more in conjunction with the strongly-arched round bow so widespread in the East. The second, which gave some stability to the bowing surface – indispensable where multistringed instruments are concerned – gradually established itself throughout Europe, where the flat bow predominated. The bow was applied to the strings roughly in the middle or the first third of its length, presumably producing, on medieval fiddles, a weak, veiled sound.

How instruments were held

The position of the instrument in performance, the fingering technique, and the bowing action, are to some extent conditioned by the structure, size, and proportions of the instruments concerned. In the East bowed instruments were almost invariably held perpendicular in front of the player's body and supported on the knee or on the floor. In medieval Europe, however, this position was restricted to waisted instruments, while pear-shaped or elliptical fiddles were either laid against the body or held out to one side. Most illustrations show the fiddle slanting steeply against the player's upper body. This position, which limits the freedom of the fingering hand, and burdens it with the double task of supporting the instrument and stopping the strings, is best suited to the production of sustained accompanying notes. However, similar practices in present-day folk music reveal that even in this position rapid passages may be achieved. During the thirteenth and fourteenth centuries, the fiddle is shown in an oblique, horizontal position across the player's body, with the bowed surface of the strings almost vertical. This presupposes the existence of a sling of some kind by which the instrument was hung round the player's neck. The modern outward position, so well adapted to executing a quick-moving melodic line, was seldom used for bowed instruments in the Middle Ages.

Then, as now, the bowed instrument was nearly always held in the left hand and the bow in the right, so that the bowing fell to the lot of the more efficient arm. Where the instrument was slanted upwards or sideways, the bow was held in the overhand grip; the underhand grip was reserved for the *a gamba* position, though even then the overhand grip was frequently used with very curved bows. Exceptionally, where on very steeply slanted instruments the lie of the strings was almost vertical, the underhand grip might be substituted.

Tunings

The earliest information we have on tuning dates from the first half of the tenth century, and refers to two-stringed instruments from Central Asia. The two strings were normally tuned to an augmented second, but might be a major third, augmented fourth, or diminished fifth apart. Around the turn of the millennium it became customary to tune the strings on bowed instruments in perfect fourths or fifths. This method, recommended by al-Fārābī, was designed to make it easier for the *rabāb* to play in consort with the lute and similar plucked instruments, which in early medieval times were tuned in fourths. The additional strings, on instruments with three or more, were not originally intended to extend the compass. Instead the strings were arranged in courses, and doubled at the unison or octave. Sets of strings in courses avoided any interruption in the music if a string happened to break, while at the same time the sound was strengthened. In addition, players used the effects of beats, with slightly 'out-of-tune' notes, in an effort to sharpen the sound. The tuning of the medieval multi-stringed fiddle was generally determined by the harmony created when all the strings sounded together, the basic pattern being key-note – fifth – octave. The illustrations reveal that the performer did not stop the strings with the ball of the finger-tip, but with the inner edge of the first and second joints. This meant that often several strings might be stopped by the same finger simultaneously. Where the normal key-note – fifth – octave tuning obtained, this fingering technique resulted in a broadening of the sound in the style of parallel organum or an organ mixture.

A characteristic feature of early bowing is a constant accompaniment of drone-strings, which provide a fixed background of sound to the melody being played on the same instrument. In view of the structure of contemporary instruments, the bow inevitably brought several or even all the strings into play at one time. Thus the sonic principles of the fiddle and hurdy-gurdy were originally the same. It was only as bowing progressed that the individual strings gradually assumed an independent musical rôle and the bow began to be used at different angles. At the outset the drone-strings and those carrying the melody did not differ a great deal. When the melody moved to a string hitherto sounding as a drone, the first string, previously stopped, took its turn to provide a drone. The non-stop sound of the fiddle drone might thus move from string to string as the circumstances demanded, running above or below the melodic line, or even through the middle of it.

There is no evidence that 'playing in positions', as it is known in modern violin technique, was practised in those early days. Obviously the compass of medieval bowed instruments was not normally fully exploited in either the high or the low notes. Besides the 'mixture tuning' (G d g d' g'), a tuning pattern (G G d c' c') is known to have been used which, on the fiddle, would not have given a consecutive scale in the first position. Clearly only the C string, doubled at the unison, was used in this case to carry the melody, with the others providing a bourdon accompaniment. The tunings indicated are identical as regards the pitch of the drone strings, which were always tuned to G and D. In the Middle Ages it was also common practice to tune the drones on the organ, bagpipe, hurdy-gurdy, and other bourdon instruments to G and D, so that it was quite possible for a group of such instruments to play together. Ensembles of this kind feature in many illustrations. Among the bowed chordophones, as among the different types of bagpipe, were some instruments which functioned exclusively as drones, while others were purely for the playing of melodies. In ensemble playing, each type complemented the other. Bowing without the continuous drone – that is to say in which the bow at times touched only stopped strings – represents a more sophisticated stage in technique by comparison with the earlier style of playing. From early in the twelfth century, however, a change may be traced in Western bowing technique. Some of the strings ran off to one side of the fingerboard, and, since their pitch could not be altered by stopping, functioned exclusively as drones. These drone strings no longer sounded continuously against the notes of the melody, but only when melody and drone formed a concordant relationship.

The hurdy-gurdy

Tenth-century Persian-Arabic sources contain references to instruments which apparently correspond to the hurdy-gurdy. The earliest undoubted illustrations of the hurdy-gurdy occur on Spanish portal sculptures dating from the first part of the twelfth century. By the second half of the same century the instrument was widely known throughout Western Europe, and reached the peak of its development and social prestige towards 1200, at the time of the Notre-Dame organum. The musical principles on which it was based – bourdon or parallel movement of parts in the style of organum, in fourths or fifths – corresponded to the essential nature of early European polyphony. Structurally, the hurdy-gurdy was an attempt to simplify the whole procedure of bowing, by avoiding the hiatus of bow changes, providing a continuity of sound, mechanizing the stopping of strings, and laying down an exactly calculated scale of notes. The hurdy-gurdy's crank wheel inevitably set all the strings vibrating simultaneously. There could be no modification in its playing technique, such as can be observed in the development of the bow. In consequence, it played a useful role in the sphere of art music only so long as European polyphony was at that stage of development.

In the twelfth century, hurdy-gurdies were large, two-man instruments with rotary keys and a resonator with waisted or incurving sides. The unwieldy key-mechanism of the early hurdy-gurdies, similar to the organ-mechanism of the time, with its individual dampers, was adequate only for a slow-moving melodic line or for long, drone-like supporting notes. From the thirteenth century, however, it was appreciably smaller in appearance, and with its practical piano-key stops it could be played by only one man. (Like the organ, which during the same period evolved into a handy one-man instrument, the portative.) These instruments with their improved mechanism combined two diametrically opposite musical elements – a quick, lively melodic line and a fixed bourdon. The number of keys shown on illustrated instruments implies that in the twelfth and thirteenth centuries the hurdy-gurdy's melodic repertoire, based on the diatonic scale, could only rarely have included tunes with a compass exceeding the octave.

The bowed rote

The bowed rote, far from representing the initial stage in the evolution of bowing, must be regarded as the final stage in the history of the European lyre. The earliest illustrations of this instrument, dating from the first part of the eleventh century, are from South-Western and Central Europe, where the bow was presumably imported by way of Spain and Byzantium. Unlike the classical lyre, the medieval instrument had its curving yoke and resonator made in a single piece. A further point of dissimilarity lies in the stringing. In the medieval lyre, the strings are secured to pegs protruding from the front or back of the peg-box. Played with the bow, the lyre's similarity to the fiddle in structure and technique becomes increasingly evident. The bowed lyre had fewer strings than its plucked version – in general not more than three or four – and the way it was tuned and held in performance also corresponded to that of the medieval fiddle. All the strings, which were stopped in harmonics, came under the bow simultaneously and were set in motion by it, since all lay at the same height above the broad, flat soundboard. The unstopped strings that had no part in the melody gave out a continuous accompanying bourdon.

Social standing and conditions of performance

As the bow became established in Europe, the social function and status enjoyed by bowing underwent a distinct change. In the East, bowed instruments were from the outset relegated to the sphere of folk music: but in medieval Europe their use was largely restricted to the members of the feudal aristocracy and to the minstrels. The fiddle was the favourite musical instrument of courtly society; and its high social standing is also reflected in the esteem it commanded among medieval writers on music. From the thirteenth century, bowed instruments were used in church music: but it is not until towards the end of the Middle Ages that vernacular literature offers any evidence that bowed instruments were on occasions also played by country folk, and even then they used nothing more sophisticated than the rebec, the pear-shaped giga, and the hurdy-gurdy. It is, however, quite possible that there were earlier examples of bowing in the world of medieval folk music as yet undocumented.

The fiddle ranked as the most versatile and promising of all the instruments then known. Anything could be played on it; and it was used on every concei-vable occasion, not only indoors but frequently in open-air performances. Its universal applicability sprang from its wide compass and its advanced technique, as well as from the cantabile quality of its melodic line. When accompanying vocal solos, bowed instruments were as a rule used only to provide the intro-duction, bridge-passages, and postludes. This helped the singer to pitch his song and in addition gave him the opportunity to rest his voice from time to time. Thus voice and instrument alternated with one another, a practice known to have been adopted in both Europe and the East in the period from the tenth to the thirteenth centuries. Medieval sources also refer to simultaneous performances by the voice and accompanying fiddle, which made considerably greater demands on the skill of the participants. The form taken by the accompaniment varied according to the nature of the vocal line and the player's own virtuosity; but the general rule seems to have been that a spirited vocal performance was backed by long supporting notes, whereas sustained cantilenas would be accompanied by rich ornamental passage-work in the fiddle part.

Much evidence shows medieval bowed instruments playing in ensembles with other instruments of widely varying tonal colour. Though it is impossible to see any specific pattern in the distribution of instruments within these ensembles, the composition of the group was clearly not always decided by chance alone, but was a matter of some consideration. Certain instruments would be selected as being more in keeping with a certain occasion and with the nature of the performance. Mention is also made from time to time in medieval sources of groups of tonally homogeneous instruments (string orchestras of up to sixty players). Here there was no attempt to achieve contrasts in timbre. The larger instrumental ensembles generally played within a compass which roughly corresponded to the middle register of the human voice. Some illustrations, which are presumably of music played in parts, show high and low-pitched instruments performing together. Ensemble playing implies a standardization of the scale system and a uniform tuning of the instruments, their drone-pipes and drone-strings.

THE BORDERLINE BETWEEN
PLUCKING AND BOWING

The problem of systematic classification

The expansion of organological studies to embrace the historical development of individual instruments and groups of instruments, including those from
outside Europe, has made it steadily more difficult to achieve a rational and
systematic classification of the entire range of instruments. Principles which emerge
in the classification of instruments of a particular period, area, or ethnic group,
frequently break down when applied to instruments of all races and times. The
classification of chordophones is a particularly intricate problem of this sort.

Erich Maria von Hornbostel, Curt Sachs, and André Schaeffner[1] had already
cast serious doubts on the old classification, used in earlier works, based on the
manner of excitation – on whether the strings were plucked, beaten, or bowed.
They discarded this system since a majority of chordophones appear as plucked,
beaten, *and* bowed in the course of their development,[2] without having undergone significant structural modification. In view of this, the classification of
chordophones adopted by Hornbostel and Sachs is no longer related to the method of playing. Instead it distinguishes on constructional grounds between
simple and compound chordophones, with appropriate sub-divisions. Karl
Geiringer has elaborated this,[3] laying greater emphasis, as a distinguishing
characteristic, on the means whereby the strings are attached, and he further
discriminates between instruments with lateral and those with sagittal pegs.

The defects of such a classification, which does not advance beyond purely
external constructional criteria, were already pointed out by Dräger in his *Systematik der Musikinstrumente*: 'The technique of playing is of primary importance,
for only through it does the instrument as played become the basis of consideration ... the whole *raison d'être* of an instrument is the production of sound.'[4]
The systematization of chordophones on purely morphological grounds has

---

[1] E. M. von Hornbostel and C. Sachs, 'Systematik der Musikinstrumente', *ZfE*, 46th Year
(Berlin, 1914), p. 556; A. Schaeffner, 'D'une nouvelle classification méthodique des instruments
de musique, *RM* XIII, Vol. II (1932), pp. 215 ff.; by the same author: 'Note sur la filiation des
instruments à cordes', *Mélanges de Musicologie offerts à M. Lionel de La Laurencie* (Paris, 1933).
T. Norlind, 'Musikinstrumentensystematik', *STMf* XIV (Stockholm, 1932), pp. 95 ff., also
adopts the basic principles of the Hornbostel-Sachs system. [2] Thus fiddle, lyre, guitar, and many
other chordophones would belong to the category of plucked as well as bowed instruments.
[3] K. Geiringer, *Die Flankenwirbelinstrumente in der bildenden Kunst*, Introduction, p. VII. [4] H.-H.

been largely rejected in more recent works, and that part of the Hornbostel-Sachs classification which relates to stringed instruments has scarcely ever been adopted.[5]

Methods transitional between plucking and bowing

Despite its obvious shortcomings, al-Fārābī's tenth-century subdivision into plucked, beaten, or bowed stringed instruments is also widely used today.[6] It has proved suitable for present-day European instruments, although here, too, overlapping occurs. As soon as the historical development of the instruments and the ethnological evidence are considered, however, the boundary between plucking and bowing becomes more and more indistinct or even totally absent. Various intermediate methods of exciting the strings combine the two opposing techniques. They are characterized by the use of the plucking stick, the beater, and the friction stick.

Instruments of the extensive lute family are comparatively rarely plucked with the fingers. As a rule a short plectrum is used, or a long plucking-stick, with which the player usually strums on all the strings at once. With a brisk movement the player draws the end of the stick or plectrum over the strings, sounding them one after another in rapid succession. The beater, on the other hand, which is still used today on instruments of very varied types, including the African musical bow,[7] the French *tambourin de Béarn*,[8] and the Hungarian *gardon*,[9] frequently excites all the strings simultaneously. Sometimes the player scrapes the stick across at right angles to the run of the strings, as well as beating them, to prolong the sound, thus combining the functions of beater and friction stick. The simplest method of exciting idiophones by friction is found on the South Sea Island of New Ireland.[10] There the *nunut* player paints his hands with rosin

Dräger, *Prinzip einer Systematik*, p. 12.   [5] The following works classify chordophones according to whether they are plucked, struck, or bowed: G. Montandon: 'La Généalogie des instruments de musique et les cycles de civilisation', *Archives suisses d'Anthropologie generale* III, fasc. I (Geneva, 1919); W. Heinitz, 'Instrumentenkunde', *Handbuch der Musikwissenschaft*, ed. E. Bücken (Potsdam, 1929); G. Kinsky, *Heyer-Katalog*; K. Nef, *Geschichte unserer Musikinstrumente*; H. Schultz, *Instrumentenkunde*; E. Valentin, *Handbuch der Musikinstrumentenkunde* (Regensburg, 1954); N. Bessaraboff, *Ancient European Musical Instruments*; cf. also J. L. Jenkins: 'A New System of Classifying Musical Instruments used in the USSR', *GSJ* XIII (1960), p. 95 f.   [6] Al-Fārābī's catalogue of musical instruments is discussed in E. A. Beichert's *Die Wissenschaft der Musik*, p. 35; a similar system is also used by Gerson *c.* 1413: 'Cantum cum pulsu fit tripliciter: aut in rotatu ut in symphonia: aut retractu, sicut in viella aut rebella: sive cum impulsu vel impulsivo quodam tractu cum unguibus vel plectro, cum virgula, ut in cithara et guiterna, lituo psalterio quoque et tympano, atque campanulis...' See Gerson, *Opera omnia*, ed. L. Ellies du Pin, Vol. III, Part II, p. 678 (Antwerp, 1706).   [7] P. R. Kirby, *The Musical Instruments of the Native Races of South Africa* (London, 1934), pp. 193 ff.   [8] T. Norlind, *Systematik der Saiteninstrumente* I, p. 167 f.   [9] O. Dincsér, *Zwei Musikinstrumente*, p. 86.   [10] A. Schaeffner, *Origine*, p. 223 f.

and rubs them over the instrument. The Kirghiz use the same method of sound production when playing their favourite instrument, the fiddle-shaped *komuz*, the tonal palette of which ranges from pizzicato and plucked tremolo to bowing. When using the *komuz* as a plucked instrument, the player rubs the flat of his hand across the strings[11] at certain points during his performance, to obtain a special effect, contrasting with the tremolo. In East Africa,[12] players sometimes use a moistened reed or a palm rib to stroke the strings, while Indian musicians[13] use a long feather. The friction stick is particularly widespread, being used among others by various African peoples and by the Colombian Motilón.[14]

In Northern China, especially in Hopei Province, the strings of the board-zither, *ya-chêng*, are rubbed either with a stem of *kao-liang* (millet), or with a piece of bamboo or wood.[15] To increase the grip of the stick on the strings, and so to increase friction, it is roughened, notched, moistened, or rubbed with rosin, or even strung with horse-hair. This completes the transition to the bow. An interesting link in the chain of plectrum – friction stick – bow, is found in Central Asia, among Sarts, Kirghiz, tribes of the Altai, and Yakuts. There a wooden stick is used to create friction on fiddle-type chordophones, but from it is suspended a loose hank of horsehair, which the musician pulls taut at will while playing.[16] The example of the notched and roughened friction stick demonstrates how the techniques of plucking and bowing merge almost imperceptibly one into the other.[17] As with a plectrum playing tremolando, each notch in a notched stick catches a string and pulls it sharply sideways. Thus the string is excited by single jerking movements at a frequency determined by the distance between the notches. The movement involved is similar to a bowing action, but the technique used to vibrate the strings is essentially that of plucking. The roughened friction stick, however, like the bow, sets up a continuous oscillation: the string clings to the stick or horsehair, moves with it slightly to the side, springs back, and is immediately caught up again. This rapid alternation between being pulled and slipping free enables bowed instruments to produce continuous sound, with prolonged and connected notes; whereas plucked or struck instruments inevitably fragment the melodic line into a series of single notes or 'notes prolonged by resonance'.[18]

As with the ethnological material cited, historical studies also show the transition from plucking to bowing. They reveal the close relationship between

[11] V. Vinogradov, *Kirgizskaja narodnaja muzyka* (Frunze, 1958), p. 173.   [12] C. Sachs, *Geist und Werden*, p. 186.   [13] C. Engel, *Researches*, p. 5.   [14] C. Sachs, *Geist und Werden*, p. 87.   [15] *Muzykal'nye instrumenty kitaja* (Moscow, 1958), p. 22 f., Russian translation from the Chinese, edited by I. Z. Alender.   [16] Cf. pp. 98–99.   [17] The question raised by G. Kinsky (*Heyer-Katalog*, Vol. II, p. 309) as to 'whether the bow evolved from the plectrum used on lute instruments, or whether it originated from the wooden or metal rubbing sticks used for certain self-sounding friction instruments and indeed still known to exist to-day among some exotic races', has been answered in various ways. C. Engel, *Researches*, p. 5, supports the theory that the bow evolved gradually from the plectrum; while F. Behn states firmly that 'no bow can possibly emerge from the plectrum; each has a totally different function'.   [18] H. Schultz, *Instrumentenkunde*, p. 82.

10*

performing techniques regarded nowadays as basically different and opposed, and the common origin provided by these for the initial stages of bowing in medieval times. It has already been established elsewhere in this work[19] that playing with the plectrum was popular during the Middle Ages. The long, sticklike plectrum, or *videlstaf*, was used at this time as plucking stick, beater, and friction stick – that is to say, its function changed at the player's discretion. Post-tenth-century illustrations increasingly portray stringed instruments played with a bow; but in every case the instrument in question had previously appeared as a plucked instrument, played in such a way that the plectrum touched several or even all the strings, always sounding groups of strings simultaneously, as in medieval fiddling. The net result in both cases is an elementary form of polyphony, such as drone-accompaniment or playing in parallel parts. If we stress the musical side of performance rather than the technical, the common features of both techniques stand out more clearly – at least in the Middle Ages – and the gulf separating the lute family (in the widest sense),[20] with all its ramifications, from the rest of the chordophones, seems wider than ever.

[19] Pp. 59ff. [20] The term 'lute' is used here in its widest sense, as in E. M. von Hornbostel and C. Sachs, 'Systematik der Musikinstrumente' *ZfE* 46 (1914), pp. 553 ff., and embraces all the various lutes with yokes, handles or necks, that is to say instruments such as the fiddle, gittern, viol, guitar, mandoline, lute, lyre, rote, etc. This family of lute-instruments is very clearly differentiated from that of the zithers and harps.

MONODY OR POLYPHONY
ON SOLO INSTRUMENTS

If we consider the music played on these medieval instruments in terms of 'monody' or 'polyphony', the word 'polyphony' should not be taken in its narrow occidental sense of a polyphony or homophony built upon harmonic relationships. 'Polyphony' here means part-music in the broadest possible meaning of the word, with all its transitional forms of an improvised character, in all the variety displayed in non-European music.[21]

Man's efforts to create music in two parts, or at least melody and drone, on the same instrument simultaneously, can be traced back to the earliest musical representations surviving from the great civilizations of the ancient world. This is most obvious for wind instruments, since the simple aerophones – vertical and transverse flutes, oboes and clarinets, horns and trumpets – are by nature firmly committed to producing single notes or single-line melodies, so that two or more parts can only be achieved by coupling two or more instruments of this type. The earliest composite forms are the double wind instruments, closely parallel or V-shaped, which occur in Near-Eastern and Egyptian representations as early as the second millennium B.C. In the majority of ancient civilizations these double wind instruments have played a leading rôle, and indicate how very widespread drone polyphony must have been. In the art music of the West, however, as for the medieval bagpipe, there was no place for them. Polyphonic playing developed only on the organ and similar composite wind instruments equipped with a key mechanism, while the simple aerophones were necessarily restricted to single notes or a single melodic line.

By contrast, polyphony has nearly always been possible on chordophones, though the manner and extent of its use has varied with the level of the culture and among different peoples.

It seems highly probable that even in ancient times – and particularly in the East – stringed instruments were made to sound two notes at a time, and a supporting chordal drone.[22] But in the West, early medieval illustrations of stringed

[21] Cf. W. Wiora, *Zwischen Einstimmigkeit und Mehrstimmigkeit*, pp. 319 ff. [22] C. Sachs reached this conclusion after examining a number of Babylonian reliefs on which harpists were shown; C. Sachs, 'Zweiklänge im Altertum', *Festschrift für Johannes Wolf* (Berlin, 1929), pp. 168 ff.; cf.

instruments – which of course nearly all come from Christian sources[23] – show no sign of two-handed playing, so customary in ancient times, of double stopping, or of similar practices that would point to 'polyphony' in the broad sense. The tendency to monodic playing, in clear contrast to the corresponding representations from antiquity, emerges very clearly in musical illustrations from the first millennium A.D., more particularly with regard to the harp, lyre, and psaltery, which were early sanctioned and recognized by the Church. In the early Middle Ages, the musician performing on these instruments generally has only one free hand, with which he always plucks one string at a time, never – or only very exceptionally – several strings together, while the other hand is used solely to support the instrument. Obviously musicians playing early Christian music consciously limited themselves to single-strand melody, without any accompanying sounds.[24] Like the choral unison of Gregorian chant, this early medieval instrumental playing is in no sense a primitive forerunner of Western harmonic polyphony as it emerged later, nor should it be looked upon simply as music that was 'not yet polyphonic'. It was rather a conscious dispensation with complex sound, a retreat from the non-monody of the surrounding world, the pagan world outside the Church, with its improvised parts and simultaneous variation (heterophony).[25]

The chordophones mentioned so far have mostly been instruments played on open strings, tuned to a standard scale and plucked with the fingers – the various types of harp and psaltery, with their many intermediate forms. Medieval illustrations show clearly how the techniques used on these instruments changed over the years. Shortly after the end of the tenth century, it became more and more common to accompany the melody with supporting notes, for which, in addition to double stopping, the musician's other hand was brought into play. Here we have the player deliberately adding notes, a practice that inevitably led to Western-style polyphony when the accompanying notes stood in a harmonic relationship to the melody.

In a second group of stringed instruments, the situation is different. Here the pitch of a string is altered, usually by pressure with the finger; and for this reason these instruments manage with fewer strings – for example, the lute, the fiddle, and also, with certain qualifications, the medieval rote. In playing these instruments, a plectrum or, after the end of the first millennium, a bow, was nearly always used. Since in the early Middle Ages (roughly until 1200) the strings usually lay in one plane, the plectrum or bow could scarcely avoid exciting some or all of the strings simultaneously, when drawn across them. In this way certain combinations of two or more sounds were produced – corres-

---

also H. Hickmann, *La musique polyphonique dans l'Egypte ancienne* (Cairo, 1952).   [23] Most of these are illustrations to theological works or ecclesiastical sculptures, showing King David with his musicians, Apocalyptic kings with musical instruments, or similar figures.   [24] In this respect folk music, attacked by the Church, occupied a special position.   [25] This theory is supported in particular by J. Quasten in *Musik und Gesang in den Kulturen der heidnischen Antike und christlichen*

ponding to the pitch of the strings – more or less accidentally and unintentionally, in contrast to the instruments previously mentioned and their technique.[26] Since only the string carrying the melody was stopped, the pitch of the other strings remained unchanged, thus providing a fixed, drone-like background of sound, against which the movement of the melody appeared in relief. Like the double clarinets and oboes, lutes and fiddle-type instruments appear relatively infrequently in early Christian paintings and sculptures, presumably because of the Church's original antipathy towards any instrument connected with drone-style playing. Though in Europe in the early Middle Ages only plucked chordophones are to be found, from the beginning of the second millennium illustrations of stringed instruments played with the bow become increasingly numerous. Significantly, however, the bow is annexed only by those instruments previously played with the type of plectrum that was often swept across several strings at once.[27] On the remaining medieval chordophones, where the player plucked one string at a time with his bare fingers, the bow was never used. Clearly, therefore, bowing represents a natural extension of that style of plucking, not strictly monodic, whereby several strings were sounded simultaneously with one sweep of the plectrum.

Frühzeit (Münster/Westphalia, 1930). [26] If the player touches only one string at a time of a multi-stringed instrument with the bow, this presupposes a highly developed bowing technique. Stopping and bowing must be accurately synchronized. [27] Curt Sachs came to the same conclusion when investigating the musical instruments of India: 'Only zithers and true, plucked lutes are played with the *mizrâb* (a steel-wire plectrum); such instruments never change to the bow. The *javá* (a long, wooden plectrum) on the other hand is only encountered in conjunction with lutes that are also bowed at certain times, or in certain places, and . . . are part of the family of bowed lutes. Thus the long wooden plectrum is not in opposition to the bow. It should rather be regarded as a rudiment from prehistory, the first step towards the fiddle bow; its length makes the gradual transition from plucking to bowing entirely comprehensible.' *Die Musikinstrumente Indiens und Indonesiens*, p. 122.

BIBLIOGRAPHY

The bibliography is limited to a selection of works from the specialist literature in musicology consulted. It does not include the general literature on history, cultural history, or the history of art drawn on in the course of this study. From the wide range of ethnomusicological writings only a few titles have been selected which furnish particularly valuable source materials and comparative evidence relating to the subject.

Abele, Hyacinth: *Die Violine, ihre Geschichte und ihr Bau* (Neuburg-on-Danube, 2nd ed., 1874).

Abert, Hermann: *Die Musikanschauung des Mittelalters und ihre Grundlagen* (Halle, 1905).

Alexandru, Tiberiu: 'Le violon comme instrument musical populaire', *Revista de folclor* (1957,) No. 3.

Ambros, August Wilhelm: *Geschichte der Musik*, Vol. II, 3rd ed., revised by Heinrich Reimann (Leipzig, 1891).

Anders, Godefroi Engelbert: 'Beitrag zur Geschichte der Violine', *Cäcilia* XIV, No. 56, pp. 247 ff.

Andersson, Otto: 'Altnordische Streichinstrumente', *Report of the 3rd Congress of the International Music Society* (Vienna, 1909), p. 252 ff.

– *Stråkharpan*, Dissertation (Helsinki, 1923) (Föreninge f. Svensk Kulturhistoria 4).

– *The Bowed-Harp, A Study in the History of Early Musical Instruments* (London, 1930), translated by Kathleen Schlesinger.

– *Musik och Musikinstrument* (*Nordisk Kultur*, Vol. 25) (Stockholm, 1934).

– 'The Shetland Gue, the Welsh Crwth, and the Northern Bowed Harp', *Budkavlen* (1954), Nos. 1–4, pp. 1 ff.

Anglès, Higino: *El Codex musical de Las Huelgas*, Vol. I, Introducció (Barcelona, 1931) (cf. esp. p. 43 ff. on musical instruments in Spain during the Middle Ages).

Apel, Willi: 'From St.-Martial to Notre Dame', *Journal of the American Musicological Society* II, 3 (1949), pp. 145 ff.

Appel, Margarete: *Terminologie in den mittelalterlichen Musiktraktaten, Ein Beitrag zur musikalischen Elementarlehre des Mittelalters*, Dissertation (Berlin, 1935. Printed in Bottrop, Westphalia, 1935).

Arro, Elmar: 'Zum Problem der Kannel', *Sitzungsbericht der gelehrten estnischen Gesellschaft* (1929), p. 158 ff.

Bachmann, Werner: 'Die Verbreitung des Quintierens im europäischen Volksgesang des späten Mittelalters', *Festschrift für Max Schneider* (Leipzig, 1955).

– 'Bilddarstellungen der Musik im Rahmen der artes liberales', *Kongreßbericht, Gesellschaft für Musikforschung, Hamburg 1956* (Cassel and Basle, 1957)

– 'Das byzantinische Musikinstrumentarium', *Anfänge des slavischen Musik*, Slowakische Akademie der Wissenschaft, Symposia I (Bratislava, 1966).

Baines, Anthony: 'Fifteenth-century Instruments in Tinctoris's De Inventione et Usu Musicae', *Galpin Society Journal* III (1950), p. 19 ff.

Balfour, Henry: *The Natural History of the Musical Bow* (Oxford, 1899).

Bedbrook, G.: 'The Nature of Medieval Music', *Music and Letters* 26 (1945), p. 78 ff.

Behn, Friedrich: 'Miszellen zur Musikgeschichte, III. Der Streichbogen', *Neue Musikzeitung* 39 (1918), No. 7.

- 'Miszellen zur Musikgeschichte, V. Mittelalterliche Terminologie der Musikinstrumente', *Neue Musikzeitung* 39 (1918), No. 9.

- 'Die Laute im Altertum und frühen Mittelalter', *Zeitschrift für Musikwissenschaft* I (1918).

- *Musikleben im Altertum und frühen Mittelalter* (Stuttgart, 1954).

Beichert, Eugen Alfred: *Die Wissenschaft der Musik bei al-Fārābī*, Dissertation (Freiburg-im-Breisgau, 1930; printed in Regensburg, 1931); reprinted in the *Kirchenmusikalisches Jahrbuch* 27 (1932).

Bel'aev, Victor: *Muzykal'nye instrumenty Uzbekistana* (Moscow, 1933).

Bergmann-Müller, Rosemarie: *Die Musikdarstellungen in der venezianischen Malerei von 1350 bis 1600 und ihre Bedeutung für die Auffassung des Bildgegenstandes*, Dissertation (Marburg, 1951).

Berner, Alfred: 'Die Instrumentenkunde in Wissenschaft und Praxis', *Kongreßbericht, Gesellschaft für Musikforschung, Bamberg 1953* (Cassel and Basle, 1954)

Bessaraboff, Nicholas: *Ancient European Musical Instruments* (Cambridge, Mass., 1941).

Besseler, Heinrich: 'Die Musik des Mittelalters und der Renaissance', *Handbuch der Musikwissenschaft*, ed. Ernst Bücken (Potsdam, 1931–34).

- 'Singstil und Instrumentenstil in der europäischen Musik', *Congress Report* (Bamberg, 1953)

- 'Spielfiguren in der Instrumentalmusik', *Deutsches Jahrbuch der Musikwissenschaft* I (1957).

Billè, Isaia: *Gli strumenti ad arco e i loro cultori* (Rome, 1928).

Bjørndal, Arne: 'The Hardanger fiddle. The tradition, music forms and style', *Journal of the International Folk Music Council* 8 (1956).

Blankenburg, Walter: 'David, König von Juda', *Die Musik in Geschichte und Gegenwart*, Vol. III.

Bonaventura, Arnoldo: *Storia del Violino, dei Violinisti e della Musica per Violino* (Milan, 1933).

Bose, Fritz: *Musikalische Völkerkunde* (Freiburg, 1953).

Bottée de Toulmon, Auguste: *Dissertation sur les instruments de musique employés au moyen-âge* (Paris, 1844).

Bowles, Edmund A.: 'Musical Instruments in the Medieval Corpus Christi Procession', *Journal of the American Musicological Society* XVII (1964).

- 'Instruments at the Court of Burgundy (1363–1467)', *Galpin Society Journal* VI (1953).

- 'Haut and Bas: The Grouping of Musical Instruments in the Middle Ages', *Musica disciplina* VIII (1954).

- 'Were Musical Instruments used in the Liturgical Service during the Middle Ages?', *Galpin Society Journal* X (1957).

- 'La hierarchie de instruments de musique dans l'europe féodale', *Revue de Musicologie* XLII (1958).

- 'Musical instruments at the medieval banquet', *Revue Belge de Musicologie* XII (1958).

Boyden, David D.: *The History of Violin Playing from its Origin to 1761* (London, 1965).

Bragard, Roger, and Ferd. J. de Hen: *Les instruments de musique dans l'art et l'histoire* (Rhode-St-Genèse, 1967).

Brancour, René: *Histoire des instruments de musique* (Paris, 1921).

Brandl, Alois:' Spielmannsverhältnisse in frühmittelalterlicher Zeit', *Sitzungsbericht der Königlich Preußischen Akademie der Wissenschaften*, phil.- hist. Klasse XLI (1910).

Bricqueville, Eugène de: *Notice sur la vielle* (2nd ed., Paris, 1911).

Buchner, Alexander: *Musikinstrumente im Wandel der Zeiten* (Prague, 1956).

Buhle, Edward: *Die musikalischen Instrumente in den Miniaturen des frühen Mittelalters. Ein Beitrag zur Geschichte der Musikinstrumente. I. Die Blasinstrumente* (Leipzig, 1903).

Buhle 'Über den Stand der Instrumentenkunde', *Report on the 2nd Congress of the International Music Society in Basle 1906* (Leipzig, 1907).
– Papers in the Staatsbibliothek, Berlin.

Bukofzer, Manfred: 'Popular Polyphony in the Middle Ages', *Musical Quarterly* XXVI, I (1940).

Cesari, Gaetano: 'Tre tavole di strumenti in un "Boezio" del X secolo', *Festschrift für Guido Adler, Studien zur Musikgeschichte* (Vienna, 1930).

Chailley, Jacques: *Histoire musicale du moyen âge* (Paris, 1950).

Claudius, Carl: 'Die schwedische "Nyckelharpa"', *Report on the 2nd Congress of the International Music Society in Basle 1906* (Leipzig, 1907).

Collaer, Paul: 'Polyphonies de tradition populaire en Europe méditerranéenne', *Acta musicologica* XXXII (1960).
– and Albert van der Linden, *Atlas historique de la musique* (Paris, 1960).

Combs, J. H.: 'Cornstalk fiddle and a buckeye bow', Folksay (1930).

Commenda, Hans: 'Die Gebrauchsschriften der alten Landlageiger', *Zeitschrift für Volkskunde* 48 (1939).

Cossacchi, Stephan: 'Musikinstrumente im mittelalterlichen Totentanz', *Die Musikforschung* VIII (1955), No. I.

Coussemaker, Edmond de: 'Essai sur les instruments de musique au moyen âge. (Instruments à cordes)', *Annales archéologiques*, ed. Didron Ainé Vol. III (Paris, 1845).
– 'On the Musical Instruments of the Middle Ages', *Journal of the British Archaeological Association* II (1846): On Stringed Instruments played with the Bow.
– *Scriptorum de musica medii aevi novam seriem a Gerbertina alteram collegit nunque primum edidit* (Paris, 1864–76).

Cserba, Simon Maria: *Hieronymus de Moravia, Tractatus de Musica*, Dissertation (Freiburg/Switzerland), 1932, printed in Regensburg, 1935).

Denis, Valentin: *De muziekinstrumenten in de Nederlanden en in Italie naar hun afbeelding in de 15e- eeuwsche kunst, I. Hun vorm en ontwikkeling* (Publications of the University of Louvain, Louvain, 1944).
– 'La représentation des instruments de musique dans les arts figurés du XVe siècle en Flandre et en Italie', *Bulletin de l'Institut historique belge de Rome* XXI (1940/41).
– 'Musical Instruments in Fifteenth-century Netherlands and Italian Art', *Galpin Society Journal* II (1949).

Dick, Friedrich: *Bezeichnungen für Saiten- und Schlaginstrumente in der altfranzösischen Literatur*, Dissertation (Giessen, 1931); *Giessener Beiträge zur romanischen Philologie*, No. 25 (Giessen, 1932).

Dincsér, Oszkár: 'Zwei Musikinstrumente aus dem Komitate Csik', *A néprajzi múzeum füzetei* 7 (Budapest, 1943).

Dohme Siedersbeck, Beatrice, and Dräger, Hans-Heinz: 'Fidel, II. Die Fidel im Abendland', *Die Musik in Geschichte und Gegenwart*, Vol. 4 (1955).

Dolejsi, R. 'Ancient viol tunings', *Violins and Violinists* II (1950).

Dolmetsch, Cecile: 'The crwth', *The Consort* 13 (1956).

Dolmetsch, Mabel: 'The history of the viol', *The Consort* 6 (1949).

Donington, Robert: 'Bow', *Grove's Dictionary of Music and Musicians*, 5th edition, ed. Eric Blom (London, 1954).

Dräger, Hans-Heinz: *Die Entwicklung des Streichbogens und seine Anwendung in Europa (bis zum Violenbogen des 16. Jahrhunderts)*. Dissertation (Berlin, 1937, printed in Cassel, 1937).
– 'Bogen', 'Drehleier' and 'Geige', *Die Musik in Geschichte und Gegenwart*, ed. Friedrich Blume (Cassel and Basle, 1949 ff.).
– 'Das Instrument als Träger und Ausdruck des musikalischen Bewußtseins', *Congress Report* (Bamberg, 1953).

Droysen, Dagmar: 'Die Darstellungen von Saiteninstrumenten in der mittelalterlichen Buch-malerei und ihre Bedeutung für die Instrumentenkunde', *Congress Report* (Cassel, 1962).
– *Die Saiteninstrumente des frühen und hohen Mittelalters (Halsinstrumente), Darstellung der Instrumenten-typen anhand ikonographischer und literarischer Quellen sowie romanischer und frühgotischer Plastik.* Dissertation (Hamburg, 1961).

Dufourcq, Norbert: 'Les instruments de musique', *La musique des origines à nos jours*, ed. N. Du-fourcq (Paris, 1946).

Edgerly, Beatrice: *From the hunter's bow. The history and romance of musical instruments* (New York, 1942).

Emsheimer, Ernst: 'Die Streichleier von Danczk', *Svensk Tidskrift för Musikforskning* 43 (1961).

Engel, Carl: *Researches into the early History of the Violin Family* (London, 1883).

Eras, Rudolf: 'Von Fiedeln, Geigen und Violen', *Instrumentenbau-Zeitschrift* 5 (1951).
– *Über das Verhältnis von Stimmung und Spieltechnik bei Streichinstrumenten in Da-gamba-Haltung,* Dissertation (Leipzig, 1958).

d'Erlanger, Baron Rudolphe: *La Musique Arabe*, Vols. 1–6 (Paris, 1930ff.).

Farmer, Henry George: 'Byzantine Musical Instruments in the ninth Century', *Journal of the Royal Asiatic Society* (1925).
– 'Ibn Khurdādhbih on Musical Instruments', *Journal of the Royal Asiatic Society* (1928).
– *Historical Facts for the Arabian Musical Influence* (London, 1930).
– 'The origin of the Arabian lute and rebec', *Journal of the Royal Asiatic Society* (1930).
– *Studies in Oriental Musical Instruments*, First Series (London, 1931) (esp. pp. 51ff., 'Ninth Century Musical Instruments', and pp. 89ff., 'The origin of the Arabian lute and rebec').
– 'Reciprocal Influence in Music 'twixt the Far and Middle East', *Journal of the Royal Asiatic Society* (1934).
– 'Rabāb', *Enzyklopädie des Islam*, ed. M. Th. Houtsma, A. J. Wensinck, W. Heffening, H. A. R. Gibb, and E. Lévi-Provençal, Vol. III (Leyden, Leipzig, 1936).
– 'The Instruments of Music in the Tāq-i-Bustān Bas-Reliefs', *Journal of the Royal Asiatic Society* (1938).
– 'Turkish Instruments of Music in the fifteenth Century', *Journal of the Royal Asiatic Society* (1940).
– *Oriental Studies, mainly musical* (London, 1953).
– 'The Music of Islam', *New Oxford History of Music*, Vol. I (London, 1957).
– 'Islam', *Musikgeschichte in Bildern*, ed. Heinrich Besseler and Max Schneider, III, 2 (Leipzig, 1966).
– 'Rebab', *Die Musik in Geschichte und Gegenwart*, Vol. 11 (1963).

Féderov, Vladimir: 'Notes sur la Musicologie Mediévale', *Polyphonie* 3 (Paris, 1949).

Fétis, François-Joseph: *Antoine Stradivari, Luthier célèbre connu sous le nom de Stradivarius* (Paris, 1856).

Ficker, Rudolf von: 'Die Musik des Mittelalters und ihre Beziehungen zum Geistesleben', *Deutsche Vierteljahresschrift für Literaturwissenschaft und Geistesgeschichte* III (1925).
– 'Grundsätzliches zur mittelalterlichen Aufführungspraxis', *Congress Report of the International Music Society* 5 (Utrecht, 1952).

Finlay, Ian F.: 'Musical Instruments in Gotfrid von Strassburg's "Tristan und Isolde"', *Galpin Society Journal* V (1952), p. 39ff.; see also *Music and Letters* 33 (1952), pp. 50ff.

Fleury, Edouard H.: *Les instruments de musique sur les Monuments du moyen-âge du Département de l'Aisne* (Laon, 1882).

Friedrich, Wilhelm: *Die älteste türkische Beschreibung von Musikinstrumenten aus dem Anfang des 15. Jahrhunderts,* Dissertation (Breslau, 1944).

Fryklund, Daniel: 'Etymologische Studien über Geige – Gigue – Jig', *Studier i modern språk-vetenskap* VI, 3 (Uppsala, 1917).

Galpin, Francis William: *Old English Instruments of Music, their History and Character* (London, 1910).

– *A Textbook of European Musical Instruments, their Origin, History and Character* (London, 1937).

Garnault, Paul: 'Les Violes', *Encyclopédie de la Musique*, ed. Albert Lavignac, part 2 (Paris, 1927).

Gavazzi, M.: 'Jadranska "lira – lirica"', *Narodna starina* IX (Agram, 1930).

Gazimihāl, Mahmud Ragib: *Asya ve Anadolu Kaynaklarında ıklığ* (The Iklij in Asiatic and Anatolian Sources), Ses ve Tel Birliği Yayinlari (Ankara, 1958).

Geiringer, Karl: *Die Flankenwirbelinstrumente in der bildenden Kunst der Zeit zwischen 1300 und 1550.* Dissertation (Vienna, 1923).

– 'Der Instrumentenname "Quinterne" und die mittelalterlichen Bezeichnungen der Gitarre, Mandola und des Colascione', *Archiv für Musikwissenschaft* 6 (1924).

– 'Der Instrumentenname "Quinterne" und die mittelalterlichen Bezeichnungen der Gitarre, Mandola und des Colascione', *Archiv für Musikwissenschaft* 6 (1924).

– 'Vorgeschichte und Geschichte der europäischen Laute bis zum Beginn der Neuzeit', *Zeitschrift für Musikwissenschaft* 10 (1927/28).

– 'Musikinstrumente', *Handbuch der Musikgeschichte*, ed. Guido Adler (2nd ed., Berlin, 1930).

– *Musical Instruments. Their history in western culture from the stone age to the present day* (New York, 1945).

Gemsage, Paul: 'Origin and Introduction of the Violin', *The Gentleman's Magazine* XXVII (London, 1757).

Gennrich, Friedrich: 'Zur Musikinstrumentenkunde der Machaut-Zeit', *Zeitschrift für Musikwissenschaft* 9.

Gerbert, Martin: *De cantu et musica sacra, a prima ecclesiae aetate usque ad praesens tempus* (St. Blasien, 1774).

– *Scriptores ecclesiastici de musica sacra potissimum* (St. Blasien, 1774, reprinted in Graz, 1905 and in Milan, 1931).

Gerhartz, Karl: 'Zur älteren Violintechnik', *Zeitschrift für Musikwissenschaft* 7 (1924/25).

– 'Die Violinschulen in ihrer musikalischen Entwicklung bis Leopold Mozart', *Zeitschrift für Musikwissenschaft* 7 (1924/25).

Gérold, Théodore: 'Les instruments de musique au moyen-âge', *Revue des Cours et Conférences* 29 (Paris, 1928) (Les instruments à cordes frottées).

– *Les Pères de l'église et la musique*, Etudes de l'histoire et de la philosophie relig., published by the Faculty of Protestant Theology of the University of Strasbourg, 25 (Paris, 1931).

– *La musique au moyen âge* (Paris, 1932).

Gerson-Kiwi, Edith: 'Migrations and mutations of oriental folk instruments', *Journal of the International Folk Music Council* 4 (1952).

Giese, Wilhelm: 'Maurische Musikinstrumente im mittelalterlichen Spanien', *Iberica, Zeitschrift für spanische und portugiesische Auslandskunde*, edited by B. Schädel, Vol. III (1925).

Ginsburg, Lev Solomonovič: *Istorija violončel'nogo iskusstvo*, Vol. I (Moscow, 1950).

Götz (Žak), Josef: 'Die Bauernfiedeln der Iglauer Sprachinsel', *Zeitschrift für österreichische Volkskunde* VI (1900), No. 3.

Gombosi, Otto Johannes: 'Ad vocem cithara, citharista', *Acta musicologica* IX (1937).

– 'Studien zur Tonartenlehre des frühen Mittelalters', *Acta musicologica* X–XII (1938–40).

Greulich, Martin: *Beiträge zur Geschichte des Streichinstrumentenspiels im 16. Jahrhundert*, Dissertation (Berlin, 1934).

Grillet, Laurent: *Les ancêtres du violon et du violoncelle, les luthiers et les fabricants d'archets*, Vol. I (Paris, 1901).

Grossmann, Wilhelm: *Frühmittelenglische Zeugnisse über Ministrels* (*c.* 1100–1400), Dissertation (Berlin, 1906).

Hamma, Fridolin: 'Der Bogen zum Streichinstrument', *Instrumentenbau-Zeitschrift* 8 (1953).

Hammerich, Angul: 'Zur Frage nach dem Ursprung der Streichinstrumente', *Report on the 2nd Congress of the International Music Society in Basle 1906* (Leipzig, 1907).

Hammerstein, Reinhold: *Die Musik der Engel, Untersuchungen zur Musikanschauung des Mittelalters* (Bern and Munich, 1962).

Handschin, Jacques: 'Die Rolle der Nationen in der mittelalterlichen Musikgeschichte', *Schweizerisches Jahrbuch für Musikwissenschaft* V (1931).

– 'Aus der alten Musiktheorie, V. Zur Instrumentenkunde', *Acta musicologica* XVI–XVII (1944/45).

– *Musikgeschichte im Überblick* (Lucerne, 1948).

Harlan, Peter: 'Vom Wesen der Musikinstrumente', *Zeitschrift für Musik* 115 (1954), No. 8.

Harris, Clement Antrobus: 'Musical animals in ornament', *Musical Quarterly* VI (1920).

Harrison, Frank, and Joan Rimmer: *European Musical Instruments* (London, 1964).

Haubensack, Otto: *Ursprung und Geschichte der Geige* (Marburg, 1930).

Hayes, Gerald R.: *Musical Instruments and their Music* (London, 1930).

Heinitz, Wilhelm: 'Instrumentenkunde', *Handbuch der Musikwissenschaft*, ed. Ernst Bücken (Potsdam, 1929).

Hemel, Victor van: *De viol: geschiedenis, bouw* (Antwerp, 1939).

Heron-Allen, Edward: *Opuscula fidicularum, I. The Ancestry of the Violin* (London, 1882).

– *Violin-Making, as it was and is* (London, New York, 1884).

– *De Fidiculis Bibliographia: Being an Attempt towards a Bibliography of the Violin and other Instruments played with a Bow* (London, 1890–94).

Heyde, Herbert: 'Polyphones Musizieren im späten europäischen Mittelalter', *Beiträge zur Musikwissenschaft* 3 (1965).

Hibberd, Lloyd: 'On "instrumental style" in early melody', *Musical Quarterly*, 32 (1946).

– 'Estampie and Stantipes', *Speculum* 19 (1944).

Hickmann, Hans: 'Eine orientalische Fidel', *Allgemeine Musikzeitung*, 64th series, No. 16.

– *Miscellanea musicologica VI, Quelques précurseurs égyptiens du luth court et du luth échancré*, Extrait des Annales du Service des Antiquités de l'Egypte, T. XLIX (Cairo, 1949).

– 'Ein unbekanntes Saiteninstrument aus koptischer Zeit', *Die Musikforschung* III (1950).

– 'Fidel I. Orientalische Vorläufer und Verwandte'. *Die Musik in Geschichte und Gegenwart*, Vol. 4 (1955).

– 'Rotta', *Die Musik in Geschichte und Gegenwart*, Vol. 11 (1963).

Högler, Fritz: 'Das Instrumentarium der Gotik', *Musikerziehung* 4 (Vienna, 1950/51).

Hüschen, Heinrich: *Textkonkordanzen im Musikschrifttum des Mittelalters*, Habilitation Thesis (Cologne, 1955).

Hughes, Dom Anselm: *Early Medieval Music up to 1300* (Oxford, 1954) (New Oxford History of Music, Vol. II).

Husmann, Heinrich: 'Singstil und Instrumentalstil in ihren Voraussetzungen', *Congress Report* (Bamberg, 1953).

Huth, Arno: *Die Musikinstrumente Ost-Turkistans bis zum 11. Jahrhundert nach Christi*, Dissertation (Berlin, 1928).

Jacob, Georg: *Der Einfluß des Morgenlandes auf das Abendland vornehmlich während des Mittelalters* (Hannover, 1924).

Jammers, Ewald: 'Anfänge der abendländischen Musik', *Sammlungen musikwissenschaftlicher Abhandlungen*, Vol. 31 (Strasbourg, 1955).

Jampol'skij, Izrail' Markovič: *Russkoe skripičnoe iskusstvo*, Vol. I (Moscow/Leningrad, 1951).

Jung, Lina: *Der Aufstieg der Violine*, Dissertation (Königsberg, 1925). Extract in the *Jahrbuch der Philosophischen Fakultät in Königsberg* (Königsberg, 1924), No. 49.

Kačulev, Ivan: 'Gdulkite v B'lgaria', *Izvestija na instituta za musika*, No. 5 (1958).

Kamiński, Wlodzimierz, 'Beiträge zur Erforschung der frühmittelalterlichen Musikinstrumente der Nordwest- und Ostslaven', *Anfänge der slavischen Musik*, Slowakische Akademie der Wissenschaft, Symposia I (Bratislava, 1966).

Kiesewetter, Rafael Georg: 'Über die musikalischen Instrumente und die Instrumentenmusik im Mittelalter', *Caecilia* XXII (Mainz, 1843).

Kinsky, Georg: *Musikhistorisches Museum von Wilhelm Heyer in Cöln, Katalog*, Vol. II, Zupf- und Streichinstrumente (Cologne/Leipzig, 1912).

— *Geschichte der Musik in Bildern* (Leipzig, 1929). Published in English as *A History of Music in Pictures* (London, 1930 and 1937, New York, 1951).

Koczirz, Adolf: 'Über die Fingernageltechnik bei Saiteninstrumenten', *Studien zur Musikgeschichte, Festschrift für Guido Adler* (Vienna, 1930).

Kolneder, Walter: 'Die musikalisch-soziologischen Voraussetzungen der Violinenentwicklung'. *Colloquium amicorum, Joseph Schmidt-Görg zum 70. Geburtstag* (Bonn, 1967).

Kotljarov, B. Ja.: *O skripičnoi kul'tur v Moldavii* (Kischinev, 1955).

Krüger, Walther: 'Singstil und Instrumentalstil in der Mehrstimmigkeit der St. Martialepoche', *Congress Report* (Bamberg, 1953).

— 'Aufführungspraktische Fragen mittelalterlicher Mehrstimmigkeit', *Die Musikforschung* IX (1956).

— 'Die authentische Klangform des primitiven Organum', *Musikwissenschaftliche Arbeiten*, No. 13 (Cassel and Basle, 1958).

Kunst, Jaap: *Ethno-Musicology* (The Hague, 1955).

Kunz, Ludvik: 'Skřipky', *Acta Musei Moraviae* XXXV (1950).

— 'Velké husle a svatebni husličky ze Srbské Lužice', *Acta Musei Moraviae* XXXVI (1951).

— 'Die Bauernfiedeln', *Zwischen Kunstgeschichte und Volkskunde, Festschrift für Wilhelm Fraenger* (Berlin, 1960).

Lach, Robert: 'Der Einfluß des Orients auf die Musik des Abendlandes', *Österreichische Monatsschrift für den Orient*, 40th series, Nos. 11/12 (1914).

Lang, Paul Henry: *Die Musik im Abendland*, Vol. I (Augsburg, 1947).

Leffler, Karl Peter: *Om Nyckelharpospelet pa Skansen* (Stockholm, 1899).

Leichtentritt, Hugo: 'Was lehren uns die Bildwerke des 14.–17. Jahrhunderts über die Instrumentalmusik ihrer Zeit?' *Sammelbände der Internationalen Musikgesellschaft* VII (1905/1906).

— 'Ältere Bildwerke als Quellen der musikgeschichtlichen Forschung', *Report on the 2nd Congress of the International Music Society in Basle 1906* (Leipzig, 1907).

Leipp, Emile: 'Étude sur les origines du violon', *Musique et Radio* 43 (Paris, 1953).

Le Prince le jeune, René: 'Observations sur l'Origine du Violon', *Journal Encyclopédique ou Universel* (Nov. 1782).

Lesser, Elisabeth: 'Zur Scordatura der Streichinstrumente mit besonderer Berücksichtigung der Viola d'amore', *Acta musicologica* 4 (1932).

Levy, Josef: 'Musikinstrumente beim Gesang im mittelalterlichen Frankreich, auf Grund altfranzösischer Texte (bis zum 14. Jahrhundert), *Zeitschrift für romanische Philologie* XXXV (1911).

Ling, Jan: 'Nyckelharpan, Studier i ett folkligt musikinstrument', *Musikhistoriska museets skrifter* 2 (Stockholm, 1967).

Machabey, Armand: *Histoire et évolution des formales musicales du Ier au XVe siècle de l'ère chrétienne* (Paris, 1928).

Marcel-Dubois, Claudine: *Les instruments de musique de l'Inde ancienne* (Paris, 1941).

Marx, Klaus: *Die Entwicklung des Violoncells und seiner Spieltechnik bis J. L. Duport*. Dissertation (Saarbrücken, 1963).

Matzke, Hermann: *Unser technisches Wissen von der Musik, Einführung in die musikalische Technologie* (Vienna, 1949).

Meyer, Kathi: 'The eight gregorian modes on the cluny capitals', *The Art Bulletin* XXXIV, No. 2 (1952).

Moberg, Carl-Allan: 'Fistula und Fidhla', *Studien zur Musikwissenschaft, Beihefte der Denkmäler der Tonkunst in Österreich* Bd. 25 (Vienna, 1962).

Möckel, Otto: *Die Kunst des Geigenbaus*, 2nd ed. revised and enlarged by Fritz Winkel (Berlin, 1954).

Montgomery, Franz: 'The Musical Instruments in "The Canterbury Tales"', *Musical Quarterly* 17 (1931).

Moser, Hans Joachim: 'Das Streichinstrumentenspiel im Mittelalter', Introduction to Andreas Moser, *Geschichte des Violinspiels* (Berlin, 1923; 2nd edition revised and enlarged by Hans-Joachim Nösselt, Tutzing, 1966).

Nef, Karl: *Geschichte unserer Musikinstrumente* (1st edition, Leipzig, 1926; 2nd edition, Basle, 1949).

– 'Gesang und Instrumentenspiel bei den Troubadours', *Festschrift für Guido Adler* (Vienna, 1930).

Nopp, Jan Mařák-Viktor: *Housle* (Prague, 1941).

Norden, Hugo: *Harmony and its application in Violin-playing* (Boston, 1937).

Norlind, Tobias: 'Beiträge zur chinesischen Instrumentengeschichte', *Svensk Tidskrift för Musikforskning* 15 (1933).

– *Systematik der Saiteninstrumente, 1. Geschichte der Zither* (Stockholm, 1936), 2. *Geschichte des Klaviers* (Hannover, 1939).

– *Musikinstrumentens historia i ord och bild* (Stockholm, 1941).

Örpen, Truls: 'Felespelet i Krödherad', *Norsk Musikgransking* (Årbok, 1947/50).

Padelford, Frederick Morgan: 'Old English musical terms', *Bonner Beiträge zur Anglistik* IV (Bonn, 1899).

Panum, Hortense: *Middelalderens Strengeinstrumenter og deres Forløbere*, 3 vols. (Copenhagen, 1915/31). Translated into English by J. Pulver, *The stringed Instruments of the middle ages* (London, 1941).

Parent, Denise: *Les instruments des musiciens au XIVᵉ siècle* (Paris, 1925).

Pek, Albert: 'Dyndáckè hudba na skřipky z Jihlavska', *Národopisný věstník českoslovanský* 32 (1952).

Persijn, Jean: *Origine du mot violon* (The Hague, 1937).

Picken, Laurence: 'Early Chinese Friction-Chordophones', *Galpin Society Journal* XVII (1965).

– 'Instrumental Polyphonic Folk-Music in Asia minor', *Proceedings of the Royal Musical Association* 80 (1953/54).

Profeta, Rosario: *Storia e letteratura degli strumenti musicali* (Florence 1942).

Pulver, Jeffrey: *A dictionary of old English Music, Musical Instruments* (London, 1923).

– 'Violin Methods old and new', *Proceedings of the Musical Association* (1923/24).

Quasten, Johannes: *Musik und Gesang in den Kulturen der heidnischen Antike und christlichen Frühzeit* (Münster/Westphalia, 1930) (Literaturgeschichtliche Quellen und Forschungen, No. 25).

Reaney, Gilbert: 'Voices and Instruments in the Music of Guillaume de Machaut', *Revue Belge de Musicologie* X (1956), fasc. 1–2; *Congress Report* (Bamberg, 1953).

Reese, Gustave: *Music in the Middle Ages, with an Introduction to the Music of Ancient Times* (London, 1941).

Regli, Francesco: *Storia del Violino* (Turin, 1863).

Reiss, Josef: 'Pauli Paulirini de Praga Tractatus de musica (c. 1460)', *Zeitschrift für Musikwissenschaft* 7 (1925).

Rettberg, R. von: 'Zur Geschichte der Musikinstrumente', *Anzeiger für Kunde der deutschen Vorzeit*, new series, 7th set (1860).

Reuter, Evelyn: *Les représentations de la musique dans la sculpture romane en France* (Paris, 1938).

Ridgeway, William: 'The Origin of the Guitar and Fiddle', *Man* VIII (1908).

Riemann, Hugo: 'Zur Geschichte der Instrumente und der Instrumentalmusik', *Präludien und Studien*, Vol. 2 (Leipzig, 1901).

Rittmeyer-Iselin, Dora: 'Das Rebec. Ein Beitrag zur Geschichte unserer Streichinstrumente', *Festschrift für Karl Nef* (Zürich, Leipzig, 1933).

Rokseth, Yvonne: 'Les femmes musiciennes du XIIᵉ au XIVᵉ siècle', *Romania* 61 (1935).

Rousseau, Jean: *Traité de la viole, qui contient une dissertation curieuse sur son origine* (Paris, 1687).

Rühlmann, Julius: 'Die Urformen der Bogeninstrumente', *Musikalisches Wochenblatt*, 5th year Nos. 30, 31, 32 (Leipzig, 17 and 24 July and 7 August 1874).

— *Die Geschichte der Bogeninstrumente* (Brunswick, 1882).

Russell, Theodore: 'The Violin "Scordatura"', *Musical Quarterly* 24 (1938).

Sachs, Curt: *Real-Lexikon der Musikinstrumente* (Berlin, 1913).

— 'Die Streichbogenfrage', *Archiv für Musikwissenschaft* I (1918).

— *Handbuch der Musikinstrumentenkunde* (1st ed., Leipzig, 1920, 2nd ed., Leipzig, 1930, 3rd ed. Leipzig, 1967) (Kleine Handbücher der Musikgeschichte nach Gattungen, 12).

— 'Der Ursprung der Saiteninstrumente', *Publication d'hommage offerte au P. W. Schmidt* (1928).

— *Geist und Werden der Musikinstrumente* (Berlin, 1929).

— *The History of Musical Instruments* (New York, 1940).

— *The Rise of Music in the Ancient World East and West* (New York, 1943).

Saint-George, Henry: *The Bow, its History, Manufacture and Use* (London, 1896).

Salmen, Walter: 'Zur Schichtung des Berufsmusikertums im mittelalterlichen Eurasien und in Afrika', *Les Congrès et Colloques de l'Université de Liège*, Vol. 19, Ethnomusicologie II (Université de Liège, 1960).

— 'Bemerkungen zum mehrstimmigen Musizieren der Spielleute im Mittelalter', *Revue Belge de Musicologie* II (1957).

— *Der fahrende Musiker im europäischen Mittelalter* (Cassel, 1960).

— 'Die soziale Geltung des Musikers in der mittelalterlichen Gesellschaft', *Studium Generale* 19 (1966).

Sandys, William, and Forster, Simon Andrew: *The History of the Violin and other instruments played on with the bow from the remotest times to the present* (London, 1864).

Schad, Gustav: *Musik und Musikausdrücke in der mittelenglischen Literatur*. Dissertation (Giessen, 1911).

Schaeffner, André: *Origine des instruments de musique, Introduction ethnologique a l'histoire de la musique internationale* (Paris, 1936).

Schering, Arnold: 'Über Musikhören und Musikempfinden im Mittelalter', *Jahrbuch der Musikbibliothek Peters* 28 (1921).

Schlesinger, Kathleen: *The Instruments of the modern Orchestra and Early Records of the Precursors of the Violin Family*, Vol. 2, *The Precursors of the Violin Family, Records, Researches and Studies* (London, 1910).

— 'Bow', 'Fiddle', 'Guitar fiddle', 'Rebab', 'Rebec', *Encyclopaedia Britannica* (11th ed., Cambridge, 1910).

— *A Bibliography of musical instruments and archaeology* (London, 1912).

Schletterer, Hans Michael: 'Die Ahnen moderner Musikinstrumente', *Sammlung musikalischer Vorträge* 46 (Leipzig, 1882).

Schlosser, Julius von: *Unsere Musikinstrumente. Eine Einführung in ihre Geschichte* (Vienna, 1922).

Schneider, Marius: 'Wurzeln und Anfänge der abendländischen Mehrstimmigkeit', *Congress Report* (New York, 1961).

– *Geschichte der Mehrstimmigkeit*, Vols. 1/2 (Berlin, 1934/35).

Schubiger, P. Anselm: *Musikalische Specilegien, Zur mittelalterlichen Instrumentalmusik*, Vol. V of the Publikationen älterer praktischer und theoretischer Musikwerke, IVth year, No. II (Berlin, 1876).

Schünemann, Georg: 'Die Musikinstrumente der 24 Alten', *Archiv für Musikforschung* I (1936).

– 'Die Violine', *Deutsches Museum, Abhandlungen und Berichte*, 12th year, No. 3 (Berlin, 1940).

Schultz, Helmut: *Instrumentenkunde* (2nd ed., Leipzig, 1954).

Schwartz, Harry Wayne: *The Story of Musical Instruments; from Shepherd's Pipe to Symphony* (New York, 1938).

Senn, Walter: 'Streichinstrumentenbau', *Die Musik in Geschichte und Gegenwart*, Vol. 12 (1965).

Serrano Fatigati, Enrique: *Instrumentos musicos en las miniaturas de los codices españoles, siglos X al XIII*. Discurso (Madrid, 1901).

Sievers, Heinrich: 'Mittelalterliche Musikinstrumente in geistlichen Spielen', *Das Musikleben* I (1948).

Simon, Alicja: 'An Early Medieval Slav Gesle', *Galpin Society Journal* 10 (1957).

Snoeck, Césare: 'Notes sur les instruments de musique en usage dans les Flandres au moyen âge', *Annales de la Fédération archéologique et historique de Belgique* (1897).

Söderbäck, Olof: 'Den svensk-estländska stråkharpan. *Vår Sång*', *Tidskrift för det folkliga Musiklivet* 22 (1949).

Sorensen, Margot Ida Sigrid: *Musik und Gesang im mittelhochdeutschen Epos*. Dissertation, University of Pennsylvania (Philadelphia, 1938, printed in Philadelphia, 1939).

Spiess, Lincoln B.: 'An Introduction to the pre-St. Martial practical sources of early Polyphony, *Speculum* (1947).

Stainer, J. F. R.: 'Rebec and Viol', *Musical Times* 41 (1900), No. 691.

Steger, Hugo: 'David rex et propheta, König David als vorbildliche Verkörperung des Herrschers und Dichters im Mittelalter, nach Bilddarstellungen des achten bis zwölften Jahrhunderts', *Erlanger Beiträge zur Sprach- und Kunstwissenschaft* VI (Nuremberg, 1961).

– 'Die Rotte, Studien über ein germanisches Musikinstrument im Mittelalter', *Deutsche Vierteljahresschrift für Literaturwissenschaft und Geistesgeschichte* 35 (1961).

Steinbauer, Othmar: 'Die moderne Vielle', *Die Musikerziehung* 4 (1951).

Steinhausen, F. Adolf: *Die Physiologie der Bogenführung auf den Streich-Instrumenten*, 5th edition, ed. by Florizel von Reuter (Leipzig, 1928).

Stephan, Rudolf: 'Einige Hinweise auf die Pflege der Mehrstimmigkeit im frühen Mittelalter in Deutschland', *Congress Report* (Lüneburg, 1950).

Stoll, Dennis: 'Music in Medieval Baghdad', *Music Review* I (1940).

Straeten, Edmund Sebastian Joseph van der: *The Romance of the Fiddle* (London, 1911).

– *History of the violin, its ancestors and collateral instruments, from earliest times to the present day* (London, Cassel, 1933).

Struve, Boris Aleksandrovič: *Prozess formirovanija viol i skripok* (Moscow, 1959).

Tolbecque, Auguste: *Notice historique sur les instruments à cordes et à archet* (Paris, 1898).

Treder, Dorothea: *Die Musikinstrumente in den höfischen Epen der Blütezeit*, Dissertation (Greifswald, 1933).

Vaeisaenen, Armas Otto: 'Kantele- ja jouhikkosävelmiä', *Suomen kansan Sävelmiä* 5 (Helsinki, 1928).

Valentin, Erich: *Handbuch der Musikinstrumentenkunde* (Regensburg, 1954).

Vertkov, K., Blagodatov, G., and Jasovizkaja, E.: *Atlas musykal'nych instrumentov narodov SSSR* (Moscow, 1963).

Vidal, Louise Antoine: *Les instruments à archet* (Paris, 1876/78).

Vinogradov, Viktor: *Kirgizskaja narodnaja muzyka* (Frunse, 1958).

Waeltner, Ernst Ludwig: *Das Organum bis zur Mitte des 11. Jahrhunderts*, Dissertation (Heidelberg, 1955).

Wagner, Peter: 'Morgen- und Abendland in der Musikgeschichte', *Stimmen der Zeit*, 58th year, Vol. 114, 2 (1927).

Walin, Stig: 'Musikinstrumenttermer i äldre svenska lexikon', *Svensk tidskrift för musikforskning* 30 (1948).

Wasielewski, Wilhelm Joseph von: *Die Violine und ihre Meister* (5th edition, Leipzig, 1910).

Weinmann, Karl: 'Ein unbekannter Traktat des Johannes Tinctoris', *Riemann-Festschrift* (Leipzig, 1909).

– *Johannes Tinctoris (1445–1511) und sein unbekannter Traktat 'De inventione et usu musicae'* (Regensburg and Rome, 1917).

Wellesz, Egon: *A History of Byzantine Music and Hymnography* (Oxford, 1949).

Werland, Peter: 'Musikinstrumente der spätromanischen Zeit', *Zeitschrift für Musik* 105 (1938).

Werner, Joachim: 'Leier und Harfe im germanischen Frühmittelalter', *Aus Verfassungs- und Landesgeschichte, Festschrift für Theodor Mayer* Vol. I (Constance, 1954).

Wewertem, J. W. F.: 'Zwei veraltete Musikinstrumente', *Monatshefte für Musikgeschichte* 13 (1881).

Wiedemann, Eilhard and Hauser, F.: 'Byzantinische und arabische akustische Instrumente', *Archiv für die Geschichte der Naturwissenschaften und der Technik* VIII (1918).

Winkel, Fritz: 'Analogien der Geigen- und Menschenstimme', *Musikblätter* (1950), No. 4.

Winternitz, Emanuel: *Die schönsten Musikinstrumente des Abendlandes*, translated by Werner Bachmann (Munich, 1966).

– 'The Visual Arts as a Source for the Historian of Music', *International Musicological Society, Congress Report* (New York, 1961), I, pp. 109/120; II, pp. 84/87.

– 'Bagpipes and Hurdy-Gurdies in their social setting', *Bulletin of the Metropolitan Museum of Art*, New Series II, 1 (1943), p. 56.

– 'Lira da braccio', *Die Musik in Geschichte und Gegenwart*, Vol. VIII.

Wiora, Walter: 'Zwischen Einstimmigkeit und Mehrstimmigkeit', *Festschrift für Max Schneider* (Leipzig, 1955).

Wolf, Johannes: 'Die Musiklehre des Johannes de Grocheo', *Sammelbände der Internationalen Musikgesellschaft* I (1899/1900).

– 'Die Tänze des Mittelalters, Eine Untersuchung des Wesens der älteren Instrumentalmusik', *Archiv für Musikwissenschaft* I (1918/1919).

Wünsch, Walter: *Die Geigentechnik der südslawischen Guslaren* (Brno, Leipzig, Vienna, 1934).

– 'Geschichte und Namen der volkstümlichen Streichinstrumente des Balkans', *Zeitschrift für Balkanologie*, Jg. 2 (1964).

Wunderlich, Friedrich: *Der Geigenbogen, seine Geschichte, Herstellung und Behandlung* (Leipzig, 1936).

Zelzer, Hugo: *Grundlage einer Strukturanalyse der europäischen Instrumentalmusik*. Dissertation (Vienna, 1952).

Special periodicals:

The Strad, London, founded 1889.
Der Geigenbauer, Berlin, founded 1925.
Violins and Violinists, Evanston, U.S.A., founded 1938.
Zeitschrift für Instrumentenbau, founded 1880.
Musikinstrumenten-Zeitung, Berlin, founded 1892.
Deutsche Instrumentenbauzeitung, 1899–1943.
Instrumentenbau-Zeitschrift, Constance, founded 1946.
Musique et instruments, Paris, founded 1909.
The Galpin Society Journal, Edinburgh, founded 1948.

PICTORIAL SOURCES

With one or two exceptions, this list is restricted to illustrations of medieval bowed instruments dating from before 1250. The published iconographic materials and the manuscript catalogues of various libraries have been systematically sifted, and inquiries have been directed to the more important libraries and museums. From the collection of good reproductions of miniatures and sculpture thus assembled, only the more instructive examples have been selected and arranged here according to topics. The numbers in brackets are those of the illustrations reproduced.

A. Illumination

Admont, Stiftsbibliothek
  MS. 3, fol. 529 and fol. 540   (50)
  MS. 4 (Vol. 1), fol. 44   (49)
  MS. 73, fol. 1
  MS. 89, fol. 65 v
Amiens, Bibliothèque municipale
  Fonds l'Escalopier, Ms. 2, fol. 2   (18)
Baltimore, Walters Art Gallery
  MS. 45, fol. 49 r
Bamberg, Staatliche Bibliothek
  MS. bibl. 46 (A-II-10), fol. 1 v
  MS. bibl. 48 (A-II-47), fol. 10 r
  MS. bibl. 59 (B-I-10), fol. 2 v   (48)
Barcelona, Museo Diocesaro
  MS. G/8011, Psalm I, Initial B   (24)
Belvoir Castle, Library of the Duke of
  Rutland, Psalter manuscript   (86)
Berlin, Deutsche Staatsbibliothek
  MS. lat. theol. fol. 358, 1 v   (94)
  MS. lat. theol. fol. 379, fol. 245 v   (52)
  MS. lat. theol. fol. 561, fol. 77, fol. 79 v
Berlin, Kupferstichkabinett
  MS. 110, fol. 14 v, 55 v, 80 r
  MS. 78 A 5, fol. 55 r
  MS. 78 A 8
  MS. 78 A 9, fol. 41 v

Boulogne-sur-Mer, Bibliothèque municipale
  MS. 2, II, fol. 190 r
Brussels, Bibliothèque Royale
  MS. 9961–62, fol. 14 r, fol. 44 r,
  fol. 57 r
Burgos, Biblioteca Provincial
  Libro de los Reyes, fol. 141
Cambridge, Fitzwilliam Museum
  MS. 330, Nr. 5
  MS. 330, Nr. 6
Cambridge, St. John's College Library
  MS. B. 18, fol. 1   (39)
  MS. D. 6, fol. 31
Cambridge, Trinity College Library
  MS. 0.4.7., fol. 112 r   (62)
Cambridge, University Library
  MS. Ff. I, 23, fol. 4 v   (92)
Chantilly, Musée Condé
  MS. 1696, fol. 14 v
Cividale de Friuli, Museo Archeologico Nazionale
  St. Elizabeth Psalter, fol. 295   (73)
Copenhagen, Kongelige Bibliotek
  Thott's Collection, MS. 108, fol. 8 v
  Collection 1606, fol. 20 v
Dijon, Bibliothèque publique
  MS. 14, Vol. III, fol. 13 v   (56)

MS. 147, fol. 2r
MS. 169, fol. 5r
MS. 633, fol. 2
Douai, Bibliothèque municipale
MS. 19, fol. 2r
MS. 23 (T. 2), fol. 3v
MS. 50, Initial B
MS. 250, Vol. I, fol. 2v   (35)
MS. 840, fol. 1r
Dublin, Trinity College Library
MS. 53, fol. 151   (34)
Florence, Biblioteca Laurenziana
MS. Plut. XVII, Cod. 3, fol. 24v   (37)
MS. Plut. XII, 17, fol. 2v
MS. Edili 125–126, II, fol. 12v
MS. Fiesol. 18, fol. 136r
Frankfurt a. M., Stadtbibliothek
Ausst. 5, fol. 150r
Glasgow, University Library
Hunterian MS. 229 (U. 3.2), fol. 21v. (60)
Grenoble, Bibliothèque municipale
MS. 41, fol. 147r
The Hague, Koninklijke Bibliotheek
MS. 76 E II (formerly y 421),   (59)
fol. 2r
Heidelberg, Universitätsbibliothek
Cod. pal. germ. 848   (66, 68)
Hildesheim, St. Godehard Bibliothek
Albani-Psalter, fol. 56v, fol. 371,
fol. 447r   (51, 54)
Ivrea, Biblioteca Capitolare
Cod. LXXXV, fol. 23v   (17)
Jerusalem, Library of the Greek Patri-
archate
Cod. Taphou, 14, fol. 100r   (6)
Cod. Taphou 14, fol. 310v   (10)
Klosterneuburg, Bibliothek des
Augustiner-Chorherrenstiftes
Cod. 987, fol. 11v   (89)
Lausanne, Bibliothèque Cant. et
Universitaire
MS. U. 964, fol. 216v
Leipzig, Universitätsbibliothek
MS. 774, fol. 31r   (30)
Leningrad, Public Library
MS. lat. Q. v. I, 67, fol. 7r
León, San Isidoro
MS. 13, fol. 133v

Leyden, Bibliotheek der Rijksuniversiteit
B.P.L. 76A, fol. 30v, fol. 78r
MS. 318, Psalm I, Initial B
London, British Museum
MS. Add. 9350, fol. 1r
MS. Add. 11695, fol. 86   (2)
MS. Add. 19352, fol. 191   (11)
MS. Add. 24686, fol. 17v
MS. Add. 28162, fol. 10v
MS. Add. 35166, fol. 4v
MS. Add. 36928, fol. 46v
MS. Add. 40731, fol. 7v
MS. Add. 42130, fol. 81v, 176r and
149   (83, 84)
MS. Add. 49999, fol. 55r
MS. Arundel 91, fol. 218v   (32)
MS. Arundel 157, fol. 71v   (53)
MS. Cotton, Tib. C. VI, fol. 30v (31)
MS. Cotton, Nero C. IV, fol. 46
MS. Harley 978, fol. 11v
MS. Harley 2799, fol. 243
MS. Harley 2804, fol. 3v   (61)
MS. Harley 4951, fol. 297v   (38)
MS. Lansdowne 383, fol. 15v
MS. Lansdowne 420, fol. 12v
MS. Lansdowne 431, fol. 64v
MS Sloane 3544, fol. 42v
London, Lambeth Palace
MS. 563, fol. 20r
London, Society of Antiquaries Library
MS. 59, fol. 38v   (81)
London, Thompson Collection
MS. 72, fol. 56r
Lunel, Bibliothèque municipale
MS. I, fol. 6   (69)
Madrid, Biblioteca Nacional
MS. Hh 58, fol. 127r   (1)
Madrid, Biblioteca de San Lorenzo
del Escorial
MS. T-i-I (Cantigas de Santa Maria) (82)
Madrid, Academia de la Historia
MS. Sig. 33, fol. 177 and 184   (3)
Milan, Biblioteca Ambrosiana
Cod. C. 128, Inf., Plate 3a   (71)
Cod. M. 47, Sup. fol. Iv
Mantua, Biblioteca Civile
MS. C. III, 20, fol. Ir   (26)
MS. C. III, 20, fol. 2

Melk, Stiftsbibliothek
  Cod. I
Mt. Athos, Vatopedi
  MS. 610, fol. 17 v
Mt. Athos, Laura
  MS. B. 26, fol. 268 v
Mt. Sinai, Monastery of St. Catherine
  Cod. 339, Initial T
Munich, Bayrische Staatsbibliothek
  Cod. germ. 51 (Cim. 27), fol. 71
  Cod. germ. 51 (Cim. 27), fol. 37 v
  Cod. lat. 835, fol. 148 v
  Cod. lat. 2599, fol. 96 v   (95)
  Cod. lat. 3900 c. p. 61, fol. 8 r
Munich, Universitätsbibliothek
  MS. 24. 4°, fol. 2 r   (85)
Naples, Biblioteca Nazionale
  Cod. V A 14   (76)
New York, Piermont Morgan Library
  MS. 429, fol. 112 r und fol. 116 v
Paris, Bibliothèque Nationale
  MS. grec. 134, fol. 127 r
  MS. suppl. grec. 1335, fol. 258 r,
  fol. 260 r
  MS. lat. 7, fol. 125 v   (33)
  MS. lat. 238, fol. 114 v and 132 v
  MS. lat. 796, fol. 235 r
  MS. lat. 1118, fol. 104 r   (91)
  MS. lat. 1987, fol. 217 v
  MS. lat. 2508, fol. II v   (23)
  MS. lat. 6755 (2), fol. A v   (58)
  MS. lat. 6819, Initial H
  MS. lat. 8846, fol. 54 v, fol. 81 v
  MS. lat. 10435, Psalm I, Initial B
  MS. lat. 10525, Plate 74/1
  MS. lat. 11509, fol. 5 r   (63)
  MS. lat. 11534, fol. 205 v and 324
  MS. lat. 11550, fol. 7 v   (25)
  MS. lat. 11565, fol. 63 and 79 v
  MS. lat. 11575, fol. 1
  MS. frc. 12473, fol. 36
  MS. nouv. acq. lat. 1392, fol. 20 and 123 v
  MS. nouv. acq. lat. 2290, fol. 56 v,
  126, 131 and 158 v
Paris, Bibliothèque de l'Arsenal
  MS. 5198, fol. 1
Paris, Bibliothèque Mazarine
  MS. 36, Psalm 1, Initial B

Paris, Le Roy Collection
  Beatus in Apocalipsin, fol. 12 r
Paris, Sainte-Geneviève
  MS. 1273, fol. 98 v
Pommersfelden, Gräflich Schönborn-
  sche Bibliothek
  Cod. 334, fol. 148 v   (29)
Prague, Národní museum
  MS. X. A. II, fol. I V
Prague, University Library
  MS. 412, fol. 72 r   (65)
Rheims, Bibliothèque municipale
  MS. 672, fol. 1
Rome, Vatican Library
  MS. graec. 1927, fol. 264 r
  MS. graec. 1947, fol. 146 r   (12)
  MS. graec. 752, fol. 3 r, 5 r, 7 v, 23 v
  and 449 v   (4, 5, 7)
  MS. graec. 372, fol. 249 r
  MS. pal. lat. 39, fol. 44 v   (57)
  MS. lat. 5729, fol. 227 v   (22)
  MS. lat. 12958, fol. 186 r
  MS. lat. 12958, II, fol. 2 v
St. Blasien, Stiftsbibliothek
  Copies of miniatures from a Codex
  destroyed by fire
St. Gall, Stiftsbibliothek
  Cod. 21, Pgm. 2°   (47)
Strasbourg, Bibliothèque du Grande
  Seminaire
  MS. 78 (I, Scr. 10), fol. 79 r   (36)
Strasbourg, Bibliothèque Municipal
  Herrad von Landsberg, Hortus
  deliciarum, copy of a miniature
  from a Codex destroyed by fire in
  1870
Stuttgart, Württembergische Landes-
  bibliothek
  Bibl., 23, 2°, fol. 125 r   (16)
Toledo, Biblioteca del Cabildo
  Bible-Ms. III, fol. 40 r
Trier, Domschatz
  MS. of the Kurfürst Kuno von
  Falkenstein, fol. 3 r
Utrecht, University Library
  Script. eccles. 484, fol. 63 v
Venice, Biblioteca Nazionale di S. Marco
  MS. gr. 17 (= 421), fol. IV v

Vienna, Österreichische National-
bibliothek
Cod. 1100 (rec. 3108), fol. 1 r
Cod. 1179, fol. 86 r   (74)
Cod. 1879, fol. 104 v
Zürich, Central Library
MS. Rh. 15, fol. 218   (87)

B. Frescoes

(Including paintings on wood and stained
glass)
Kiev, Cathedral of St. Sophia, North
Tower, Fresco   (8)
Madrid, Academia de la Historia,
Reliquary Triptych, Painting on
wood   (75, 88)
Niederhaslach, Florentiuskirche,
Stained glass   (72)
Palermo, Capella Palatina, Fresco   (21)
Rheims, Cathedral, West Rose window,
Stained glass
Rome, S. Urbano alla Caffarella, Crypt,
Fresco   (28)
St. Denis, Abbey Church, Stained
glass
Troyes, Lady Chapel, Stained glass

C. Stone and wood carvings

Aguero, Eremita de San Jaime, Portal
Amiens, Cathedral, West door
Aulnay-de-Saintonge, Saint-Pierre-de-la
Tour, Portal
Barcelona, Monastery of Santa Maria
del Estany, Capital
Bordeaux, Cathedral of Sainte-Croix,
West door, inner archivolt
Canterbury, Crypt, Capital in the
South-east Chapel
Carboeiro, Church, West door
Chartres, frontal pillar between the
central door and left side-door
Cluny, Abbey Church of St. Pierre,
Capital (Musée Ochier)
Dourade, Monastery, Capital in the
transept (Toulouse, museum)   (40)

Ely, Cathedral, South door, right-hand
pillar
Erfurt, Cathedral, Choirstall   (67)
Estella (Navarra), San Miguel, North
door
Foussais, Cathedral, West door
Fünen, Gamtofte Church
Cologne, Walraff-Richartz-Museum,
relief
León, Colegiata de San Isidoro, West
door
Meillers, Church, West door   (42)
Moissac, Saint-Pierre, Main door   (43, 44)
Oloron, St. Mary's Cathedral, West
door   (64)
Paris, Notre-Dame, St. Anne door   (79)
Parma, Baptistry, West door   (70)
Parthenay, Notre Dame-de-la-Couldre,
Central door
Pronvins, Saint-Ayoul, portal
Ripoll (Gerona), Monastery of Santa
Maria, portal in the West front
Rouen, Abbey of St. Georges-de-
Boscherville, Capital   (77)
Rouen, Cathedral, bookseller's door
St. Denis, Abbey Church, Central
West door   (45)
Santiago de Compostela, Cathedral,
Puerta de Platerias
Santiago de Compostela, Cathedral,
Pórtico de la Gloria   (80)
Santiago de Compostela, Palacio de
Gelmirez, Archbishop's Palace
St.-Vivien, Apse
Soria, Santo Domingo, West door   (78)
Tauriac, Church, Consoles on the
West front
Toro (Zamora), Cathedral, North
door
Toulouse, Saint-Sernin, portal in side
nave   (41)
Trondheim, Cathedral, portal sculp-
ture   (97)
Vermenton (Yonne), Church, Portal
Vézelay, Abbey Church, south row
of pillars
Vienne, Cathedral, capital on a pillar
on the North side   (46)

INDEX